KHAN'S TUTORIAL
Digital SAT Grammar Study Guide

Douglas S. Kovel, Ed.M.

Copyright © 2023 CosmicPrep, LLC
All rights reserved.

No part of this work may be reproduced, stored in a retrieval system, or transmitted in any form or by any means, including electronic, mechanical, photocopy, or recording, without the written permission of the author. For more information, please email cosmicprep@gmail.com.

ISBN- 9798865460312

Table of Contents

Unit 1: Building a Foundation (Grammar Vocabulary) 5
- Lesson 1: Basic Parts of Speech Overview 5
- Lesson 2: Sentence Structure Basics 17
- Lesson 3: Coordination and Subordination 23

Unit 2: Sentence Structure 39
- Lesson 4: Sentence Boundaries 39
- Lesson 5: Modifier Placement 65
- Lesson 6: Verb Tense 74
- Structure Unit Quiz 84

Unit 3: Usage 92
- Lesson 7: Possessive Determiners 92
- Lesson 8: Pronoun Agreement 98
- Lesson 9: Subject-Verb Agreement 106
- Usage Unit Quiz 122

Unit 4: Punctuation 129
- Lesson 10: End-of-Sentence Punctuation 129
- Lesson 11: Within-Sentence Punctuation 133
- Lesson 12: Items in a Series 147
- Lesson 13: Possessive Nouns and Pronouns 151
- Lesson 14: Restrictive and Nonrestrictive Punctuation 160
- Lesson 15: Unnecessary Punctuation 174
- Punctuation Unit Quiz 187

Unit 5: Expression 194
- Lesson 16: Transitions 194
- Lesson 17: Rhetorical Synthesis 201
- Expression Unit Quiz 215
- Key 226
  - Lesson 1: Basic Parts of Speech 226
  - Lesson 2: Sentence Structure 227
  - Lesson 3: Coordination and Subordination 228
  - Lesson 4: Sentence Boundaries 230
  - Lesson 5: Modifiers 235
  - Lesson 6: Verbs 237
  - Structure Unit Quiz 239
  - Lesson 7: Possessive Determiners 240

Lesson 8: Pronouns 241
Lesson 9: Subject Verb Agreement... 242
Usage Unit Quiz... 245
Lesson 10: End of Sentence Punctuation 246
Lesson 11: Within Sentence Punctuation.. 247
Lesson 12: Items in a Series.. 249
Lesson 13: Possessives.. 250
Lesson 14: Restrictive and Nonrestrictive Punctuation... 252
Lesson 15: Unnecessary Punctuation 255
Punctuation Unit Quiz.. 258
Lesson 16: Transitions 259
Lesson 17: Rhetorical Synthesis 260
Expression Unit Quiz.. 261

Unit 1: Building a Foundation (Grammar Vocabulary)

Lesson 1: Basic Parts of Speech Overview

Nouns are words that name people, places, things, and abstract ideas (e.g., *Minh, girl, dog, Paris, freedom, kindness*).

1) **Common nouns** are general nouns that don't refer to specific people, places, things, and ideas.
2) **Proper nouns** refer to specific people, places, things, and ideas.

Common Noun Examples	Proper Noun Examples
author	Jules Verne
restaurant	Pete's Pizza
building	Eiffel Tower
person	Kenny
president	President of the United States

Pronouns are words that stand for nouns.

1) **Personal pronouns** refer to people, things, places, and ideas.
   - **He** wrote a research paper.

"He" refers to a specific male.

   - Shiloh saw **it** in the window.

"It" refers to something that is not a person, such as an item or an animal.

Personal Pronouns are classified by **person** and **number**.

Point of view	Singular (one)	Plural (two or more)
First Person (the speaker)	I/me	we/us
Second Person (the audience)	you	you
Third Person (all others)	he/him she/her it	they/them

2) **Reflexive pronouns** are followed by "self" or "selves" *(myself, yourself, himself, herself, ourselves, themselves, itself)*. These are used when the subject and object of the verb are the same thing (the performer of the action and the recipient of the action are the same).
- Reflexive: Ari bought **herself** a shirt.

Ari is both the person who bought the shirt and the recipient of the shirt.

Reflexive pronouns can also act as intensive pronouns. An intensive pronoun emphasizes the noun to which it refers.
- Abby wrote the book **herself.**

"Herself" is not used as a substitute for a specific noun. It emphasizes that Abby was the person who wrote the book.

- That infraction **itself** won't disqualify him from playing.

"Itself" emphasizes the infraction, but it is not used as a substitute for any specific noun.

3) **Possessive pronouns** show ownership *(mine, yours, hers, his, ours, theirs)*.
- The money on the counter is **hers.**
- The time is **yours** to use as you wish.

4) **Indefinite pronouns** don't stand for any specific person, thing, or amount.

Singular Indefinite Pronouns

another	little
anybody	much
anyone	neither
anything	nobody
each	no one
either	nothing
enough	one
everybody	other
everyone	somebody
everything	someone
less	something

- Can you give me **something** for my headache?
- **One** might disagree with that assessment.

Plural Indefinite Pronouns

both	others
few/fewer	several
many	they

- **Both** are good options.
- **Several** are located there.

Indefinite Pronouns That Take Plural and Singular Forms

all	any	more/most
none	some	such

- There are **none** for you to take home.
- **Some** are still waiting.

5) **Demonstrative pronouns** (*this, these, that, those*) stand for specific nouns.
   - I read about **that**.
   - Put **those** away!

Adjectives are words that modify, or describe, nouns (e.g., *big, wealthy, smart, generous*). Questions answered by adjectives include the following:

1) What kind?
   - An **old** house.
   - A **gym** membership.

2) How many?
   - **Five** horses.
   - I have a **few** books.

3) Which one? When demonstrative pronouns precede nouns, they act as demonstrative adjectives.
   - **This** calendar is from last year.
   - **These** people are friendly.

4) Whose? Possessive adjectives include *my, your, his, her, our, their*, and *its*.
   - **Darcy's** dress is over there.
   - **My** locker is on the top row.

Verbs are words that indicate action or states of being.

1) **Action verbs** indicate what nouns do.
   - I **gave** him a gift.
   - He **dove** off the diving board.

2) **Linking verbs** provide information about a noun. Specifically, they express states of being (*be, appear, seem, feel, remain, taste, smell, sound, look, etc.*).
   - The plate **is** on the table.
   - You **are** thirsty.
   - The task **seems** easy.
   - The pillow **feels** soft.
   - You **look** cold.

3) **Helping verbs** are verbs that are paired with action verbs in sentences.
    a. **Primary helping verbs** are generally variations of the words "be" (*am, is, are, was, were*), "do" (*do, does, did*), and "have" (*have, has, had*).
        - He **is** going to the movies.
        - She **did** know about the plan.
        - I **have** not revealed your secret.

    b. **Modal helping verbs** modify the main verb's meaning to express possibility, permissibility, obligation, ability, probability, desire, or necessity (*can, could, may, might, will, would, shall, should, must, ought*).
        - Possibility: He **might** call you.
        - Permissibility: You **may** enter.
        - Ability: She **can** read in three different languages.
        - Obligation: We **ought to** follow the rules.
        - Necessity: You **must** stay calm.
        - Desire: I wish you **would** listen to your mother.
        - Probability: The plan **should** go as expected.

Verbs are **conjugated** (change form) depending on the **subject** of the sentence and the **tense** of the verb. The subject is the noun performing the action of the verb or whose state of being is described. The tense is the time period in which the verb is acting.

When a regular verb refers to something happening in the present, add an "-s" at the end of the verb when the subject is **singular** and in the **third person**. In most cases, if a verb ends in "-y," change the "-y" to "-ies" for third person singular subjects.

I walk.	I study.
You walk.	You study.
He/She **walks.**	He/She **studies.**
We walk.	We study.
They walk.	They study.

When a regular verb refers to an action happening in the past, add "-ed" to the end of the verb. For verbs ending in "-y," change the "-y" to "-ied."
- I/You/He/She/We/They **walked.**
- I/You/He/She/We/They **studied.**

The verb "to be" is irregular in both the present and past tense.

Present	Past
I am.	I was.
You are.	You were.
He/She is.	He/She was.
We are.	We were.
They are.	They were.

Irregular verbs do not conjugate normally. In some cases, they change form in the past tense.
- Irregular Present: I **buy** groceries.
- Irregular Past: I **bought** groceries.

Some irregular verbs change form in the perfect tenses (tenses where the verb is preceded by *have*, *has*, or *had*). The perfect tense also applies when "not" follows *have*, *has*, or *had*.
- Regular Verb: We **argued**/We **have argued**.
- Irregular Verb: The bell **rang**/The bell **has rung**.

Some Common Irregular Verbs

Verb	Past	Perfect (has, have, had + verb)
Begin	Began	Begun
Blow	Blew	Blown
Break	Broke	Broken
Choose	Chose	Chosen
Come	Came	Come
Draw	Drew	Drawn
Drink	Drank	Drunk
Drive	Drove	Driven
Eat	Ate	Eaten
Fall	Fell	Fallen
Forgive	Forgave	Forgiven
Freeze	Froze	Frozen
Give	Gave	Given
Go	Went	Gone
Grow	Grew	Grown
Know	Knew	Known
Ride	Rode	Ridden
Ring	Rang	Rung
Rise	Rose	Risen
Run	Ran	Run
See	Saw	Seen
Shake	Shook	Shaken
Sing	Sang	Sung
Sink	Sank	Sunk
Speak	Spoke	Spoken
Steal	Stole	Stolen
Swim	Swam	Swum
Take	Took	Taken
Write	Wrote	Written

Adverbs are words that modify verbs, adjectives, or other adverbs. Adverbs often end in "–ly" (e.g., *strongly, kindly, newly, and beautifully*).
- He thought **carefully** about his decision.

The adverb "carefully" modifies the verb "thought."

- He ran **very fast.**

The adverb "fast" modifies the verb "ran," and the adverb "very" modifies the adverb "fast."

- It is **terribly** cold outside.

The adverb "terribly" modifies the adjective "cold."

Prepositions are words that show relationships of time and place. They also can reveal more details about a noun.

Relationships of Time (prepositions in **bold**)	Relationships of Place (prepositions in **bold**)	Details about a noun (prepositions in **bold**)
<ul><li>I will call you **by** 2:00.</li><li>Let's reconvene **on** Wednesday.</li><li>The festival happened **during** the night.</li></ul>	<ul><li>I walk **to** the mall.</li><li>The iPad is **in** my hand.</li><li>The markings **along** the trail were bright yellow.</li></ul>	<ul><li>The experience **of** skydiving is thrilling.</li><li>The anecdote **about** the sea turtles amused the children.</li><li>The agenda **for** the conference is posted online.</li></ul>

Common Prepositions

about	before	for	onto	under
above	behind	from	opposite	underneath
across	below	in	outside	unlike
after	beneath	inside	over	until
against	beside	into	past	upon
along	between	like	since	via
among	beyond	of	through	with
as	by	off	toward	within
at	except	on	towards	without

A **phrase** is a group of words that functions as a single part of speech.

1) **Prepositional phrases** are strings of words beginning with a preposition. They often act as adjectives or adverbs.
   - He delivered the speech **with confidence**.

"With confidence" modifies the verb "delivered."

   - The increase **in prices** was concerning.

"In prices" modifies the noun "increase."

2) **Participial Phrases** are phrases that contain participles, verbs functioning as adjectives. The **present participle** ends in "-ing" (e.g., *parking, writing, winning*) and the **past participle** typically ends in "-ed," "-en," "-d," "-n," or "-t" (e.g., *quoted, written, known, bent*).

   - **Having succeeded in cracking the code,** the cryptologist was pleased with his accomplishment.

The participial phrase modifies the noun "cryptologist."

   - **Located between the café and the laundromat**, the supermarket attracts a lot of customers.

The participial phrase modifies the noun "supermarket."

Sometimes a participial phrase will appear at the end of a sentence.
   - The company experienced a major setback after the scandal, **losing even its most loyal customers.**

The participial phrase modifies the noun "company."

3) **Appositives** are words or phrases that rename a noun or pronoun.
   - My uncle, **a man of few words,** shocked everyone with his friendly behavior at the party.

The appositive "a man of few words" functions as a noun that renames "my uncle."

   - The experimental group, **or treatment group**, is exposed to a drug during clinical trials. On the other hand, the control group receives a placebo.

The appositive "treatment group" is another term for the "experimental group."

Drill 1

For questions 1-20, select the part of speech of each underlined word or phrase.

1. The article included many <u>advanced</u> words.
   A) pronoun
   B) adjective
   C) adverb
   D) preposition

2. I was <u>thoroughly</u> impressed by your analysis.
   A) noun
   B) adjective
   C) verb
   D) adverb

3. The snow <u>is</u> falling quite rapidly.
   A) preposition
   B) noun
   C) verb
   D) adverb

4. The students had a discussion <u>about economic policy</u> that lasted for several hours.
   A) noun
   B) participial phrase
   C) prepositional phrase
   D) appositive

5. What did <u>they</u> tell you about the competition?
   A) noun
   B) pronoun
   C) preposition
   D) verb

6. Vanna has <u>six</u> rings in her jewelry box.
   A) noun
   B) pronoun
   C) adjective
   D) adverb

7. Howard examined the slide <u>himself</u>.
   A) preposition
   B) adverb
   C) adjective
   D) pronoun

8. Please <u>introduce</u> me to your friend.
   A) noun
   B) verb
   C) adverb
   D) pronoun

9. <u>Smoke</u> was coming out of the chimney.
   A) noun
   B) pronoun
   C) adjective
   D) adverb

10. There is a box <u>underneath</u> the couch.
    A) preposition
    B) noun
    C) pronoun
    D) verb

11. We have a special <u>bond</u>.
    A) noun
    B) preposition
    C) verb
    D) adjective

12. You solved the puzzle <u>extremely</u> quickly.
    A) adjective
    B) adverb
    C) preposition
    D) verb

13. I went <u>to</u> your house last night.
    A) adverb
    B) preposition
    C) pronoun
    D) verb

14. <u>Working for days on end</u>, Delia finally finished the paper.
    A) appositive
    B) participial phrase
    C) prepositional phrase
    D) adjective

15. My dog, an energetic creature, loves to play fetch.
    A) participial phrase
    B) prepositional phrase
    C) appositive
    D) adjective

16. The need for improved working conditions was the subject of the petition.
    A) prepositional phrase
    B) adverb
    C) participial phrase
    D) appositive

17. The heat of vaporization, or heat of evaporation, is the amount of heat required to change a quantity of a liquid into a gas without a change in temperature.
    A) preposition
    B) adverb
    C) verb
    D) appositive

18. I am quite concerned about your behavior.
    A) adjective
    B) adverb
    C) noun
    D) pronoun

19. He is so gullible; he will believe anything you tell him.
    A) noun
    B) adverb
    C) preposition
    D) pronoun

20. Renowned for its unintended tilt to one side, the Leaning Tower of Pisa is a freestanding bell tower in Italy.
    A) prepositional phrase
    B) participial phrase
    C) appositive
    D) noun

For questions 21-32, select the correct verb form.

21. They _____ about everything.
    A) complain
    B) have complain
    C) complains
    D) complaining

22. Miriam _____ about that all the time.
    A) talk
    B) have talk
    C) has talks
    D) talks

23. The application process has _____
    A) begin.
    B) began.
    C) begun.
    D) beginning.

24. We have _____ the artifact carefully.
    A) examine
    B) examines
    C) examining
    D) examined

25. You _____ responsible for knowing that information.
    A) is
    B) are
    C) am
    D) was

26. Kelly had _____ the glass.
    A) broke
    B) break
    C) broken
    D) breaks

27. I have _____ for one mile.
    A) swum
    B) swim
    C) swam
    D) swimming

28. Craig____ not telling the truth.
    A) were
    B) was
    C) be
    D) being

29. Have you____ your homework?
    A) did
    B) do
    C) does
    D) done

30. I have _____ on an excursion through New Zealand.
    A) go
    B) went
    C) gone
    D) going

31. We have not_____ here before.
    A) drove
    B) drive
    C) drived
    D) driven

32. The batteries had_____ out of power before the exam, so he had to borrow a calculator.
    A) ran
    B) run
    C) runs
    D) running

Lesson 2: Sentence Structure Basics

A **main (independent) clause** has all the elements of a complete sentence.
A **complete sentence** contains a subject and a predicate verb, and it expresses a complete thought.
- A **subject** is the noun that performs an action or whose state of being is described.
- A **predicate verb** is a word that indicates what the subject is doing or reveals information about the occurrence of something or the subject's state of being.

- Independent Clause: Dan ran on the boardwalk.

The subject is "Dan," and the predicate verb is "ran." The sentence expresses a complete thought, so it is an independent clause.

- Independent Clause: He was at the concert.

The subject is "he," and the predicate verb is "was," which expresses the subject's state of being. The sentence expresses a complete thought.

Many predicates also contain **objects** on which verbs act. **Direct objects** can be thought of as recipients of actions, and **indirect objects** (if they exist) receive the direct object.
- Willy gave Claude a new bike.
- Polly enjoys comic books.

In the first example, the subject is "Willy," the performer of the action. The direct object is "a new bike," the item Claude received. Claude himself is the indirect object. "Gave Claude a new bike" is the predicate. In the second example, "Polly" is the subject (who the sentence is about). "Comic books" is the direct object (the recipient of Polly's enjoyment). "Enjoys comic books" is the predicate with the verb "enjoys."

A **dependent clause (subordinate clause)**, like an independent clause, contains a subject and a verb. *Unlike an independent clause*, a dependent clause does not express a complete thought. Put another way, a dependent clause cannot stand alone as a complete sentence. A dependent clause connected to an independent clause forms a complex sentence.
- Dependent Clause: **Even though** I was tired.

The above clause is dependent because it cannot stand alone.

- Complete Sentence: I was tired.

Removing "even though" generates an independent clause.

- Complete Complex Sentence: **Even though** I was tired, I still attended the party.

When the dependent clause is connected to an independent clause, the sentence becomes complete.

While you are not responsible for identifying the types of dependent clauses by name, it is useful to know some of the different forms dependent clauses take. The dependent clause in each sentence is in **bold**.

1) **Adverbial clauses** are dependent clauses that function as adverbs. They answer questions such as "why?," "how?," "where?," "when?," "to what extent/degree?," "under what conditions?," and "with what goal/result?"
   - Cause: **Since it was raining,** she wore boots.
   - Purpose: I practiced **in order to improve my skills.**
   - Place: **Wherever there is trouble,** Carl is found.
   - Time: I listened to music **while I exercised.**
   - Condition: **Unless you follow the recipe precisely,** the cake will not come out edible.
   - Concession: **Although I wanted to attend the event,** I had another obligation.
   - Degree: I studied **until I memorized the material.**

Common words found in adverbial subordinate clauses include *after, although, as, as soon as, because, before, even though, given that, if, in order to, once, provided that, since, though, unless, until, when, whenever, wherever, whether,* and *while.*

2) **Relative (adjective) clauses** are dependent clauses that function as adjectives. They answer questions such as "what kind?" and "which one?" They include relative pronouns *(who, which, whose, that, whom)* and relative adverbs *(when, where, why).*
   - The convention was attended by people **who like comic books.**
   - I liked the shirt **that had green stripes.**
   - I attended the university, **where I studied philosophy.**
   - Yesterday is **when I read the book.**

3) **Noun clauses** are clauses that stand for nouns. They function similarly to personal pronouns. Common pronouns included in noun clauses are *that, whichever, whatever, whoever,* and *whomever.*
   - **Whoever was at the game** had a good time.
   - I will eat **whatever you recommend.**
   - **That you called in advance** was important.

Note that the word "that" can sometimes mean "the fact that" when it begins a sentence. In this case, "the fact" was important.

Miscellaneous

1) **"Verb + That" clauses** occur when "that" follows a verb used to report something (e.g., *say that, admit that, indicate that, note that*) or a verb used to show a mental process (*wish that, hope that, believe that, think that, feel that*).
   - Adriano *said* **that he was sorry.**
   - We *noted* **that the study had a small sample size.**
   - Franca *admitted* **that she was lying.**

The above examples above report on states of affairs.

   - I *wish* **that you would tell me the truth.**
   - Bela's professor *hopes* **that she enjoys learning linear algebra.**
   - You *think* **that you are an expert on rap music.**

The above examples report on mental processes.

2) **"Adjective + That" clauses** occur when "that" follows an adjective, often to report opinions or feelings.
   - I am *certain* **that you are a fine candidate for the job.**
   - It is *important* **that people listen to the advice of those with more wisdom.**
   - Pia is *happy* **that she won a prize for her rhubarb pie at the country fair.**

The above examples report on opinions and emotions of the speaker or the subject.

Sentence Types

Now that you are familiar with independent and dependent clauses, we will briefly touch on the three most basic types of sentences. This will make mastering some of the material in later chapters a little easier, especially as we dive into fragments, run-ons, and punctuation.

1) **Simple Sentence:** A simple sentence is a sentence that contains **one independent clause** and **no dependent clause**. They may contain phrases, however (see the first lesson for common phrase types: prepositional, appositive, participial). Examples of simple sentences are shown below.
   - Sanjay loves completing tangram puzzles.
   - The ocean looks peaceful this time of day.
   - Kali went to the lecture, hoping to learn more about astronomy.

All the sentences have one independent clause and no dependent clauses. Note that "hoping to learn more about astronomy" in the last sentence is a participial phrase, not a dependent clause.

> *A subtle distinction*: Phrases are similar to dependent clauses in that they cannot stand alone, meaning they must be connected to an independent clause in order for a sentence containing a phrase to be complete. A key difference is that dependent clauses **usually** have a subject and a verb while phrases need not have both. The table of contrasting examples below illustrates this more concretely. For each pair along each row, pay attention to the differences in the underlying grammatical structure despite similar surface features in terms of content.
>
> | Phrase | Dependent Clause |
> |---|---|
> | Yielding the right of way. | While Deshawn yielded the right of way. |
> | A loyal friend. | That she is a loyal friend. |
> | Wanting to work together. | Because we want to work together. |

2) **Complex Sentence**: A complex sentence contains one independent clause and **one dependent clause**. The dependent clauses below are in bold.
   - **While the author had strong sales,** her works were not well received by critics.
   - Xavier studied at the local university, **where he received a degree in art.**

3) **Compound Sentence:** A compound sentence contains **two independent clauses**. The independent clauses are often connected by a FANBOYS conjunction (these conjunctions include the following: *for, and, nor, but, or, yet,* and *so*) following a comma. Each independent clause is underlined, and each FANBOYS conjunction is bolded.
   - <u>Paulina was overwhelmed by her math homework</u>, **so** <u>she took a break.</u>
   - <u>Miss Xiao enjoys gardening</u>, **and** <u>she runs a botany club in her town.</u>

Alternatively, semicolons can also separate independent clauses in compound sentences, as we will study in Lessons 3 and 4.
   - The venue for Kailash's birthday party was **magnificent**; however, some of her guests felt it was too fancy.
   - Costa Rica has a thriving tourism **industry**; visitors can enjoy its beautiful beaches, botanical gardens, national parks, and cloud forests.

Drill 1

Part 1: Identify whether each clause is independent (I) or dependent (D).

Clause	Write (I) or (D)
1. Because the explanation was so long.	
2. The giraffe eats.	
3. That is an interesting fact.	
4. That you think the speech was good.	
5. Whichever one you choose.	
6. Whom the detective interviewed.	
7. Which was on the table next to the napkins.	
8. We dialed the number.	
9. In order that they improve their odds of being chosen.	
10. Once the decision was made.	
11. Where I discovered my talent.	
12. The tea is excellent.	
13. Unless you decide to change your mind.	
14. Whatever is going to make you happy.	
15. It is intriguing.	
16. Who attempted to contact me yesterday.	
17. While we went hiking in the rain.	
18. I enjoyed the show.	
19. We should celebrate.	
20. Until you scan the document.	

Part 2: Identify if each sentence is simple (S), compound (CD), or complex (CX).

21. While Ximena loves studying European history, she found the reading load excessive.

22. Ichiro is an avid outdoorsman, and he frequently goes on hiking expeditions with his friends.

23. We wanted you to attend the college information session, but you insisted you play video games instead.

24. Daniela was overwhelmed by the chaotic bustle of the big city.

25. Although the two populations of moss share a common ancestor, they are on their way to diverging into distinct species.

26. Eli's grandma will not let him have dessert until he finishes his lima beans.

27. The results of the experiment were not statistically significant, so the scientist failed to reject the null hypothesis.

28. Unless property values decline, Harrison will not buy a condo in that neighborhood.

29. Having wanted to go skydiving for many years, Kiel finally achieved his goal.

30. It was not surprising Landy did not get hired for his dream job, as he lacked the requisite experience and educational credentials.

Lesson 3: Coordination and Subordination

Coordinating and Correlative Conjunctions

Coordinating conjunctions, the FANBOYS conjunctions **(for, and, nor, but, or, yet, so)**, connect two equal parts of a sentence (words, phrases, or clauses).

Conjunction	Relationship	Example
And	Continuation Addition	He is kind **and** smart. People will come **and** go into the building.
But, Yet	Contrast	The stew was visually appealing, **but** it had an unpleasant taste. The stew was visually appealing, **yet** it had an unpleasant taste.
Or	Alternative (when at least one alternative is true or happens)	I will order either the chicken **or** the fish.
Nor	Alternative (when each alternative is untrue or does not happen)	I will not eat the chicken, **nor** will I eat the fish.
So	Effect (result)	I was cold, **so** I put on a jacket.
For	Cause	I put on a jacket, **for** I was cold.

Note: "Nor" is used instead of "and" when the noun or pronoun in the second independent clause follows a helping verb (e.g., *do, did, can, could, will, would*).

- I did not eat, **and** I did not drink.
- I did not eat, **nor did I** drink
- I will not go today, **and** I will not go tomorrow.
- I will not go today, **nor will I** go tomorrow.

When **FANBOYS** conjunctions connect independent clauses, a compound sentence is made. For compound sentences, a comma must precede the conjunction.

Simple Sentences with Compound Subjects	Simple Sentences with Compound Objects	Simple Sentences with Compound Predicates	Compound Sentences
• My aunt **or** my uncle will give me a ride. • Bandicoots **and** Australian possums are marsupial omnivores.	• Feng will cook chili **or** pasta. • I will lend you a protractor **and** a calculator.	• We will go kayaking on the lake **and** surfing in the ocean. • They will be gracious to their friends **but** cold to their rivals.	• I will fly to Ireland, **or** I will take a cruise to Alaska. • Alvaro prepared hard, **yet** he still doubted himself.

Note how only in the last column did the conjunctions connect two independent clauses.

Correlative conjunctions appear in word pairs and connect equal grammatical items (words, phrases, clauses).
1) either…or
   - We will watch **either** a comedy **or** an action movie.

2) neither…nor
   - The explanation was **neither** accurate **nor** intelligible.

3) not only…but also
   - **Not only** do I think you made a great impression at the meeting, **but** I **also** think you will be given many exciting opportunities in the future.

4) both…and
   - Golden Retrievers are known for being **both** gentle **and** friendly.

5) whether...or
   - I wasn't sure **whether** you would attend the lecture **or** listen to the recording.

6) at once...and
   - The drink is **at once** refreshing **and** delightful.

7) between…and
   - The competition was **between** the juniors **and** the seniors of the high school.

Drill 1: Select the coordinating conjunction or correlative conjunction that most logically completes the text.

1. Venture capitalists provide funding to startup companies,____ they help these companies grow in the process.
   A) and
   B) or
   C) nor
   D) for

2. Despite its name, a kangaroo-rat is neither a kangaroo____ a rat.
   A) or
   B) and
   C) nor
   D) but

3. We will either go to the park___ do a jigsaw puzzle.
   A) and
   B) or
   C) but
   D) nor

4. Kristina complained that she had a headache,____ she decided to rest until she felt better.
   A) but
   B) so
   C) and also
   D) yet

5. Ben did not want to go on the roller coaster,____ did he want to ride the carousel.
   A) and also
   B) and
   C) nor
   D) yet not

6. The professor claims that the artist avoids tackling social issues in her work,____ some critics believe that her paintings subtly criticize the social order.
   A) so
   B) and
   C) for
   D) yet

7. Cleo had to sell her house, ___ she got a new job in a different state.
   A) yet
   B) but also
   C) or
   D) for

25

8. Sandy was required to complete forty hours of community service,___ she volunteered at a soup kitchen.
    A) or
    B) so
    C) but
    D) for

9. The lecturer was clearly prepared, and he distilled the major concepts discussed in the complicated text,_____ he could have done more to hold his students' attention and promote dialogue.
    A) but
    B) so
    C) but also
    D) and also

10. The documentary about the meat industry was both informative_____ disturbing.
    A) yet
    B) and
    C) nor
    D) and also

Conjunctive Adverbs

Conjunctive adverbs often connect two independent clauses. Within a sentence, conjunctive adverbs follow semicolons when introducing a new independent clause.

- The scientist was praised for conducting a comprehensive study; **however**, some of his colleagues were skeptical of his conclusions.

- The chemicals in the laboratory are extremely toxic; **therefore**, employees are trained in basic safety procedures.

Both sentences contain an independent clause before and after the semicolon.

In addition, a single conjunctive adverb can be set off by commas *in the middle of an independent clause* to create a pause for effect. In such cases, conjunctive adverbs act as **interrupters.**

- Unprovoked wild deer are generally not aggressive towards humans. I do not, **however,** recommend that you approach one.

- There are many ways to become involved in local government. You can, **for example**, create a petition or campaign for politicians who hold your views.

When the conjunctive adverbs above are deleted, the sentences still make sense.

Conjunctive adverbs can **begin** or **end** a sentence for emphasis or dramatic effect.

- All the details about the new company policy were explained in an email. Employees must attend the meeting going over this same information, however.

- Priya met her state senator to advocate for the passage of an educational funding bill. Priya's political activism didn't end with this meeting, though: she also registered voters and organized peaceful protests.

- The leaders of the large corporation were thrilled to land a deal to build a new mall. Nevertheless, they were concerned about the optics of this development, as the mall would replace a beloved historical landmark.

- The weather is known to be quite fickle in Bangladesh. Therefore, you should pack clothing appropriate for a variety of weather conditions before you travel there.

Common Conjunctive Adverbs

Addition	*furthermore, in addition, moreover, also, likewise, besides:* used to show additional information. • I have a dog; in addition, I have a cat. • I was busy during the concert; besides, I didn't want to go anyway.
Contrast	*conversely, on the other hand, by contrast, on the contrary*: used to show opposites. • Sekou is tall; conversely, Clay is short. *however, still*: used to present a fact that is contrary to another or seems to contradict something previously said. • Latasha was born in New York; however, she grew up in Illinois. • Lara campaigned hard for the position of class president; still, this was not enough to get her enough votes to win. *nevertheless, nonetheless:* used to present a fact that is contrary to another **and** that is surprising or unexpected. • Mike was cut from his high school's baseball team; nevertheless, he managed to become the star player of his college's baseball team. *instead:* used to show an alternative. • Don't go on an extreme diet; instead, make healthier choices.
Cause and Effect	*as a result, accordingly, consequently, thus, therefore*: used to show the result of a reason provided in the previous clause. • Pandas only digest a small portion of their food; therefore, they need to feed constantly in order to meet their nutritional needs.
Time	*first, next, now, then, subsequently, thereafter, finally, ultimately, at last*: used to show sequence. • I wrote the essay; subsequently, I edited it. *in the meantime, meanwhile*: used to show actions happening simultaneously. • He is cooking dinner; meanwhile, his brother is playing outside.
Emphasis	*indeed, certainly, of course, in fact*: used to emphasize a more surprising or important point related to a point previously mentioned. • Getting a Ph.D. is no easy feat; in fact, many people spend years in school before completing the requirements of their degree programs.
Example	*for example, for instance*: used to show examples or evidence. • Cell membranes perform many important functions; for example, they protect cells from their surroundings.
Clarity/ Summary	*in other words, that is, all in all, in summary:* used to specify what is meant by an earlier clause. • The teacher is not infallible; in other words, she can make mistakes. *then:* used to show the way something appears in order to sum up a point or to show a conclusion. • Pippa didn't want to reflect on her own responsibility for her team's poor progress because it would cause her too much guilt. Her tendency to deflect blame to her group members, then, was self-serving.

Drill 2: Select the conjunctive adverb that most logically completes the text.

1. Many people mistakenly think that the koala is a bear; _____ it is a marsupial.
   A) therefore,
   B) however,
   C) finally,
   D) additionally,

2. It was snowing all day; _____ the weather was not severe enough to close school.
   A) consequently,
   B) likewise,
   C) in addition,
   D) still,

3. Tony wrote an outstanding research paper; _____ he was given an award and asked to present his findings at a conference.
   A) in other words,
   B) consequently,
   C) despite this,
   D) nonetheless,

4. Some animals that seem innocuous can actually harm humans; _____ magpies, birds that are harmless most of the year, sometimes attack humans during nesting season.
   A) nevertheless,
   B) as a result,
   C) next,
   D) for instance,

5. Charles Dickens made his first trip to the United States in 1842; _____ he recorded his impressions in a travelog.
   A) besides,
   B) otherwise,
   C) subsequently,
   D) therefore,

6. In order to become an expert at playing a musical instrument, you must spend time perfecting your craft; _____ you must spend a significant amount of time practicing.
   A) conversely,
   B) on the other hand,
   C) nonetheless,
   D) in other words,

7. "Strict constructionists" argue that the Supreme Court should be bound by the words and original intentions of the Constitution's framers; _____ "broad constructionists" argue that the Supreme Court should take into account the values of modern times and the needs of the nation.
   A) similarly,
   B) on the contrary,
   C) accordingly,
   D) indeed,

8. E-learning has become an increasingly popular field in the internet age; _____ many educational institutions offer degrees in instructional design and e-learning.
   A) conversely,
   B) likewise,
   C) in fact,
   D) then,

9. The scientist did not expect to encounter so much ridicule as a result of his unconventional hypothesis; _____ he continued to advance his views at academic conferences.
   A) nevertheless,
   B) despite,
   C) furthermore,
   D) moreover,

10. The exercise program has helped many people get into shape. It is still, _____ recommended that you seek approval from a doctor if you have any major health issues before signing up for this program.
    A) in addition,
    B) however,
    C) yet,
    D) despite,

Subordinating Conjunctions

Subordinating conjunctions are conjunctions that make one clause dependent.

When a dependent clause precedes an independent clause, a comma is generally needed.
- **While** I like apples, I also like oranges.

A dependent clause that follows an independent clause does NOT necessarily require a comma.
- I did not speak to the professor **after** class ended.

Common Subordinating Conjunctions

Contrast	*whereas, while*: used to show opposites. • While Bob is tall, Clay is short. *although, even though, though*: used to present a fact that is contrary to another. • Although Latasha was born in New York, she grew up in Illinois. • Even though I had a cold, I did not go to the doctor. *rather than:* used to show alternatives. • Rather than complain, I will make the best of the unpleasant situation. **despite, notwithstanding:* means "without being affected by; in spite of." • Notwithstanding your efforts to cheer me up, I am still sad. • Despite my better judgment, I will heed your advice. *These words are prepositions, but they are sometimes tested with conjunctions.
Cause and Effect	*because, since, as*: used to show a reason for a result. • Since I had to finish my homework, I did not go out with my friends. • She works at the camp, as her name tag indicates. *in order to, in order that, so, so that:* used to show goals. • The scientist spent hours in the lab in order to make a fruitful discovery. • He worked a summer job so that he could make money. *whereby:* means "by means of which or through which." • The students use a system whereby they can communicate electronically. Note that the adverb *thereby* means "by means of that" or "for that reason" and is frequently used before a participle. • Enrico conducted a professional research study, thereby earning his professor's admiration.

Time/Place	*once, before, after, as soon as, by the time*: used to show sequence or timing. • As soon as I get the directions, I will read them. *when, whenever*: used to show timing in which events happen. • Whenever I write an essay, I edit it. *where, wherever*: used to emphasize location. • Wherever you go to school, you will learn a great deal. • I saw Bethel at the mall, where she works. *until:* used to emphasize the time up to when something happens or is possible. • I won't go until you talk to me. *while*: used to show actions happening simultaneously. • While he is cooking dinner, his brother is playing outside.
Condition	*provided that, as long as, so long as, if*: used to show a condition that must be satisfied for something else to happen. • As long as you answer the questions honestly, you will not get in trouble. *unless:* used to introduce a case in which something is made not to be true or valid. • Unless you answer the questions honestly, you will get in trouble. *given that, granted that:* used when judging one thing based on something else being true. • Given that the law was unpopular, it was expected that there would be efforts to repeal it. *even if, even when, whether or not*: used to emphasize a condition that will not change an outcome. • Even if you speak to him nicely, he will give you an attitude. *now that:* used to show a situation that is true and allows for other possibilities. • Now that I have arrived, the meeting can begin.

More Correlative Conjunctions (Word Pairs)

1) no sooner…than
   - **No sooner** had I started working **than** it started snowing.

2) rather…than
   - The earth revolves around the sun in an elliptical orbit **rather than** a circular one.

3) more/less/greater/fewer…than
   - There are **more** people in the swimming class **than** in the cycling class.

4) as…as
   - The writer was **as** capable **as** his contemporaries.

5) so/such...that
   - The author wanted **so** much to make her fans happy **that** she decided to write a sequel.
   - We had **such** a nice time **that** we decided to meet again.

6) not so much…as
   - It was **not so much** a fight **as** a disagreement.

7) until...that (*NOT* until...when!!!!).
   - It was not **until** I arrived at the store **that** I realized I forgot my wallet.

8) just as….so ("just as" means "in the same way that").
   - **Just as** Chopin was a musician, **so** was Mendelssohn.

Drill 3: Select the subordinating conjunction that most logically completes the text.

1. _____ I did not agree with all of Elan's suggestions, I found some of his advice helpful.
   A) Because
   B) While
   C) Unless
   D) If

2. _____ water is heated to a high enough temperature, it boils.
   A) When
   B) Although
   C) Until
   D) In case

3. _____ the experience was frustrating for me at times, I am pleased that it taught me valuable lessons about overcoming adversity.
   A) Though
   B) Since
   C) Just as
   D) When

4. I will accompany you to the museum_____ you remind me to clear my schedule for the day.
   A) until
   B) so
   C) in order that
   D) as long as

5. Beethoven's Ninth Symphony is sometimes called "Choral Symphony" _____ its final movement includes four vocalists and a chorus.
   A) because
   B) even though
   C) in order to
   D) unless

6. It was not until the prototype for the app had been designed _____ the engineer noticed the glitch.
   A) that
   B) when
   C) unless
   D) while

7. The plot of the police drama was not so much copied from an actual news story_____ it was loosely inspired by true events.
   A) while
   B) as
   C) until
   D) although

8. The invention of medicinal penicillin was as important to the treatment of diseases _____ the development of the telephone was to the enhancement of interpersonal communication.
   A) while
   B) though
   C) as
   D) provided that

9. You talked at such a low volume_____ I could not hear you.
   A) although
   B) until
   C) then
   D) that

10. _____Pablo Picasso painted rather somber paintings during his "Blue Period" between 1901 and 1904, he subsequently painted much happier paintings with warmer colors during his "Rose Period" between 1904 and 1906.
    A) Although
    B) Given that
    C) As long as
    D) Since

Drill 4: Select the choice that most logically completes the text while conforming to the conventions of standard written English.

1. The scholar criticized the law not only for its political implications_____ for its constitutionality.
   A) though
   B) but also
   C) despite
   D) and

2. The novel is not only a riveting tale of mystery and intrigue_____ an incisive critique of modern politics.
   A) but
   B) but also
   C) and also
   D) and

3. _____Ghalen is a respected physician, it is no surprise that the other doctors heed his advice.
   A) In order that
   B) Even so
   C) Given that
   D) Despite that

4. I was at once surprised_____ disappointed that you decided not to enter the contest.
   A) but
   B) yet
   C) and
   D) although

5. Just as running requires endurance, _____does boxing.
   A) also
   B) as well
   C) so
   D) and

6. The Luddites were opposed to technological advancements during the Industrial Revolution,_____ they thought the machinery would take jobs away from laborers.
   A) so
   B) yet
   C) thus
   D) for

7. The Yellow Sea is located between the mainland of China_____ the Korean Peninsula.
   A) and
   B) and also
   C) but also
   D) moreover

8. _____the gliding ant can safely glide off the ground after a fall, it can avoid being crushed by animals walking on the ground.
   A) Even though
   B) So
   C) Since
   D) While

9. The singer is not afraid to voice his political beliefs. His latest song, _____ criticized what he saw as abusive government practices.
   A) however,
   B) instead,
   C) for example,
   D) thereafter,

10. Pablo Neruda gained fame for his poetry_____ he was still a teenager.
    A) despite
    B) accordingly
    C) and
    D) while

11. _____you manage to pass the written exam, you will not necessarily pass the class.
    A) Even if
    B) As long as
    C) Granted that
    D) So

12. The disgruntled executive claimed that_____ her best efforts, the company is still struggling to make a profit.
    A) although
    B) yet
    C) even so
    D) despite

13. Aerobic respiration is a process_____ many organisms obtain energy from organic compounds.
    A) from which
    B) whereby
    C) so that
    D) by when

14. _____ his professional responsibilities, Esufunle still has time for his family.
    A) Notwithstanding
    B) Provided that he has
    C) Due to
    D) Given that he has

15. The tree obstructed my view; _____ I was prevented from witnessing the commotion.
    A) however,
    B) despite,
    C) thus,
    D) for example,

16. The actor is known exclusively for being a comedic genius. She recently excelled in a dramatic role and, _____ shocked her fans.
    A) for example,
    B) therefore,
    C) however,
    D) nevertheless,

17. Shannon's family told her not to enroll in law school. She, _____ decided to pursue her law degree anyway.
    A) for example,
    B) thus,
    C) hence,
    D) nevertheless,

18. The administrator received so much pushback for his new policy prohibiting students from bringing their backpacks to _____ he reversed his decision.
    A) class as
    B) class that
    C) class to where
    D) class, yet

Unit 2: Sentence Structure

Lesson 4: Sentence Boundaries

A complete sentence contains a subject and a predicate verb. It also expresses a complete thought. A sentence **fragment** is an incomplete sentence. There are several variations of fragments.

Subject and Verb-Related Fragments

1) **Error: Missing Subject**

If the subject is missing, the result is a fragment.
- Incorrect: Also recommends Claude talk to his guidance counselor.

There is no subject. *Who* also recommends that Claude talk to his guidance counselor? It is not clear from this sentence.

- Correct: Claude's teacher also recommends that he talk to his guidance counselor.

2) **Error: Object in Improper Form**

The object of a sentence (what a verb acts on) must be a noun or pronoun.
- Incorrect: The company had significant **growing.**
- Incorrect: The company had significant **grows.**
- Correct: The company had significant **growth**.

The noun "growth" is the object of "had," not the gerund "growing" or the verb "grows."

3) **Error: Missing Verb**

If the main verb is missing, the result is a fragment.
- Incorrect: The hotel next to the doctor's office.

There is no verb to clarify the meaning of the sentence.

- Correct: The hotel **is** next to the doctor's office.
- Correct: The hotel next to the doctor's office **has** a pool.

4) **Error: Incomplete (Nonfinite) Verb**

If the main verb inappropriately ends in "-ing," replace the verb with one that can act as a main verb. You can also add a helping verb such as "is," "are," "were," or "was."
- Incorrect: Saira **walking** to the store.
- Correct: Saira **is walking** to the store.
- Correct: Saira **walks** to the store.

Past participles (verbs ending in "-ed," "-en," "-d," -t," or "-n") CANNOT act as main verbs unless they are attached to helping verbs.
- Incorrect: The book situated on the desk.
- Correct: The book **is** situated on the desk.

"Situated" describes the book's state of being, so a helping verb like "is" is needed.

- Correct: The man **situated** himself on the bench.

In this case, "situated" functions as the past tense of the action verb "situate," so no helping verb is needed.

Infinitive verbs (verbs preceded by "to," such as *"to run"* or *"to eat"*) cannot act as main verbs. They can create a dependent clause after an independent clause with a main verb.
- Incorrect: Emile **to work** at a private research lab.
- Correct: Emile **left** her job at the university **to work** at a private research lab.

Complete Thought Fragments

A sentence with a subject and a verb does not necessarily express a complete thought.

1) **Error: Dependent Clause Not Connected to an Independent Clause**

When a dependent clause stands alone, add more information to the sentence to complete the thought. Alternatively, remove the subordinating conjunction.
- Incorrect: **Once** Megan arrived home.

Possible Revisions
- Correct: Once Megan arrived home, she went to her room.

The addition of the independent clause completes the sentence.

- Correct: Megan arrived home.

The removal of the subordinating conjunction results in an independent clause.

2) **Error: Relative Clause Not Connected to an Independent Clause**

A relative clause contains a **relative pronoun** such as *that, who, whom,* or *which,* or a **relative adverb** such as *where, when,* or *why*.

Sample Relative Clauses
- **Where** he learned to fish.
- **Who** called me for help.
- **Which** is found in the Midwest.

A verb that is part of a relative clause cannot act as a main verb.
- Incorrect: The person **who biked on the street.**

The verb "biked" is part of the bolded relative clause and cannot function as the main verb.

- Correct: The person **who biked on the street is my neighbor**.

The addition of "is my neighbor" completes the sentence. When the relative clause is removed from the sentence, the result is a complete sentence ("The person is my neighbor.")

- Incorrect: That the judges have tough standards, **which caused the contestants anxiety**.

The sentence has no main verb due to the presence of "which." Note that in this case, "that" means "the fact that."

- Correct: That the judges have tough standards **caused the contestants anxiety**.

"Caused" acts as the main verb when "which" is removed.

3) **Error: Illogical Subordinating Conjunction or Adverb Used**

Be careful when using "where" or "when" to define subjects.
- Incorrect: A regular polygon is **when a polygon has equal sides and equal angles**.

A polygon is a "what," not a "when." No time relationship is indicated.

- Correct: A regular polygon is a polygon **that has equal sides and equal angles.**
- Correct: A regular polygon is a polygon **with equal sides and equal angles**

The first sentence connects the independent clause to a relative clause, and the second connects the independent clause to a prepositional phrase.

4) **Error: Sentence is Not Complete When Nonessential Terms Removed**

Nonessential terms are words, phrases, and clauses (relative clauses, participial phrases, appositives, etc.) that are NOT needed in a sentence. Nonessential terms in the middle of a sentence are typically set off by commas or dashes. The nonessential clauses in the two sentences below are in **bold**.
- The building, **which was recently renovated,** is now open for business.
- The child, **who was wearing a red shirt,** goes to school with my sister.

When nonessential terms are removed from a sentence, the result is a complete sentence.
- Incorrect: The Capitol Building, **which is located in Washington, D.C.,** where the legislature meets.

When the nonessential relative clause ("which is located in Washington, D.C.") is removed, the resulting sentence is not complete. Instead, the sentence contains a subject connected to a relative clause beginning with "where."

- Correct: The Capitol Building, **which is located in Washington, D.C.,** is where the legislature meets.

The above sentence is correct. When the nonessential clause is removed, the result is a complete sentence ("The Capitol Building is where the legislature meets.")

5) **Error: Coordinating Conjunction Follows a Dependent Clause**

A coordinating conjunction should not be used after a dependent clause.
- Incorrect: **While** the presentation was informative, **but** it was not interesting.

"While" and "but" are both contrast conjunctions. Only one is needed.

- Correct: **While** the presentation was informative, it was not interesting.
- Correct: The presentation was informative, **but** it was not interesting.

6) **Error: Relative Clause Follows a Dependent Clause**

A sentence containing a dependent clause followed by a relative clause is not complete.
- Incorrect: **When** I play board games with Stephen, **who** is always very competitive.

There is no independent clause. Either the subordinating conjunction or the relative pronoun should be removed. Alternatively, add an independent clause.

- Correct: **When** I play board games with Stephen, he is always very competitive.
- Correct: I play board games with Stephen, **who** is always very competitive.
- Correct: **When** I play board games with Stephen, **who** is always very competitive, I **have fun.**

The first sentence makes the opening clause dependent and the second independent. The second sentence makes the opening clause independent and the second dependent. The third sentence makes the second dependent clause a nonessential element between commas and adds a new independent clause at the end.

7) **Error: A predicate (main verb + object indicating the subject's action or state of being) follows an independent clause by a comma.**

- Incorrect: Amara studied the owner's **manual, figured** out what was wrong with her car.

There is no clear subject for the predicate "figured out what was wrong with her car."

- Correct: Amara studied the owner's manual **and** figured out what was wrong with her car.

Simply adding "and" makes clear that Amara is the subject. "Studied" and "figured" function as compound verbs.

- Correct: Amara studied the owner's **manual, and she** figured out what was wrong with the car.

This change is slightly different from the first revision. In this case, a comma is added before "and," while "she" is added after "and." In this case, a compound sentence is made by creating a second independent clause. "She figured out what was wrong with the car" could stand alone as a second sentence. When a FANBOYS conjunction connects two independent clauses, a comma is needed before it.

Understanding when to use commas with "and" can be a little confusing, but the chart below can clarify examples of when commas are and are not needed between similar sentences.

Compound Predicate: NO COMMA	Compound Sentence: COMMA
<ul><li>Joel played bassoon in the band **and was** the running back on the football team.</li><li>Loggerhead turtles weigh an average of 250 pounds **and live** primarily in subtropical climates.</li><li>The task was not difficult **but** tedious.</li></ul>	<ul><li>Joel played bassoon in the band, **and he was** the running back on the football team.</li><li>Loggerhead turtles weigh an average of 250 pounds, **and they live** primarily in subtropical climates.</li><li>The task was not **difficult, but it was** tedious.</li></ul>

Miscellaneous

1) When a modifying phrase (participial phrase, appositive, etc.) follows an independent clause, it is acceptable to use a comma.
    - The farmer spent hours working on the farm, an arduous undertaking indeed.

An "arduous undertaking indeed" describes the work that the farmer did.

- The unscrupulous judge was accused of running a **kangaroo court**, a court that ignores the principles of justice and operates dishonestly.

The definition of "kangaroo court" appropriately follows the comma.

Sample Question

> The Navajo Cultural Arts _____ to raise awareness about traditional arts practices in Navajo culture in both educational and community outreach settings, allowing for intergenerational bonding between artists.
>
> Which choice completes the text so that it conforms to the principles of Standard English?
> A) Program, seeking
> B) Program, which seeks
> C) Program seeks
> D) Program to seek

The convention being tested is sentence boundaries. In this case, "Navajo Cultural Arts Program" is the main subject. In order for the sentence to be complete, a main verb is needed. Only Choice C has a main verb, so **Choice C is correct.** Choice A connects a subject to a participial phrase, so this sentence is a fragment. Choice B connects a subject to a relative clause, so this sentence is a fragment. Choice D connects the subject to a dependent clause beginning in an infinitive verb, so this sentence is a fragment.

Drill 1: Select the choice that best completes each blank to conform to standard written English.

1. The Saint Lawrence River _____ part of the boundary between New York and Canada.
   A) forming
   B) being
   C) forms
   D) having formed

2. _____ a great effort to appear impartial.
   A) Made
   B) Is making
   C) She made
   D) She making

3. Sound waves _____ fast through solids because the particles in solids are close together and collide quickly.
   A) traveling
   B) travel
   C) being traveled
   D) have traveling

4. The new mathematics curriculum at the school _____ more innovative teaching techniques.
   A) encouraging teachers to use
   B) have encouraging teachers to use
   C) encourages teachers to use
   D) encouraging teachers using

5. Research has shown that coffee _____ some health benefits, especially when consumed in moderation.
   A) having
   B) has
   C) it having
   D) having had

6. Preventable _____ resources to implement disease control programs are limited.
   A) diseases, especially common in certain places because
   B) diseases are especially common in places where
   C) diseases, being that they are especially common in certain places due to
   D) diseases, especially common in certain places and

45

7. After studying the effects of beams of light shined on metals, scientists _____ that the number of electrons metals emit is proportional to the frequency of the light that is shined on them.
   A) concluding
   B) being concluded
   C) having concluded
   D) concluded

8. Some of Isabel Allende's works, such as *House of Spirits*, _____ elements of magical realism.
   A) incorporate
   B) being incorporated by
   C) incorporating
   D) thus incorporating

9. _____ NASA's Kepler space telescope found a "super earth" located about 180 light years away from Earth.
   A) Using
   B) By using
   C) A team of astronomers using
   D) Having used

10. Booker never took a college mathematics class, _____ advanced calculus.
    A) while he can performing
    B) but he can perform
    C) however, he can perform
    D) as he performs

11. In light of new studies, _____ that parents feed infants foods containing peanuts to prevent them from developing allergies.
    A) doctors recommending
    B) recommend
    C) doctors recommend
    D) has been recommended

12. If enough people disapprove of the initiative, the board _____ give a speech addressing the public's concerns.
    A) members, who will
    B) members, which will
    C) members will
    D) members who

13. A park in Manhattan _____ after James Madison, who was the fourth American president.
    A) named
    B) naming
    C) who was named
    D) is named

14. Electric cars, already available in the United States, _____ to cleaner air in cities.
    A) which contribute
    B) having contributed
    C) and contribute
    D) contribute

15. George _____ before he became president.
    A) Washington, who served as a general during the Revolutionary War,
    B) Washington served as a general during the Revolutionary War
    C) Washington, which served as a general during Revolutionary War,
    D) Washington, serving as a general during the Revolutionary War,

16. _____ outside the doors of the busy bakery, which is known for its delicious cupcakes.
    A) Usually a crowd of people that is waiting
    B) A crowd of people usually waits
    C) Since a crowd of people usually waiting
    D) That a crowd of people usually wait

17. In order to encourage customers to buy their products, a number of stores _____ free gifts to people who make purchases.
    A) which offer
    B) who offer
    C) which offering
    D) offer

18. My grandmother, a long-time educator, _____ me many important lessons.
    A) and she teaches
    B) and she has taught
    C) teaches
    D) who teaches

19. One of the most famous athletes of the twentieth century, Jesse Owens _____ four gold medals for track and field in the 1936 Olympics.
    A) who was known for winning
    B) he was known for winning
    C) was known for winning
    D) who was being known to win

20. Episodes of *The Twilight Zone* _____ from fantasy stories with happy endings to dark morality tales.
    A) which ranged
    B) that ranged
    C) ranging
    D) ranged

21. _____ turns on the illumination to a comfortable level, rotates the objective lens, rotates the eyepiece diopter ring, and adjusts the interpupillary distance.
    A) When the scientist
    B) Since the scientist
    C) While the scientist
    D) The scientist

22. A concerto _____ musical composition for a solo instrument or instruments accompanied by an orchestra.
    A) is when a
    B) being a
    C) which is a
    D) is a

23. The professor, who is passionate about history, _____ in traditional garb for a Civil War reenactment.
    A) dressed
    B) dressing
    C) who dresses
    D) being dressed

24. Philosophic subfields, areas of study that explore fundamental problems, _____ ethics, metaphysics, epistemology, and logic.
    A) and include
    B) include
    C) including
    D) which include

25. During the hibernation period of the Arctic ground squirrel, a species known for its beige and tan coat, _____ sub-zero abdominal temperatures for more than three weeks.
    A) its body can maintain
    B) body maintaining
    C) body can maintain
    D) body maintains

26. Although Van Gogh is widely regarded as one of the most acclaimed _____ he did not gain much fame for his works until after his death.
    A) painters, but
    B) painters,
    C) painters, despite that
    D) painters, yet

27. Because the leaders of the two countries did not speak the same _____ a translator was present during their meeting.
    A) language, therefore
    B) language,
    C) language:
    D) language, so

28. Because yawning increases the oxygen supply to the _____ some researchers believe that one purpose of yawning is to cool the brain.
    A) brain, accordingly
    B) brain, therefore,
    C) brain, so
    D) brain,

29. The Akkadian _____ earliest attested Semitic language, a type of language originating in Western Asia.
    A) language, the
    B) language, it is the
    C) language is the
    D) language, which is the

30. Smoking bans have been passed throughout history, _____ San Luis Obispo, California, became the first city to ban smoking in all public places.
    A) but not until 1990 when
    B) it was not until
    C) however, it was not until when
    D) but it was not until 1990 that

31. That Revanth is an excellent _____ is not debated.
    A) writer which
    B) writer that
    C) writer this
    D) writer

32. The common poorwill is a nocturnal bird that will often pick a spot under a rock or rotten log to _____ practice that can last for up to five months.
    A) hibernate. A
    B) hibernate, a
    C) hibernate; a
    D) hibernate; which is a

33. The archaeologist's research was based on a very small sample of artwork from the ancient civilization and, as a result, _____ many questions unanswered.
    A) leaving
    B) which left
    C) having left
    D) left

34. Testing confirmed that a neurotoxin produced by blue-green algae, not epizootic hemorrhagic disease, _____ responsible for the mysterious elk deaths in New Mexico.
    A) being
    B) was
    C) it was
    D) it were

35. The conductor originally planned on overseeing all of her orchestra's rehearsals, but upon noticing her students' issues playing certain difficult musical _____ bring in a guest clinician to work with the ensemble.
    A) passages, deciding to
    B) passages decided to
    C) passages, she decided to
    D) passages, and deciding to

36. The bell rang at 7:55 every _____ the start of first period for the students at the small rural high school.
    A) morning, signaled
    B) morning. Signaled
    C) morning; signaling
    D) morning and signaled

37. The employees who frequently show up late receive _____ in their pay.
    A) deducting
    B) deductions
    C) subtracting
    D) subtracts

50

Run-On Sentences

Run-on sentences are sentences that contain two or more independent clauses that have been improperly combined.

A **fused sentence** is a type of run-on that occurs when two or more independent clauses are separated by no punctuation. Fused sentences are occasionally tested on the SAT.
- Incorrect: I had never given a speech **before I** was nervous.
- Incorrect: It was sunny **out she** swam in the lake.

The original sentences are fused sentences, as they contain two independent clauses separated by no punctuation.

A **comma splice** is a type of run-on that occurs when two independent clauses are separated by a comma. This is the type of run-on tested more often on the SAT.
- Incorrect: I had never given a speech **before, I** was nervous.
- Incorrect: It was sunny **out, she** swam in the lake.

The sentences inappropriately contain two independent clauses that are only separated by commas.

There are several ways to correct run-ons. Below are some of the most common methods.

1) **Method 1: Create two complete sentences by placing a period between the independent clauses (adjusting the capitalization in the second sentence as needed).**
   - I had never given a speech before. I was nervous.

   - It was sunny out. She went swimming in the lake.

2) **Method 2: Place a semicolon between the independent clauses.**
Note that when a semicolon is used, the clauses before and after the semicolon must be independent. That is, both clauses should be able to stand alone as complete sentences. In some cases, add a conjunctive adverb after the semicolon in order to clarify the relationship between the clauses.

   - I had never given a speech before; I was nervous.
   - I had never given a speech before; **therefore,** I was nervous.

   - It was sunny out; she went swimming in the lake.
   - It was sunny out; **thus,** she went swimming in the lake.

3) **Method 3: Add a subordinating conjunction to make one of the clauses dependent.**
   - **Since** I had never given a speech before, I was nervous.

   - **Because** it was sunny out, she went swimming in the lake.
   - She went swimming in the lake, **as** it was sunny out.

4) **Method 4: Add a coordinating conjunction (*for, and, nor, but, or, yet, so*) after a comma that separates the independent clauses.**
    - I had never given a speech before, **so** I was nervous.

    - It was sunny out, **and** she went swimming in the lake.
    - It was sunny out, **so** she went swimming in the lake.

5) **Method 5: Change one independent clause into a modifying phrase, a phrase that provides more details about a noun.**
    - **Having never given a speech before,** I was nervous.

In this case, the first independent clause is turned into a participial phrase.

    - **On a sunny day**, she went swimming in the lake.

In this case, a prepositional phrase is used to introduce the independent clause.

Conjunctive Adverbs and Run-ons

1) A conjunctive adverb introducing a second independent clause at the end of a sentence **MUST** follow a semicolon.
    - Incorrect: Lucky's painting was a portrait, **however**, Judd's was an abstract.

The sentence contains a comma splice.

    - Correct: Lucky's painting was a portrait; **however**, Judd's was an abstract.

The semicolon appropriately separates two independent clauses.

Reminder: Conjunctive adverbs can appear between commas when they INTERRUPT an independent clause. Notice the differences between the pairs of sentences in the table. Though they are similar in terms of the content they discuss, they are very different grammatically.

Conjunctive Adverb Interrupts an Independent Clause (Between Commas)	Conjunctive Adverb Begins a Second Independent Clause (Between Semicolon and Comma)
Manners are important. You should not, **for example**, disturb someone who is sleeping for no reason.	Manners are important; **for example**, you should not disturb someone who is sleeping for no reason.
The hiring committee was not impressed with Shaun's interview answers. They decided, **however**, to give him the job based on his stellar credentials.	The hiring committee was not impressed with Shaun's interview answers; **however**, they decided to give him the job based on his stellar credentials.

Notice how in the left column, the bolded conjunctions interrupt each independent clause. When the bolded portion is ignored in each sentence, the result is an independent clause (e.g., "You should not disturb someone who is sleeping for no reason.") In the right column, the conjunctions each introduce the second independent clause. The semicolons are needed after the first independent clauses to prevent run-on sentences.

2) When an adverb is put at the end of an independent clause for dramatic effect, introduce any subsequent independent clauses with a semicolon.
    - The art professor gave his students rough guidelines for their final project, but he purposely left the instructions vague, **though;** he wanted to give his students freedom to be as creative as possible without constraining their artistic choices.
    - A study showed that bees were able to learn how to play a version of football by watching other bees demonstrate how to play. The observer bees didn't merely copy what they saw other bees do, **however;** they actually improved on the strategies employed by the demonstrator bees.

Miscellaneous Important Points

1) A coordinating conjunction between two independent clauses **should not** follow a semicolon.
    - Incorrect: Hieroglyphics were a system of writing that used pictures to represent words and sounds**; and** they were deciphered by Jean-François Champollion.
    - Correct: Hieroglyphics were a system of writing that used pictures to represent words and sounds**, and** they were deciphered by Jean-François Champollion.

2) An independent clause **should not** follow nonessential terms that are set off by commas in the middle of a sentence.
    - Incorrect: Herodotus, **who was a Greek historian**, he wrote about the Persian Empire.
    - Correct: Herodotus, **who was a Greek historian**, wrote about the Persian Empire.

The first sentence separates a subject from an independent clause inappropriately. The corrected sentence is complete when the bolded relative clause is ignored.

3) Independent clauses usually cannot function as nonessential terms that are set off by commas. Phrases that contain a main verb with no subject should not be set off by commas.
    - Incorrect: *Saturday Night Live*, **it is a television show known for its comedic sketches**, has entertained audiences for decades.
    - Incorrect: *Saturday Night Live*, **is a television show known for its comedic sketches**, has entertained audiences for decades.

The first sentence uses an independent clause in the middle of a sentence, and the second uses a phrase with a main verb.

- Correct: *Saturday Night Live*, **a television show known for its comedic sketches**, has entertained audiences for decades.
- Correct: *Saturday Night Live*, **which is known for its comedic sketches**, has entertained audiences for decades.
- Correct: *Saturday Night Live*, **known for its comedic sketches**, has entertained audiences for decades.

The first sentence has a nonessential appositive, the second has a nonessential relative clause, and the third has a nonessential participial phrase. The bolded portions interrupt otherwise correct and complete sentences.

4) Creating a relative clause by changing a noun or pronoun to an appropriate relative pronoun *(who, whom, which)* can sometimes eliminate a comma splice.
   - Incorrect: I called my friend, **he** gave me advice.
   - Correct: I called my friend, **who** gave me advice.

The first sentence is a comma splice. The second separates an independent clause from a dependent relative clause by a comma.

5) It is acceptable to only have one comma before the final independent clause in complex sentences in which the opening dependent clause has a compound predicate.
   - While phonics instruction is supported by many reading **researchers and** many schools embrace this practice, others continue to teach a whole language approach to reading.
   - While phonics instruction is supported by many reading **researchers, and** many schools embrace this practice, others continue to teach a whole language approach to reading.

Both versions are grammatically acceptable. The first suggests the two introductory points are equally important. Despite phonics being both supported by reading *and* despite it being embraced by some schools, other schools teach a different approach to reading. The second sentence suggests that the second point ("many schools embrace this practice") is nonessential information that is not as important to the writer's argument. When it is removed from the sentence, a complex sentence remains ("While phonics instruction is supported by many reading **researchers,** others continue to teach a whole language approach to reading.")

6) Creating a prepositional phrase with "of which" (when discussing non-humans) or "of whom" (when discussing humans) before the main verb can sometimes eliminate a comma splice. These phrases often follow indefinite pronouns (*all, both, each, many, most, some, etc.*)
   - Incorrect: The students gave presentations, **most of them** were excellent.
   - Correct: The students gave presentations, **most of which** were excellent.

Adding "of which" makes the second clause dependent, correcting the comma splice.

- Correct: The students gave presentations, **most of them excellent**.

Alternatively, simply delete the verb "were" so that a phrase follows the independent clause. **However, you cannot both delete the verb and add "of which."** "The students gave presentations, most of which excellent" is NOT correct.

Let's look at another example of a run-on, followed by a chart with corrections.
- Run-on (Incorrect): The sports psychologist has ten **clients, all of them are** under age 45. The sentence has two independent clauses separated by a comma.

Method of Correcting	Example
Adjust the punctuation.	- The sports psychologist has ten **clients; all of them are** under age 45. - The sports psychologist has ten **clients. All of them are** under age 45.
Keep the punctuation, and remove the main verb "are."	- The sports psychologist has ten clients, **all of them** under age 45.
Keep the punctuation and main verb, and make the second clause dependent by changing "of them" to "of whom."	- The sports psychologist has ten clients, all **of whom are** under age 45.

Sample Question

Puerto Rican fiber artist Alyson Vega, whose work was described by a reviewer for the *New York Times* as having a "magical effect," frequently uses everyday materials to reflect the beauty and order she perceives in an otherwise chaotic world. In 2019, she constructed a green salad bowl out of fabric, resin, and_____ in 2022, she created a sculpture of a garden in an antique basket consisting of wet felted wool and hand-dyed wool.

Which choice completes the text so that it conforms to the principles of Standard English?
   A) fiber;
   B) fiber, later
   C) fiber, later,
   D) fiber,

Choice A correctly separates what can stand alone as complete sentences with a semicolon. The other choices all result in comma splices. **Choice A is correct.**

Mini Active Learning Activity

For each bolded sentence or pair of sentences, answer the questions that follow (answers may vary; see key for possible responses).

People from all over the state lined up hours in advance for the opening of the new water park, they were not disappointed.

1. Why is the sentence incorrect?

2. Propose at least two changes to the underlined portion that would correct the error.

When a polar vortex is strong and healthy, cold air is kept farther north. When the Arctic polar vortex weakens, part of this low-pressure system can break off; causing temperatures to plummet as far south as Florida.

3. Why is the underlined portion grammatically incorrect?

4. Propose a change to the underlined portion that would make the sentence grammatically correct.

Some of the students presented prototypes for educational interventions grounded in emotion research, others proposed areas for future research in the field, highlighting gaps in the literature.

5. Why is the underlined portion grammatically incorrect?

6. Propose at least two changes to the underlined portion that would make the sentence grammatically correct.

Economic growth, an integral feature of the global economy, has long fascinated scholars; and they have proposed many theories for this phenomenon.

7. Why is the underlined portion grammatically incorrect?

8. Propose at least two changes to the underlined portion that would make the sentence grammatically correct.

One of the sentences below contains an error.

Sentence 1: The game show app proved to be quite popular, in fact, it had over three million subscribers.

Sentence 2: The game show app, in fact, is quite popular.

9. Is the underlined portion of Sentence 1 grammatically correct? Explain why or why not.

10. Is the underlined portion of Sentence 2 grammatically correct? Explain why or why not.

11. Suggest a revision to the underlined portion of the sentence you chose as incorrect.

Although Lila's ideas about how to run her company were met with skepticism by her naysayers, yet she proved them wrong when her unorthodox ideas increased her profits.

12. Why is this sentence incorrect?

13. Propose at least two changes to the sentence that would correct the error.

Drill 2: Select the choice that best completes each blank to conform to standard written English.

1. The talk show host apologized for her on-air _____ many viewers believed the apology was insincere.
   A) gaffe, however,
   B) gaffe; however,
   C) gaffe; but
   D) gaffe; despite the fact that

2. There were several markings along the_____
   A) trail, each was clearly labeled.
   B) trail; each being clearly labeled.
   C) trail, each were clearly labeled.
   D) trail, each of which was clearly labeled.

3. The institute provides funding for budding startup _____ to spur entrepreneurship among young college graduates.
   A) companies, it aims
   B) companies, this aims
   C) companies; as it aims
   D) companies; it aims

4. It has long been unknown why some people are better navigators than _____ researchers in London have recently discovered that the entorhinal region of the brain is responsible for the strength of "homing signals" that give people a sense of direction.
   A) others,
   B) others, but
   C) others, however,
   D) others; yet

5. The novel became an instant_____ and the plot is compelling.
   A) success, the characters are relatable
   B) success, the characters being relatable
   C) success; the characters relatable
   D) success because the characters are relatable

6. Napoleon Bonaparte, whose army suffered a crushing defeat at Waterloo,_____ his throne a few days later.
   A) he abdicated
   B) abdicating
   C) abdicated
   D) and abdicated

7. Famed photographer Edward Ranney is known for his photographs of the Nazca _____ a series of ancient geoglyphs located on an arid plateau in Peru.
   A) lines, they are
   B) lines;
   C) lines,
   D) lines, being

8. _____ on a safari before, I was excited for the adventure.
   A. I had never gone
   B. I never went
   C. Having never gone
   D. Never did I go

9. William "Marcy" _____ ran a ring of corrupt city officials, was known as "Boss Tweed."
   A) Tweed, he
   B) Tweed, who
   C) Tweed, being that he
   D) Tweed

10. There was a delay in the shipment of Roberto's _____
    A) order, the reason is that he did not enter his address correctly.
    B) order, he is not correctly entering his address.
    C) order because he did not enter his address correctly.
    D) order, the address was not entered correctly.

11. Useful in both the home and the workplace, _____ increasingly important.
    A) smartphones, they are becoming
    B) smartphones being
    C) smartphones are becoming
    D) smartphones which are

12. The harlequin filefish has the ability to detect the scent of the coral reefs _____ to avoid detection by predators.
    A) on which it feeds, this trait allows it
    B) that provide food for them, thus, this trait allowing it
    C) that they feed on and this trait is allowing it
    D) on which it feeds, a trait that allows it

13. I opened up the _____
    A) box, after I looked inside, I read the directions for assembling the equipment.
    B) box, after I looked inside; I read the directions for assembling the equipment.
    C) box. After I looked inside, I read the directions for assembling the equipment.
    D) box, and, after I looked inside, I read the directions. For assembling the equipment.

14. Ruth Benedict, _____ that different temperaments are glorified by different cultures.
    A) she was an American anthropologist, argued
    B) being that she was an American anthropologist who argued
    C) an American anthropologist, argued
    D) was an American anthropologist, argued

15. Isak Dinesen was the Danish author of *Out of* _____ 1914 to 1931, she lived on a coffee plantation in Kenya.
    A) *Africa*, from
    B) *Africa*. From
    C) *Africa* from
    D) *Africa,* in the period of

16. _____ his studies on pea plants, Gregor Mendel enhanced scientists' understanding of genetic inheritance.
    A) He is celebrated for
    B) He is being celebrated for
    C) Celebrated for
    D) They celebrated him for

17. The Battle of Verdun was the longest battle of _____ 300 days.
    A) World War I, it lasted
    B) World War I, lasting
    C) World War I, and lasting
    D) World War I; lasting

18. Emily Brontë is best known for her novel *Wuthering* _____ only published novel.
    A) *Heights*. Being her
    B) *Heights*. Which is her
    C) *Heights*, her
    D) *Heights;* and it was her

19. 1925 saw the release of _____ influential silent film directed by Sergei Eisenstein.
    A) *Battleship Potemkin*, it was an
    B) *Battleship Potemkin*; it being an
    C) *Battleship Potemkin*; which was an
    D) *Battleship Potemkin*, an

20. There are 17 species of penguins, _____ live in warm climates.
    A) some of them
    B) some penguins
    C) some of which
    D) some

21. The Angora rabbit, one of the oldest types of domestic rabbits, is known for its silky _____ popular among French royalty in the eighteenth century.
    A) wool, it was
    B) wool and was
    C) wool was
    D) wool and being

22. Lions_____ throughout sub-Saharan Africa, hunting for a variety of prey.
    A) traveling in packs are found
    B) traveling in packs they are found
    C) traveling in packs finding
    D) that travel in packs, where they are found

23. The professional sumo wrestler wore a kimono,_____ is a traditional Japanese garment.
    A) this
    B) it
    C) which
    D) that

24. Memorizing chemical nomenclatures and functional groups is needed to be successful in organic _____ one also needs a deeper understanding of the underlying chemical reactions.
    A) chemistry, however
    B) chemistry, however;
    C) chemistry. However,
    D) chemistry however

25. The park contains several paths, each one _____ for several miles, and they are suitable for hikers and bikers alike.
    A) stretches
    B) stretched
    C) stretching
    D) which by stretching

26. Inspired by tales of how dogs help military veterans cope with trauma, the lawmakers advanced a bill to fund training for service_____ that these dogs will provide veterans and their families with something forward-looking on which to focus.
    A) dogs they believe
    B) dogs, believing
    C) dogs, they believe
    D) dogs; and they believe

27. More people are relying on public transportation and services such as Uber and Lyft. Several studies confirm this shift, _____ that younger people have less interest in automobile ownership.
    A) they show
    B) it shows
    C) showing
    D) shows

28. A survey found that many people believe that private space companies would be _____ they doubt that such companies would minimize human-made space debris.
    A) profitable, however,
    B) profitable, but
    C) profitable,
    D) profitable and

29. Benito decided to visit his brother and cousin, _____ live in New Mexico.
    A) both
    B) both men
    C) both of which
    D) both of whom

30. A crime that carries significant penalties is counterfeiting_____ a form of fraud that has serious societal consequences, such as undermining trust in currency.
    A) money, it is
    B) money, being
    C) money,
    D) money;

31. Westin spent hours researching boutique life science consulting_____ to earn a job at one of them after graduation.
    A) companies, hoped
    B) companies, he hoped
    C) companies, hoping
    D) companies; hoping

32. The spring came early this_____ reservoirs behind dams filled too early and vegetation dried out.
    A) year, this means
    B) year, meaning
    C) year, means
    D) year; meaning

33. Usagi spent many hours volunteering at the local animal _____ she hoped, perhaps somewhat selfishly, that she would find a suitable pet for herself in the process.
    A) shelter: where,
    B) shelter, where,
    C) shelter; where
    D) shelter, where

34. Nadya couldn't decide which of her two favorite gowns to wear to the _____ in her favorite color.
    A) prom; both of which were
    B) prom, both were
    C) prom, both
    D) prom; both

35. Before the experiment began, some subjects were asked to focus on the genders of the faces in pictures they were _____ others were asked to identify the faces' emotional expressions.
    A) shown, however,
    B) shown,
    C) shown, meanwhile,
    D) shown, while

36. Although the workout regimen is_____ it is relatively inexpensive, it requires a vast amount of discipline.
    A) effective,
    B) effective and
    C) effective;
    D) effective, however,

37. While scholars can debate the precise role that the cultural identity of judges plays in judicial rulings, _____ some argue that diversity allows judges to see certain cases from unique lenses that benefit society and the law, most agree that adherence to sound legal principles is crucial to a functioning society.
    A) even so,
    B) and
    C) consequently,
    D) thus,

38. Hedy Lamarr is perhaps best known for her starring roles in many European films during the 1930s, but her talents weren't limited to _____ she was also an inventor, and her work provided the basis for modern cellular phone technology.
    A) acting; however
    B) acting, however;
    C) acting, however,
    D) acting however

39. The students used advanced technology to construct models of biomes, including those of the arctic tundra,_____ them at the science fair.
    A) displayed
    B) they displayed
    C) and displayed
    D) they then displayed

Lesson 5: Modifier Placement

Modifying phrases are phrases that describe nouns. In each example, the modifying phrase is in **bold** and the noun being modified is in *italics*.

Participial Phrases are phrases that contain participles, verbs functioning as adjectives. The **present participle** ends in "-ing" (e.g., *parking, running*), and the **past participle** typically ends in "-ed," "-en," "-n," "-d," or "-t" (e.g., *quoted, written, known, bent*).
- **Walking through the woods,** the *hiker* admired the beautiful scenery.
- **Delayed in its implementation,** the *new curriculum* was not taught in schools for another year.

Adjectival Phrases are phrases that begin with an adjective.
- **Uncomfortable with her boss's unethical request,** *Maura* decided to quit her job rather than comply.
- **Happy with his progress,** *Simian* decided to continue his martial arts studies.

Prepositional Phrases are phrases that begin with prepositions.
- **As a member of the band,** *I* helped compose the song.
- The *children* went to the amusement park, **with the most daring riding the fastest roller coaster.**

Appositive Phrases are phrases that rename a noun.
- *Pinball*, **an activity requiring great skill**, has lost popularity in recent years.
- **One of the best consultants in the electronics industry,** *Ana* was hired to help the fledgling business.
- **A document that indicates the rules of the organization,** *the charter* was signed by the company's founder last year.
- The 18th century saw the rise of the *French Salon*, **a gathering of men and women for intellectual and social exchange.**

Dangling Modifiers

The noun that an introductory phrase describes must immediately follow the modifying phrase in order to avoid a dangling modifier.
- Incorrect: **Wanting to do well on his exam,** every night for a week *Kyle* studied.

The sentence inappropriately suggests that "every night" wanted to do well on his exam.

- Correct: **Wanting to do well on his exam,** *Kyle* studied every night for a week.

The noun "Kyle" correctly follows the participial phrase.

- Correct: Wanting to do well on his exam, *the ambitious Kyle* studied every night for a week.

In this case "ambitious" helps describe Kyle. It is still clear that Kyle is the noun being modified.

- Incorrect: **Selected for their keen sense of smell,** police investigations often use *dogs* to detect crime evidence.

The sentence inappropriately suggests that the police investigations have a keen sense of smell.

- Correct: **Selected for their keen sense of smell**, *dogs* are often used in police investigations to detect crime evidence.

The revision corrects the dangling modifier by clarifying that dogs are being described.

<u>Important Points</u>

1) Incorrect answer choices will often include the possessive form (a noun followed by an apostrophe to show belonging) of the modified noun after the modifying phrase.
    - Incorrect: **Respected for his kindness,** the volunteer's time was spent working with children.

The modifying phrase is supposed to describe the volunteer. As the sentence is written now, it appears that the *time* of the volunteer was respected for its kindness.

- Correct: **Respected for his kindness,** *the volunteer* spent his time working with children.

2) Occasionally, the modifying phrase itself must be changed to correctly modify a given noun. For example, a present participle is sometimes (incorrectly) used when a past participle is needed. Such confusion usually occurs when one noun is acting on another.
    - Incorrect: **Using it to promote relaxation,** *the product* has grown popular in recent years.

In this case, "using it" seems to describe people using the product. Since "the product" follows the comma, the result is a dangling modifier.

- Correct: **Used to promote relaxation**, *the product* has grown popular in recent years.

The modifying phrase describes the product.

- Incorrect: **After electing him as class president,** *Herb* was honored that his classmates supported him.

In context, "electing him" describes the classmates (they were the ones who elected Herb).

- Correct: **Having been elected as class president**, *Herb* was honored that his classmates supported him.

"Having been elected" clearly describes Herb, the person who was elected.

3) When a modifying phrase follows an independent clause, the noun before the comma does NOT have to be the modified noun (though it should be clear which noun is being modified).
    - Incorrect: The *painting* was beautiful, **it complemented** the ambiance of the room.

The sentence above contains a comma splice.

- Correct: The *painting* was beautiful, **complementing** the ambiance of the room.

The second independent clause is changed to a modifying phrase that modifies "the painting."

- Incorrect: *Flying squirrels* glide between trees, **many are found** in coniferous habitats.

The sentence above contains a comma splice.

- Correct: *Flying squirrels* glide between trees, **many found** in coniferous habitats.

The second independent clause is changed to a modifying phrase that modifies flying squirrels. "Many found in coniferous habitats" is a participial phrase, so there is no comma splice.

4) When a relative pronoun *(who, whom, which, that)* or adverb *(where)* follows a comma, it usually must refer to a noun that precedes it (generally the noun right before the comma).

- Incorrect: *Bold colors* were used by the artist in many of his works, **which** made his work visually appealing.

The sentence inappropriately suggests that "which" refers to the works.

- Correct: In many of his works, the artist used *bold colors*, **which** made his work visually appealing.

The sentence correctly indicates that "which" refers to bold colors.

- Incorrect: The photographer went to the *park* every weekend, **where** he took pictures of the scenery.

"Where" can only describe the park. However, it seems to describe the weekend.

- Correct: Every weekend, the photographer went to the *park*, **where** he took pictures of the scenery.

Moving "park" before "where" makes the sentence clearer.

- Correct: *The photographer* went to the park every weekend, **taking pictures of the scenery.**

Changing the relative clause to a participial phrase that describes the photographer also corrects the original error.

Sample Question

> Verena Puehringer-Sturmayr conducted a study to better understand why birds fly in a V-formation. By tagging the northern ibises with GPS trackers, _____
> The team found that flying in V-formation likely takes advantage of aerodynamic principles and conserves the birds' energy during migrations.
>
> Which choice completes the text so that it conforms to the principles of Standard English?
> A) Puehringer-Sturmayr and her team were able to track the location of these birds.
> B) the location of these birds was able to be tracked by Puehringer-Sturmayr and her team.
> C) tracking the location of these birds was achieved by Puehringer-Sturmayr and her team.
> D) these birds' locations were tracked by Puehringer-Sturmayr and her team.

The introductory modifying phrase includes the participle "tagging." This opening phrase describes Puehringer-Sturmayr and her team, as they are the people who tagged the ibises. Thus, "Puehringer-Sturmayr and her team" should follow the comma. **Choice A is correct.** The other choices are dangling modifiers suggesting that the location (in Choice B), tracking (in in choice C), and birds' locations (in choice D) tagged the ibises rather than the researchers.

Mini Active Learning Activity

Answer the questions about each sentence.

Having ascertained that the skincare product did not violate any existing patent protections, consumers would have it determined for them by the company the best way in which to market it to them.

1. The bolded phrase is supposed to describe _____, but as it is written now, it seems to be describing _____

2. Rewrite the underlined portion with an acceptable revision.

Recognizing the importance of having a student body from diverse communities, students from remote communities have been subject to recruitment efforts by many colleges and universities.

3. The bolded phrase is supposed to describe _____, but as it is written now, it seems to be describing _____

4. Rewrite the underlined portion with an acceptable revision.

Noticing that stars in the Andromeda galaxy were moving in unexpected ways, the conclusion of astronomer Vera Rubin was that "dark matter" must exist in the universe.

5. The bolded phrase is supposed to describe _____, but as it is written now, it seems to be describing _____

6. Rewrite the underlined portion with an acceptable revision.

Knowing him as the Great Communicator, Ronald Reagan is often celebrated as a model of effective presidential communication.

7. In what way does the sentence above contain a dangling modifier?

8. How should the underlined portion be changed to correct the dangling modifier?

69

Drill 1: Select the choice that best completes each blank to conform to standard written English.

1. Walking along the path,_____
   A) Elizabeth's shoelaces became untied, which caused her to trip.
   B) Elizabeth's shoelaces became untied; thus, she tripped.
   C) Elizabeth tripped after her shoelaces became untied.
   D) having become untied, the shoelaces caused Elizabeth to trip.

2. Located in a remote part of town, _____
   A) it has been years since the old cabin was last maintained.
   B) years have passed since the old cabin was last maintained.
   C) maintenance on the old cabin has not been done in years.
   D) the old cabin has not been maintained in years.

3. Hired as the chief engineer of the Golden Gate Bridge,_____
   A) Joseph Strauss has been credited with designing over 400 drawbridges.
   B) credit is given to Joseph Strauss for designing over 400 drawbridges.
   C) over 400 drawbridges have been credited with being designed by Joseph Strauss.
   D) the number of drawbridges designed by Joseph Strauss is credited to be 400.

4. Known for his explorations, _____is celebrated for its detail and impact on cartography.
   A) Marco Polo's travelog
   B) the travelog of Marco Polo
   C) Marco Polo wrote a travelog that
   D) the travelog Marco Polo wrote

5. Seeking to safeguard benefits for retirees,_____
   A) a massive spending bill was voted on by the legislature to protect the pension plans of workers.
   B) pension plans for workers were protected by a massive spending bill on which the legislature voted.
   C) votes were cast by the legislature on a massive spending bill to protect the pension plans of workers.
   D) the legislature voted on a massive spending bill to protect the pension plans of workers.

6. _____for his confident demeanor, Tim, a capable spy, shocked everyone when he expressed nervousness about the upcoming mission.
   A) Knowing him
   B) He is known
   C) He has a reputation
   D) Known

7. Large enough to be seen from outer space, _____
   A) Anca Petrescu designed the Palace of Parliament when she was only 28 years old.
   B) having designed the Palace of Parliament, 28 years old was the age of Anca Petrescu.
   C) 28-year-old Anca Petrescu designed the Palace of Parliament.
   D) the Palace of Parliament was designed by Anca Petrescu when she was only 28 years old.

8. Home to famous architectural sites such as the Delphi and the Parthenon, _____
   A) Greece attracts millions of tourists each year.
   B) millions of tourists each year are attracted to Greece.
   C) tourists go in millions to Greece each year.
   D) each year, millions of tourists go to Greece.

9. A calculation tool that was used before the invention of the numeral system, _____
   A) schools today often use the abacus as a teaching aid.
   B) the abacus is still used as a teaching aid in schools.
   C) schools today are still using the abacus as a teaching aid.
   D) used today by schools as a teaching aid is the abacus.

10. _____ to speak at the conference, Jacqueline spent hours preparing a speech.
    A) After choosing her
    B) Having been chosen
    C) They chose her
    D) Choosing her

11. Although competitive and fast-paced, _____
    A) you can learn how to be resilient from the company's environment.
    B) resilience can be learned by you due to the company's environment.
    C) the company's environment can teach you to be resilient.
    D) you become resilient due to the environment of the company.

12. A pioneer in the field of psychology, _____
    A) Sigmund Freud's theory of psychoanalysis remains influential in some forms of therapy.
    B) psychoanalysis, one of Sigmund Freud's theories, remains influential in some forms of therapy.
    C) Sigmund Freud developed the theory of psychoanalysis, which remains influential in some forms of therapy.
    D) some forms of therapy today are influenced by Freud's theory of psychoanalysis.

13. Founded by Maria Montessori in 1907, _____ to provide a stimulating and child-centered education.
    A) the aim of the Children's House in Rome was
    B) the Children's House in Rome aimed
    C) the Children's House's aims in Rome were
    D) in Rome the Children's House was aiming

14. By wearing gloves when walking in the cold,_____
    A) it can better prevent frostbite.
    B) you can better prevent frostbite.
    C) frostbite can be better prevented.
    D) prevention of frostbite occurs.

15. Failing to anticipate the public outcry, _____
    A) the ad run by the company during the Super Bowl offended many people.
    B) the Super Bowl ad that the company ran offended many people.
    C) the company ran an ad during the Super Bowl that offended many people.
    D) many people were offended by the Super Bowl ad that the company ran.

16. _____ biofeedback devices worn on the chest vibrate when one slouches.
    A) Designing it to improve people's posture,
    B) They designed it to improve people's posture,
    C) Designed to improve people's posture,
    D) It was designed to improve people's posture,

17. Yesterday's boring guest lecturer contrasted with_____ was clearly passionate about her field.
    A) today, who
    B) today's lecturer, who
    C) the lecture given today, who
    D) today, the lecturer

18. A chameleon is a master of disguise,_____ effortlessly into its environment.
    A) which blend
    B) it blends
    C) and blending
    D) blending

19. According to a report, a typical washing machine generates 300 loads of laundry per year,_____12,000 gallons of water.
    A) this uses
    B) which using
    C) using
    D) it uses

20. The penguin has a sharp beak, _____ it to eat prey without teeth.
    A) this allowing
    B) which allows
    C) this is allowing
    D) therefore this allows

21. The Amazon rainforest is home to hundreds of species of_____
    A) mammals, some are found in trees.
    B) mammals, some found in trees.
    C) mammals; and some reside in trees.
    D) mammals, finding some in trees.

22. Scientists use various methods to study ancient artifacts, _____ from stratigraphy to radiocarbon dating.
    A) these range
    B) which range
    C) ranging
    D) and ranging

23. Babylon was a city in ancient Mesopotamia,_____ for its hanging gardens.
    A) it was renowned
    B) renowned
    C) who was renowned
    D) being that it was renowned

24. A career field resistant to being replaced by automation,_____
    A) the career prospects for strategy management are favorable.
    B) there are favorable career prospects for strategy managers.
    C) strategy management holds favorable career prospects.
    D) strategy managers have favorable career prospects.

25. Ever since_____ to several ancient nations, cinnamon has been a highly regarded spice.
    A) introducing it
    B) they introduced it
    C) it had been introduced
    D) introducing it

26. A group of flowers was found outside the_____ in rows.
    A) building, which were placed
    B) building, placed
    C) building, it was placed
    D) building, placing it

27. _____ where we watched a comedy show.
    A) We went to the Apollo Theater last year during our vacation,
    B) On our vacation we went to the Apollo Theater last year,
    C) On our vacation last year, the Apollo Theater was visited by us,
    D) On our vacation last year, we visited the Apollo Theater,

Lesson 6: Verb Tense

Verb tense is the time in which a verb is acting. In the introductory lesson, we reviewed the basics of how verbs are conjugated. We will now examine the contexts in which different verb tenses are used.

Simple Tenses

The most basic tenses are the present, past, and future tenses. When determining the most appropriate verb in a sentence, pay attention to clues about the ***time period*** (e.g., *today, yesterday, tomorrow, next week*) to analyze when the sentence took place.

Simple Tenses		
Present Tense	Past Tense	Future Tense
<ul><li>To show a present action or state of being.<ul><li>The house is clean.</li><li>I see the sign.</li></ul></li><li>To show a habitual action.<ul><li>I play baseball weekly.</li><li>He meets me every day after school.</li></ul></li><li>To indicate a future time.<ul><li>The restaurant closes at ten.</li></ul></li><li>To state a general truth.<ul><li>The Super Bowl is always on Sunday.</li></ul></li></ul>	<ul><li>To show a completed action or state of being.<ul><li>He swam one mile.</li><li>Yesterday, she went to the zoo.</li></ul></li></ul>	<ul><li>To show an action that will or won't happen in the future.<ul><li>Tomorrow, I will return her call.</li><li>Starting next month, the restaurant will offer discounts on select items.</li></ul></li></ul>

Perfect Tenses

Perfect tenses are tenses that require the helping verb *have, has,* or *had* followed by a **past participle.** Past participles are verbs ending in "-ed," "-d" "-t," "-n," or "-en" (e.g., *spoken, asked, known, taught*).

Perfect Tenses		
The **present perfect** tense generally describes actions that are currently happening and that started in the past. The present perfect takes the form of *have + past participle* and *has + past participle*.	The **past perfect** tense indicates an action that was completed in the past before another past action or time period. The past perfect takes the form *had + past participle*.	The **future perfect** tense refers to actions that will be completed before another action or time period in the future. The future perfect takes the form *will have + past participle*.
<ul><li>I **have been** studying Spanish since 6th grade.</li><li>He **has written** an article for the newspaper every week since the beginning of the year.</li><li>I **have been** here for three weeks.</li></ul>	<ul><li>After I **had gone** to the show, I received your message.</li><li>We **had completed** the paper by the deadline.</li><li>The students **had had** no previous instruction in computer programming languages before the summer program started.</li></ul>	<ul><li>I **will have finished** my final exams by the end of June.</li><li>He **will have** completed his hike before the storm.</li></ul>

The present perfect is also sometimes used to describe actions that will happen before another action in the future is completed.
- The bus will not leave until attendance **has been** taken.

The present perfect is often used in sentences with the simple present tense or simple past tense to highlight a change over time.
- You **have grown** so much since I last **saw** you.
- The amount of time people **spend** commuting **has increased** in recent years.

The past perfect is often confused with the past tense. Note that the past perfect is used to describe an action COMPLETED before a past event or action, and it is often (but not always!) paired with "before," "after," or "by the time." **Note that "until" is generally used with the regular past tense.**
- Past: Scott **watched** the game **until Mirabella arrived**.
- Past Perfect: Scott **had finished** watching the game **before Mirabella arrived**.

The past perfect is only needed in the second case since Scott completed watching the game (the first event) before Mirabella arrived (the second event). In the first sentence, the first event ended at the same time as the second happened.

Progressive Tenses

The **progressive tense** is used to describe actions that were, are, or, will be in progress. The progressive tense requires the use of a helping verb followed by a **present participle**, participles ending in "-ing."

The **present progressive** tense shows actions in progress now.	The **past progressive** tense shows actions that were in progress.	The **future progressive** tense shows actions that will be in progress.
- Currently, I **am walking** through the botanical garden. - She **is writing** a letter now.	- I **was walking** through the botanical garden last weekend. - She **was writing** a letter yesterday.	- I **will be walking** through the botanical garden later. - She **will be writing** a letter tomorrow.

Modal Verbs: The Case of "Would"

"Would" is a special helping verb that is frequently tested in verb tense questions. Although this word has a lot of different functions, we will review the three most common ones.

1) To show repeated actions in the past.
    - Every weekend, **I would** wake up early to go canoeing on the lake.
    - Each time the student wrote a research paper, he **would** go to the library.

2) To show the future from the perspective of the past.
    - The scientist suggested that her team employ a new methodology so that they **would** get more accurate measurements.
    - The artist worried that people **would** misinterpret her painting's message.

3) To express probability or possibility (**conditional tense**). Note that "will" is used for hypotheticals that have realistic future outcomes. "Would" is used with unreal conditions in the past and their probable results in the past or present (in other words, "what could have happened") or unreal conditions in the present and their unreal results in the past or future (in other words, "what would be different if conditions were different").

Conditional Situation	Example
Hypothetical Future with Probable Outcome	<ul><li>If I save money, I **will** be able to afford the trip.</li><li>If Paola's boss gives her time off, she **will** be able to go to the music festival.</li></ul>
Hypothetical With Unreal Past Condition	<ul><li>Had I saved more money, I **would** have been able to afford the trip.</li><li>Paola **would** have gone to the music festival had her boss let her have time off.</li></ul>
Hypothetical With Unreal Present Condition	<ul><li>If I were better at saving money, I **would** have been able to afford the trip.</li><li>If Paola's boss were more understanding, Paola **would** be at the music festival now.</li></ul>

Switching Verb Tenses

1) A sentence cannot switch between verb tenses without reason.
   - Incorrect: Because I **was** scared, I **scream.**

This sentence inappropriately shifts from the past to the present tense without reason. To correct this sentence, change "scream" to "screamed" so that the entire sentence is in the past tense.

2) Between sentences, verb tense must remain consistent unless there are clues in a sentence that indicate a time shift.
   - Incorrect: During the conference, I **presented** a proposal to the committee. I then **listen** to the committee's feedback.

There is no reason for the sentence to switch to the present tense. "Listened" should follow "then." In order for the present tense to be correct, the writer needs to add more information that clarifies a change in time period.

   - Correct: **Earlier today**, I presented a proposal to the committee members. **Now**, I am listening to their feedback.

The addition of "earlier today" and "now" clarify that there was a time shift.

Miscellaneous Reminders

1) "Would" and "could" are often used with the past tense and are paired with other verbs.
   - Correct: My grandfather **told** me stories so that I **would be** entertained.
   - Correct: I **got** my homework done early so that I **could go** outside.

2) "Can" and "will" are often used in sentences that include the present tense.
   - Correct: My grandfather **tells** me stories so that I **will be** entertained.
   - Correct: I **am doing** my homework early so that I **can go** outside later.

3) When reporting on an action in the past tense, the second verb often takes the present tense form.
   - Incorrect: I **heard** him **said** that he was sorry.
   - Correct: I **heard** him **say** that he was sorry.

Sample Question

> Octavia Butler was one of the most prolific Black science fiction writers of her time, producing seminal works such as *Patternmaster* and *Fledgling* that explored important themes, such as identity, marginalization, and power. Until her writing career took off, Butler _____ fiction at two or three in the morning before heading to her day job.
>
> Which choice completes the text so that it conforms to the principles of standard English?
> A) will write
> B) would write
> C) had written
> D) can write

The sentence describes a repeated action in the past, so the modal "would" is needed. **Choice B** is correct. Choice A suggests that events described will happen in the future. Choice C incorrectly uses the past perfect, which describes actions completed before another action (note that the past perfect would not be used with "until"). Choice D implies that the sentence discusses hypothetical events related to the present.

Drill 1: Select the choice that best completes each blank to conform to standard written English.

1. The amount of time people_____ listening to the radio has decreased since five years ago.
   A) spend
   B) spent
   C) have spent
   D) will spend

2. Painters during the Renaissance in the 1300s_____ an interest in Greco-Roman culture.
   A) revived
   B) have revived
   C) had revived
   D) revive

3. The project_____ completed by the time you arrive next month.
   A) was
   B) had been
   C) has been
   D) will have been

4. According to Chinese records, rice farming_____ over 4,000 years ago.
   A) begins
   B) began
   C) have begun
   D) has begun

5. The morning bell_____ at 7:55 every weekday since the new schedule was implemented.
   A) rang
   B) rings
   C) had rung
   D) has rung

6. Dutch ovens, which are found in many retail stores, _____ in use for hundreds of years.
   A) were
   B) have been
   C) had been
   D) will be

7. Carrie Nation _____ an advocate for abstinence from alcohol before she appeared on vaudeville.
   A) has been
   B) had been
   C) will have been
   D) is

79

8. The claims of the research study _____ disproved by the time the scientist publicly acknowledged his errors.
   A) are
   B) has been
   C) had been
   D) will be

9. They will not be permitted to register for classes until they_____
   A) have paid.
   B) paid.
   C) had paid.
   D) paying.

10. Experts predict that the interest rates of the bonds_____ next month.
    A) rose
    B) rises
    C) will rise
    D) have risen

11. It was not until the 1970s that scientists_____ acid rain as a serious environmental problem.
    A) view
    B) viewed
    C) will view
    D) have viewed

12. There_____ things you can do to determine which summer job is right for you.
    A) are
    B) were
    C) have been
    D) had been

13. When the author was a child, his family _____ a cabin in the woods every summer, inspiring his first novel.
    A) have rented
    B) will rent
    C) would rent
    D) had rented

14. The number of people who report working from home_____ over the past five years.
    A) increases
    B) has increased
    C) will have increased
    D) had increased

15. _____ at the hospital, the patient was given an antibiotic to prevent infection.
    A) After treating the wound
    B) After the wound has been treated
    C) After the wound had been treated
    D) After treating it

16. According to the scientist, the chemical reaction produced a precipitate, which _____ at the bottom of the beaker.
    A) settles
    B) will settle
    C) have settled
    D) settled

17. Aaron decided to run errands so he_____ have to babysit his brother.
    A) cannot
    B) will not
    C) would not
    D) may not

18. After the host of the popular program quit, many viewers_____ concerned that his replacement would not be as entertaining.
    A) are
    B) were
    C) will be
    D) had been

19. The storm produced a large amount of snow, which then _____ on the roads, making conditions treacherous.
    A) pile
    B) piled
    C) had piled
    D) have piled

20. Defying expectations that she would study law, Shiloh instead _____ to become an artist.
    A) chose
    B) chooses
    C) will choose
    D) had chosen

21. The chef argues that people should use dry heat when cooking tender steaks, since other methods_____ steak a less rich flavor.
    A) gave
    B) give
    C) have given
    D) will give

81

22. Although the suspect_____ his role in the crime before DNA evidence was uncovered, he later admitted his guilt.
    A) has denied
    B) will have denied
    C) had denied
    D) denies

23. Some of the author's works deal with issues that seem outdated to contemporary readers, but others_____ relevant in modern times.
    A) remaining
    B) remain
    C) remained
    D) had remained

24. Some people do not adapt as well to stressful situations as others_____
    A) did.
    B) do.
    C) will.
    D) have done.

25. Raja began working as a research assistant for an evolutionary biologist because he thought this position_____ him more competitive for graduate school admissions.
    A) will make
    B) can make
    C) is making
    D) would make

26. Sharonda_____ her friend was a generally trustworthy person until she caught him in an obvious lie riddled with nonsensical contradictions.
    A) had believed
    B) believed
    C) will believe
    D) has believed

27. Since its founding over 30 years ago, the company_____ itself on its forward-thinking mission and quality service.
    A) prided
    B) had prided
    C) has prided
    D) prides

28. Benjamin List and David W.C. Macmillan received the Nobel Prize in Chemistry in 2021 after independently developing a tool _____ molecules using asymmetric organocatalysis, revolutionizing the field of medicine.
    A) building
    B) to build
    C) build
    D) built

Structure Unit Quiz

Shrinking ice caps make it more difficult for polar bears to hunt seals, increase negative human-polar bear interactions on land, and expose young polar bears to more threats due to the weakened integrity of their den sites. Other dangers polar bears_____ include contaminants, such as hydrocarbons, pollutants, and heavy metals.

1. Which choice completes the text so that it conforms to the principles of standard English?

    A) face
    B) having faced
    C) faced
    D) will face

When shopping, why are you drawn to some items and not others? According to some scientists, you may be "programmed" to have positive responses to certain products. Neuromarketing is a field_____ brain imaging and eye tracking technologies to study the brain's responses to marketing stimuli.

2. Which choice completes the text so that it conforms to the principles of standard English?

    A) to use
    B) that uses
    C) uses
    D) it uses

Evidence has emerged that Neanderthals painted on cave walls 65,000 years ago, which was before modern humans existed. Thus, some experts _____ that Neanderthals are the first examples of artists, not humans.

3. Which choice completes the text so that it conforms to the principles of standard English?

    A) to contend
    B) having contended
    C) contend
    D) contending

A 2022 study found evidence that many planets have more water than was previously believed, but it does not seem that this water is free-flowing, as it is on _____ it is likely embedded within rocks.

4. Which choice completes the text so that it conforms to the principles of standard English?

   A) Earth, rather,
   B) Earth, rather;
   C) Earth; rather,
   D) Earth, rather

Joan of Arc was a peasant woman who has since become a patron saint and cultural and feminist icon. Heartened by her faith and sincerity, _____ Because of Arc's influence, the tides turned against the British.

5. Which choice completes the text so that it conforms to the principles of standard English?

   A) the liberation of Orléans that changed the course of the Hundred Years' War occurred when French armies found courage.
   B) courage was found by the French armies to liberate Orléans, changing the course of the Hundred Years' War.
   C) the French armies found the courage to liberate Orléans, changing the course of the Hundred Years' War.
   D) the course of the Hundred Years' War was changed when the French armies found the courage to liberate Orléans.

Enheduanna was a unique figure in Mesopotamian history: she was a priestess who also wrote myths and hymns, employing sophisticated rhetorical devices— techniques that writers use to make their writings more persuasive— such as appeals to logic and emotion. Today, Enheduanna _____ considered the first writer by some scholars.

6. Which choice completes the text so that it conforms to the principles of standard English?

   A) was
   B) is
   C) will be
   D) had been

Sarah Sze is a multidisciplinary artist known for her immersive constructions that make use of household objects. In 2016, she created a multisensory sculpture incorporating flashing lights and clicking objects to capture the flow of information people are inundated with each _____ in 2020, she continued her exploration of time when she made an installation that incorporated video projection displays on a massive structure, giving her construction the appearance of a planetarium.

7. Which choice completes the text so that it conforms to the principles of standard English?

    A) day, later
    B) day;
    C) day and later
    D) day,

Guatemalan-born Luis von Ahn is an entrepreneur and professor known for his pioneering work in crowdsourcing. Considered one of the most important figures in improving the world through modern technology,_____

8. Which choice completes the text so that it conforms to the principles of standard English?

    A) von Ahn cofounded Duolingo, an app that provides free language education.
    B) Duolingo was cofounded by von Ahn, which is an app that provides free language education.
    C) free language education is provided by Duolingo, a company von Ahn cofounded.
    D) as a result of von Ahn cofounding the free app Duolingo, free language education is available.

The theory of embodied cognition—a theory that maintains cognition is fundamentally intertwined with sensory and motor systems—has found support in part from experiments that show irrelevant sensory features of an object affect mental _____ some critics argue that most elements of the theory are either poorly defined or offer few valuable scientific insights.

9. Which choice completes the text so that it conforms to the principles of standard English?

    A) reasoning but
    B) reasoning, however,
    C) reasoning
    D) reasoning, but

Singer Nina Simone initially balked at performing songs that had political themes. When Martin Luther King Junior was arrested in 1963 after taking part in a nonviolent demonstration against segregation, pressure mounted on Simone to use her voice for activism. Ruminating on the advice of trusted confidant and playwright Lorraine Hansberry to use her platform for justice,_____

10. Which choice completes the text so that it conforms to the principles of standard English?

    A) it was then that Simone decided to mix politics with music.
    B) politics was then added to Simone's music.
    C) Simone decided to mix her music with politics.
    D) a decision was made by Simone to incorporate politics into her music.

Scientists are growing alarmed by the changing behavior of bears in Lake Tahoe. These bears normally hibernate during the winter to get through the cold season when food is more scarce, but they have become accustomed to plentiful food supply from human garbage,_____ them to forgo hibernation.

11. Which choice completes the text so that it conforms to the principles of standard English?

    A) this prompts
    B) to prompt
    C) prompted
    D) prompting

The first automatic clothes dryer, developed by African American inventor George T. Sampson, which consisted of a frame suspended over a stove, not only allowed for fast drying of clothes but also protected them from _____ to his invention, people would hang their clothes near open flames, resulting in clothes that smelled smoky and that were covered in soot.

12. Which choice completes the text so that it conforms to the principles of standard English?

    A) fires and prior
    B) fires. Prior
    C) fires, prior
    D) fires prior

When coral reefs become overheated, they experience bleaching events that expel their algae, turn them white, and endanger other organisms in their marine ecosystems that depend on them. Scientists in Australia proposed the possibility of developing technology that can manipulate clouds to be more reflective. Doing so would cool the ocean waters and _____ heat stress on corals.

13. Which choice completes the text so that it conforms to the principles of standard English?

   A) reduces
   B) reduced
   C) reduce
   D) reducing

The Society of Asian Scientists (SASE) is a student-run organization at Texas A&M University, dedicated to bringing together aspiring engineers and scientists to learn about career opportunities. Despite its name, the program is open to students of all backgrounds, who can bond over their love of science while eating Asian food and learning more about different cultures. With only around 30 members upon its founding in 2013, the organization _____ its membership by 2015.

14. Which choice completes the text so that it conforms to the principles of standard English?

   A) doubles
   B) had doubled
   C) has doubled
   D) will double

In her analysis of Toni Morrison's novel *Jazz* (1992), a college student noted that the work "is definitively the story of the City, of the twenties and of jazz, the music that gave voice to the African-American_____ a fitting observation given that the book was set during Jazz Age, a period that saw a flourishing of Black music that helped promote civil rights causes and share poignant stories of the Black experience.

15. Which choice completes the text so that it conforms to the principles of standard English?

   A) experience"
   B) experience,"
   C) experience";
   D) experience" and

In 1922, archaeologist Howard Carter discovered the tomb of King Tut in the Valley of the Kings, a remote location west of the Nile River. Tut's tomb contained many interesting treasures, including a chest _____ into its structure was a translucent quartz gemstone, giving the chest plate an ethereal quality.

16. Which choice completes the text so that it conforms to the principles of standard English?

    A) plate built
    B) plate; built
    C) plate, built
    D) plate and built

Despite being safe, recyclable, and made of renewable materials, _____ they must be kept at high temperatures to work and require constant energy consumption.

17. Which choice completes the text so that it conforms to the principles of standard English?

    A) some drawbacks are associated with salt batteries:
    B) salt batteries have some drawbacks, as
    C) there are some drawbacks of salt batteries, which are that
    D) salt batteries' problems are that

First Lady Dolley Madison hosted weekly drawing room parties in which she welcomed guests of all social classes. Politicians with opposing political ideologies socialized at these parties and strengthened their bonds. As a result, they were able to work together more _____ a precedent for the importance of cooperation amongst government officials with different political beliefs.

18. Which choice completes the text so that it conforms to the principles of standard English?

    A) effectively, this set
    B) effectively, setting
    C) effectively; setting
    D) effectively; which set

George Washington Carver was a famous botanist and inventor of over 100 products. He altered farming practices in ways that improved farmers' lives. By encouraging farmers to plant soil-enriching crops, such as peanuts and cowpeas, _____

19. Which choice completes the text so that it conforms to the principles of standard English?

    A) poor farmers who could not afford traditional fertilizers were able to increase crop yields thanks to Carver.
    B) crop yields for poor farmers who could not afford traditional fertilizers increased because of Carver's help.
    C) the help that Carver offered poor farmers who could not afford traditional fertilizers allowed them to increase crop yields.
    D) Carver helped farmers increase crop yields without the use of traditional fertilizers that poor farmers could not afford.

The "nanoworld" refers to substances at the scale of one billionth that of what humans can perceive. Many objects take on different properties in the nanoworld than they do in the "macroworld" humans experience. For example, salt is generally inflexible in the _____ it is highly flexible in the microworld, often stretching to more than twice its length.

20. Which choice completes the text so that it conforms to the principles of standard English?

    A) macroworld. While
    B) macroworld: while
    C) macroworld, while
    D) macroworld while

How ordinary work tasks are framed can have tremendous implications for employee satisfaction: employees are more likely to tolerate mundane, seemingly unimportant tasks when they reflect on how these tasks fit within a larger goal, a phenomenon research Jaewon Yoon and colleagues dub "superordinate framing." They tested this idea by having employees list unimportant tasks in their _____ some subjects were instructed to reflect on how their mundane work tasks fit "like a puzzle" into broader goals, participants in the control group were not given such instructions.

21. Which choice completes the text so that it conforms to the principles of standard English?

    A) work, while
    B) work. While
    C) work; while,
    D) work while

Although memoirist and civil rights activist Maya Angelou is perhaps most famous for her works of prose—including seven acclaimed autobiographies—she was also quite the prolific_____ over 167 completed poems during her lifetime, many of which explore universal themes.

22. Which choice completes the text so that it conforms to the principles of standard English?

    A) poet—producing
    B) poet producing
    C) poet, producing
    D) poet: producing

Traditionally, astronomers have only been able to view a limited number of celestial objects, such as those that emit as much light as_____ the aid of microlensing techniques, though, astronomers have been able to detect objects that emit little to no light.

23. Which choice completes the text so that it conforms to the principles of standard English?

    A) stars with
    B) stars with;
    C) stars. With
    D) stars, with

Unit 3: Usage

Lesson 7: Possessive Determiners

Your vs. You're
"Your" is a possessive word that shows belonging.
- I will need to see your identification card.
- Your efforts are commendable.

"You're" means you are.
- You're good at playing tennis.
- I think you're on the right track.

Its vs. It's
"Its" is the possessive pronoun meaning something belongs to it. "Its" is used with **owners** that are singular (non-human) nouns.
- The house is beautiful, but water leaks from its roof.

The roof belongs to the house, so "its"= "the house's."

"It's" means "it is."
- It's time to go home.

Their vs. They're vs There
"Their" is a possessive pronoun that shows belonging. "Their" is used with **owners** that are plural nouns (human or non-human).
- Celia and Carson were elated that their science fair project won first place.

The project belongs to Celia and Carson, so "their"="Celia and Carson's.".

"They're" means "they are." "They're" is used with plural nouns.
- They're running around the track.

"There" is frequently used as an adverb that refers to a location (concrete or abstract) or the existence of something.
- The book is over there.
- There is a lot to do today.

Whose vs Who's
"Whose" is the possessive determiner for people or things.
- Whose dog is that?
- The flowers whose petals are purple are in the garden.

"Who's" means "who is."
- Who's going to testify?
- I know who's being honest and who's lying.

Sample Question

> Korean artist Do Ho Suh challenged popular conceptions of what "home" really means through various drawings, installations, sculptors, and films. With _____ glaring displays of the practical aspects of home—such as appliances, door knobs, and other fundamental furnishings—the artworks prompt viewers to consider what physical and emotional structures constitute a home.
>
> Which choice completes the text so that it conforms to the principles of standard English?
> A) its
> B) it's
> C) there
> D) their

The displays belong to the artworks, a plural noun. Thus, the plural possessive determiner "their" is needed. **Choice D is correct.** Choice A incorrectly uses a singular possessive determiner. Choices B and C are not possessive.

Drill 1: Select the choice that best completes each blank to conform to standard written English.

1. _____ important that you handle the artifact carefully.
   A) It's
   B) Its
   C) Their
   D) There

2. All of _____ ideas will be given careful consideration.
   A) you're
   B) your
   C) there
   D) they're

3. I don't know _____ advice you have been taking.
   A) who's
   B) who
   C) whom
   D) whose

4. _____ is uncertainty over the authorship of *Beowulf*, though the story likely has German, Scandinavian, and Anglican influences.
   A) There
   B) Their
   C) They're
   D) They

5. It is not clear _____ going to win the election, so both candidates should continue to campaign as if they expect to lose.
   A) who's
   B) who
   C) whom
   D) whose

6. _____ record for public service is outstanding, so it is no wonder you were honored with an award.
   A) You're
   B) Your
   C) There
   D) They're

94

7. We are going _____ for dinner after we attend the conference on Incan art.
   A) their
   B) they're
   C) there
   D) they are

8. The town has _____ own unique culture that seems eccentric to visitors.
   A) it's
   B) its
   C) their
   D) there

9. I find _____ arguments intriguing, but not compelling, as there is little empirical evidence to support their veracity.
   A) their
   B) there
   C) they're
   D) you're

10. _____ about to embark on an exciting journey as you start the next chapter in your career.
    A) Your
    B) You're
    C) Their
    D) There

11. The Silver Maple is a type of tree known for _____ soft wood, which is used for lumber.
    A) their
    B) there
    C) its
    D) it's

12. I believe that _____ is more than one way to solve that problem, so it is important to think flexibly and consider multiple perspectives.
    A) they
    B) their
    C) they're
    D) there

13. Make sure you can defend _____ thesis with specific examples and logical reasoning.
    A) you're
    B) your
    C) you
    D) it's

14. After speaking to the executives, I think_____ going to publish her article, which had a powerful message.
    A) they're
    B) your
    C) their
    D) there

15. Many hotels in Bora Bora, a small island in the South Pacific, are known for_____ overwater bungalows.
    A) its
    B) it's
    C) their
    D) there

16. The company demonstrated_____ capacity to adapt to the vicissitudes of the market.
    A) their
    B) there
    C) its
    D) it's

17. The performance of solar panels in areas with a lot of shade is compromised, thus limiting_____ appeal to some consumers.
    A) its
    B) it's
    C) there
    D) their

18. Overuse of herbicides in conventional farming methods limits_____ effectiveness.
    A) their
    B) there
    C) its
    D) they're

19. _____ many reasons to learn a new language, from developing your mind to being more cultured.
    A) They're is
    B) There are
    C) They're are
    D) They are

20. The organization offers services that are distinctive from those offered by_____ competitors.
    A) its
    B) it's
    C) their
    D) there

Lesson 8: Pronoun Agreement

Pronouns must agree with their **antecedents,** the nouns (people, places, things, ideas) for which they stand. The pronouns and antecedents must agree in **gender** (male or female), **number** (singular or plural), and case (**subjective or objective**). For the Digital SAT, you will NOT be tested on case errors (e.g., the difference between "I" and "me" or "we" and "us").

Pronouns acting as possessive determiners (*my, your, his, her, its, our, their*) must also agree with the nouns that possess something.

When the antecedent is a singular noun, the pronoun must be singular. When the antecedent is a plural noun, the pronoun must be plural.

Pronouns	Singular	Plural
Personal	I, me, he, him, she, her, you, it	they, them, we, us
Reflexive	myself, yourself, himself, herself, itself	ourselves, themselves
Possessive pronouns	mine, yours, his, hers	ours, yours, theirs
Possessive determiners	my, your, his, her, its	your, our, their

Pronouns can also be classified by case, but you will not be tested on differentiating between subjective and objective pronouns.

Subjective	Objective
I, you, he, she, we, they, who	me, you, him, her, us, them, whom

Subjective pronouns are the subjects of sentences. Typically, they refer to nouns that perform actions.
- **He** went to the convention for fans of superhero comics.
- **They** saw a flock of blue jays.
- **I** am standing outside the gazebo.

Subjective pronouns often precede linking verbs.
- **She** is kind to everyone she meets.
- **I** was chosen to present my research to a committee.

Objective pronouns replace the objects of a verb or preposition in a sentence. They often function as recipients of actions.
- His sister called **him** on the phone.
- The documentary was seen by **them**.
- The ceiling is above **me**.

Pronoun Tips

1) Use singular pronouns when referring to one noun and plural pronouns when referring to multiple nouns.
    - I read the story, and I really enjoyed **it**.

"It" refers to the singular noun "story."

- The campers appreciate when their counselors give **them** candy.

"Them" refers to the plural noun "campers."

2) Use singular possessive determiners when the **owner** is a singular noun and plural possessive determiners when the **owner** is a plural noun.
    - **Samson** did **his** homework.
    - The **students** did **their** homework.

Even though "homework" (the thing "owned") is singular, it is irrelevant to whether a singular or plural possessive determiner is needed. In the first sentence, the singular owner (Samson) requires the singular possessive determiner "his." In the second sentence, the plural owners (students) require the plural possessive determiner "their."

3) Use singular possessive determiners when "each" is used (**each=each one**).
    - **Each** of the snowflakes has **its** own unique pattern.

Each individual snowflake has a unique pattern.

4) Use singular possessive determiners when joining more singular nouns by "or" or "nor."
    - Either Britney **or** Azha did **her** homework.
    - Neither Britney **nor** Azha did **her** homework.

The singular female pronouns joined by "or" and "nor" require the singular possessive determiner "her."

5) Use plural possessive determiners when joining more than one noun by "and."
    - Gene **and** Sonia wear **their** uniforms.

Gene and Sonia are the owners of the uniforms, so the plural possessive determiner "their" is needed.

In many sentences, the pronoun will not be located right next to the antecedent.
- Incorrect: The **iguana**, known for **their** vegetarian **diets**, resides in the canopies of rainforests.

"Iguana" is a singular noun and "their" is a plural possessive determiner.

- Correct: The **iguana**, known for **its** vegetarian **diet**, resides in the canopies of rainforests.

The singular possessive determiner "its" agrees with the singular owner noun "iguana."

- Correct: **Iguanas**, known for **their** vegetarian **diets**, reside in the canopies of rainforests.

The plural possessive determiner "their" agrees with the plural owner noun "iguanas."

- Incorrect: The workers demanded improved benefits for **himself or herself**.
- Correct: The workers demanded improved benefits for **themselves.**

The plural pronoun "themselves" is needed to refer to the plural antecedent "workers."

6) Use "this" for singular words close in location ("these" for plural) and "that" for singular words far in location ("those" for plural)
   - **This** is the restaurant LaCienega raved about to me.
   - **These** cups on the table are the ones Ilya ordered online.
   - **That** was a good point that Jedediah made last night.
   - Many resources can help you with your research project, including **those** found in libraries.

7) Recall that **indefinite pronouns** are pronouns that do not stand for any specific noun. Possessive determiners must agree in number with indefinite pronouns (see fundamentals lesson).
   - **Everyone** is in **her** seat.
   - **Each** gives **his** opinion.
   - **One** must own up to **his or her** mistakes in order to learn from them.

8) Reflexive pronouns are used when the performer(s) and the recipient(s) of the action are the same subject(s).
   - **Opal** treated **herself** to a spa day.
   - **They** taught **themselves** to sew.

Sample Question

> Many psychologists create computational models that can highlight the relationship between factors modulating learning behaviors in children. Though these models—which often employ sophisticated statistical techniques— can help clarify mechanisms underlying the nature of learning mechanisms, _____ still subject to serious limitations: many are too simple, too complex, or too reductionist.
>
> Which choice completes the text so that it conforms to the principles of standard English?
>   A) they are
>   B) it is
>   C) that is
>   D) one is

The plural antecedent is "models," so the plural pronoun "they" is needed. **Choice A is correct.** The other choices incorrectly suggest that the antecedent is singular.

Mini Active Learning Activity

Answer the questions about each bolded sentence.

Although many people would like to take luxury vacations regularly, their huge expense keeps it out of reach for many.

1. To what antecedent is the underlined pronoun **supposed** to refer?

2. To what should the underlined portion be changed to correct the agreement error?

The stripes of zebras are thought by some scientists to provide it with a means of keeping cool in hot temperatures.

3. To what antecedent is the underlined pronoun **supposed** to refer?

4. To what should the underlined portion be changed to correct the agreement error?

Louisa May Alcott and other female authors like Violet Paget and Mary Ann Evans have penned some of her works under male pseudonyms.

5. To what antecedent is the underlined possessive determiner **supposed** to refer?

6. To what should the underlined portion be changed to correct the agreement error?

For more than a decade after their invention in 1992, the smartphone was not widely used, though it is now an ubiquitous feature of modern life.

7. To what antecedent is the underlined possessive determiner **supposed** to refer?

8. To what should the underlined portion be changed to correct the agreement error?

Most plants move slowly, but the Venus flytrap can change their position quickly.

9. To what antecedent is the underlined possessive determiner **supposed** to refer?

10. To what should the underlined portion be changed to correct the agreement error?

The observers of the baby loggerhead turtles going to sea knew he or she would always cherish that memory.

11. To what antecedent is the underlined possessive determiner **supposed** to refer?

12. To what should the underlined portion be changed to correct the agreement error?

Drill 1: Select the choice that best completes each blank to conform to standard written English.

1. One function of the kidneys is to filter the blood that passes through_____
   A) them.
   B) which.
   C) it.
   D) one.

2. The brains of toddlers are extremely adaptable:_____ can change in response to learning experiences.
   A) its neural pathways
   B) his or her neural pathways
   C) their neural pathways
   D) one's neural pathway

3. Famous for_____ in the 1933 film *King Kong,* the Empire State Building is one of the tallest skyscrapers in the world.
   A) their appearance
   B) its appearance
   C) it's appearance
   D) their appearances

4. The anthology contains several stories, each of which_____ plots and themes.
   A) is unique in their
   B) is unique in its
   C) being unique in their
   D) are unique in their

5. Known for_____ flagrant, colorful blooms, the Empress Tree is one of the fastest growing trees.
   A) its
   B) one's
   C) their
   D) our

6. Math and science, though challenging for some students, are_____ the most important disciplines.
   A) one of
   B) some of
   C) being one of
   D) any of

7. The rustic town is known for using cobblestone to pave_____ streets.
   A) its
   B) one's
   C) their
   D) whose

8. The mossy leaf-tailed gecko is named for_____ tail that resembles a leaf.
   A) their
   B) they're
   C) whose
   D) its

9. The oldest examples of flutes that have been discovered are over 40,000 years old. Because_____ precise function in society is not completely understood.
   A) they are so old, its
   B) it is so old, its
   C) they are sold old, their
   D) it is so sold, their

10. Each of their sons received a watch for_____ birthday.
    A) their
    B) its
    C) your
    D) his

11. Though the cable company charges reasonable usage fees, _____not offer many channels that are popular with viewers.
    A) they do
    B) it does
    C) one does
    D) he does

12. Abraham Lincoln delivered the Gettysburg Address at the end of the Civil War, one of_____ most prominent speeches.
    A) their
    B) our
    C) his
    D) one's

13. There are several different restaurants on the busy street, _____
    A) each with their own cuisines.
    B) each with their own cuisine.
    C) each with its own cuisine.
    D) each having their own cuisine.

14. While many people have difficulty understanding works of abstract art, in reality,_____ open to interpretation: all that is needed is a little imagination.
    A) it is
    B) one is
    C) they are
    D) we are

15. Although electronic books have only recently been offered by the textbook company,_____ in greater numbers than the hardcover textbooks.
    A) they have been sold
    B) they are selling it
    C) it has been sold
    D) it is selling it

16. A jury that does not consider all the evidence presented has not done _____ civic duty.
    A) their
    B) one's
    C) whose
    D) its

17. Peregrine falcons were once an endangered species due to pesticide use, but_____ in large numbers thanks to recovery efforts.
    A) it now exists
    B) they now exist
    C) them now existing
    D) who now exist

18. Many mentors will find_____ in challenging situations; thus, it is important that they establish positive relationships with the children they mentor.
    A) himself or herself
    B) ourselves
    C) themselves
    D) them

19. All individuals have_____ own ways of coping with stressful situations.
    A) their
    B) one's
    C) his or her
    D) one's

20. Many plants, including_____ found in the ocean, absorb harmful carbon dioxide.
    A) this
    B) that
    C) those
    D) these

21. _____ to other pricing methods, cost-plus pricing is the simplest method.
    A) If they are being compared
    B) If you compare them
    C) When comparing it
    D) Compared

Lesson 9: Subject-Verb Agreement

Singular subjects require singular forms of verbs, and plural subjects require plural forms of verbs. **Note that for regular present tense verbs, the plural form in the third person does NOT end in "s," while the singular form DOES end in "s."**

Singular
- The **child talks.**
- The **committee has** voted.

Plural
- The **children play.**
- The **people have** voted.

When there are multiple subjects, the verb will be plural if the subjects are linked by the word "and."
- The **dog and the cat run.**

When "or" and "nor" join more than one subject, the verb must agree with the noun closest to the verb.
- Either the plate **or the forks are** on the table.
- Either the forks **or the plate is** on the table.

When phrases that suggest two nouns are being combined (*along with, joined to, combined with, in addition to, together with* and *as well as*) connect two nouns, the first noun determines whether a singular or plural verb is needed. Generally, the noun(s) that is(are) NOT the subject(s) will be placed in between commas or dashes.
- **Palacio Real**, along with La Concha, **is** a popular tourist destination in Spain.

In this case, "Palacio Real" is the subject, so "is" is needed.

When connecting multiple subjects with "and," a plural verb is needed.
- **Palacio Real and La Concha are** popular tourist destinations in Spain.

In this case, both "Palacio Real" and "La Concha" are subjects, so "are" is needed.

When singular indefinite pronouns are used, singular verbs are needed. When plural indefinite pronouns are used, plural verbs are needed.
- **Each** of the cars **is** traveling over the speed limit.
- **Both** of you **have** improved a great deal.

When collective pronouns (pronouns standing for groups of people) act as subjects (e.g., *audience, jury, committee, company, organization, government, family, etc.*), singular verbs are generally used.
- The family *sits* at the table.
- The company **has** a forward-thinking mission.

Subject-Verb Inversion

Sometimes, the verb will appear before the subject for a poetic effect. Most commonly, the subject-verb inversion will follow a prepositional phrase.
- Incorrect: In the story **exist** a world of mystery and intrigue.
- Correct: In the story **exists** a world of mystery and intrigue.

The singular subject "world" requires the singular verb "exists." "In the story" is a prepositional phrase and does not contain the subject. The singular subject is "world," so the singular verb "exists" is needed.

- Incorrect: On the cot **was** a pillow and a blanket.
- Correct: On the cot **were** a pillow and a blanket.

The subjects and verbs are inverted. "On the cot" is a prepositional phrase. The two subjects joined by "and" ("pillow" and "blanket") require the plural verb "were."

When "that" begins a sentence, it sometimes means "the fact that." Clauses beginning with "that" function as singular subjects.
- **That (The fact that)** they are struggling with the decision **is** obvious.

"That they are struggling with the decision" is a noun clause. "That" acts as a singular subject for the main verb "is" that follows the clause. Within the clause, the plural pronoun "they" agrees with the plural verb "are."

- Among the researcher's findings **was that** disruptions in sleep patterns can be harmful to the body.

In this case, the subject and verb are inverted. "Among the researcher's findings" is a prepositional phrase that does not contain the subject. The noun clause ("that disruptions in sleep patterns can be harmful to the body") is the subject, and "was" is the singular verb. "That (the fact that) disruptions in sleep patterns can be harmful to the body **was** among the researcher's findings" is another way of wording this sentence.

Miscellaneous

1) Singular verbs are used with units representing distance, time, or money that act as subjects.
   - **$100 is** expensive.
   - The barn **is five miles** away.
   - It **is 3:00**.

2) Phrases starting with gerunds ("-ing" verbs) that function as nouns act as singular subjects.
   - **Learning** new musical instruments **is** a favorite pastime of mine.
   - **Knowing** how to communicate with others and take constructive criticism **is** important.

3) "What" and "whether" always act as singular subject clauses.
   - **What is important is** that you learn from your mistakes.
   - **Whether or not I should go to the concert is** my decision.

4) "Here is" and "there is" precede singular subjects. "Here are" and "there are" precede plural subjects.
   - **Here is** the file/**Here are** the files.
   - **There is** the file/ **There are** the files.

5) "A number of" is plural, but "the number of" is singular.
   - **A number** of people **have complained** about the new law.
   - **The number** of people in the village **has remained stable.**

6) "Every," "each," and "many a" require the use of singular verbs.
   - Every piece of evidence **was** examined.
   - Each response to the prompt **is** thoughtful.
   - Many a tourist **has** visited the idyllic town.

Drill 1: Select the correct verb in each set of parentheses.

1. Radiocarbon dating **(is/are)** a useful technique for estimating the age of rocks.
2. In the 19th century, fairy tales **(was/were)** frequently read to children.
3. Aqueous solutions and precipitates **(is/are)** the products of many double replacement chemical reactions.
4. A salt is formed when either an acid or a base **(neutralizes/neutralize)** the other.
5. Each of the children **(is/are)** responsible for completing the assignment.
6. A number of studies **(has/have)** been conducted on the connection between neuroscience and consumer behavior.
7. Whether or not pets are allowed in apartments **(depends/depend)** on the regulations of the particular building.
8. Planting flowers **(is/are)** a popular activity in the community.
9. The number of people attending college **(has/have)** increased in recent years.
10. There **(is/are)** several reasons for the collapse of the business deal.
11. That scientific findings are peer reviewed before being published in respected journals **(helps/help)** ensure that there is a quality control process in the dissemination of scientific information.
12. There **(is/are)** many applications of radioisotopes.
13. Inside the cupboard **(was/were)** flour and sugar.
14. Many a person **(has/have)** struggled to solve the puzzle.
15. Joaquin, along with Andre, **(sings/sing)** in the chorus.
16. A few people **(has/have)** written positive reviews about the new restaurant.
17. Next to the gas station **(was/were)** a cinema that has since been torn down.
18. All of the books **(contains/contain)** important information to study.
19. Each of the pictures **(looks/look)** completely different.
20. Neither Damian nor Max **(plays/play)** chess.
21. Across the hall **(is/are)** large doors leading into the auditorium.
22. Making napping a part of corporate culture **(is/are)** thought to enhance productivity.

The subject is not always next to the verb. In context, determine which noun is performing the action (in the case of action verbs) or is being described (in the case of linking verbs).

Advanced Subject-Verb Agreement

1) **Subject + Prepositional Phrase + Verb**

When a prepositional phrase is found between the subject and the verb, the subject before the prepositional phrase must agree with the verb.
- Incorrect: The **need** *for better education and job training programs* **are** responsible for the activist's demand for change.
- Correct: The **need** *for better education and job training programs* **is** responsible for the activist's demand for change.

The singular subject is "need," which requires the use of the singular verb "is." Although the plural word "programs" appears next to "is," it is part of the prepositional phrase "for better education and job training programs."

- Incorrect: The **affordability and practicality** *of the invention* **accounts** for its popularity with consumers.
- Correct: The **affordability and practicality** *of the invention* **account** for its popularity with consumers.

The compound subjects are "affordability" and "practicality." The plural verb is "account." The prepositional phrase is "of the invention."

Mini Active Learning Activity

Part 1: Identify all prepositional phrases in the sentences.
1. Beatriz loves spending days on the lake kayaking and paddle boarding with her family.
2. Critics said that the lead actor's performance in the production of *Hamlet* deserved an award.
3. The cake with the cherry on top is your sister's.
4. Return the toys to their drawers when you are done playing.
5. A hole in the pipe was responsible for the leak.
6. College student development theory is a body of scholarship that seeks to explain ways students learn, grow, and develop so that professionals in higher education can serve students' needs.

Part 2: Answer the questions about each bolded sentence.

Political scientists were not surprised that voter turnout in many states <u>hovers</u> under 50%, meaning that around half of eligible voters do not vote.

7. What prepositional phrase appears between the true subject and the underlined verb?

8. What is the true subject, and is it singular or plural?

9. How should the underlined verb be revised, if at all?

During the college orientation for new students at the small liberal arts college, one of the first events <u>were</u> the dean's welcoming speech.

10. What prepositional phrase appears between the true subject and the underlined verb?

11. What is the true subject, and is it singular or plural?

12. How should the underlined verb be revised, if at all?

As a result of the economic stimulus package, the proliferation of new jobs <u>has</u> given many residents in the city hope for a better future.

13. What prepositional phrase appears between the true subject and the underlined verb?

14. What is the true subject, and is it singular or plural?

15. How should the underlined verb be revised, if at all?

Some citizens told politicians they were concerned that the uses of 3D printing <u>has</u> expanded to include production of dangerous objects, such as weapons that look like toys.

16. What prepositional phrase appears between the true subject and the underlined verb?

17. What is the true subject, and is it singular or plural?

18. How should the underlined verb be revised, if at all?

A group of botanists argued that the wide rows in the farmer's vegetable garden <u>were</u> conducive to growing vegetables that grow over prolonged periods, like lettuce, but not to growing large vegetables, like tomatoes.

19. What prepositional phrase appears between the true subject and the underlined verb?

20. What is the true subject, and is it singular or plural?

21. How should the underlined verb be revised, if at all?

Other Ways of Separating Subjects and Verbs

1) **Subject + Nonessential Elements + Verb**

Nonessential elements in the middle of a sentence (e.g., relative clauses and appositives) are typically set off by commas. A verb that appears after nonessential terms must agree with the subject that comes before the nonessential terms.
- Incorrect: The **diet program**, *which has been purchased by thousands of people*, **were** featured on the talk show.
- Correct: The **diet program**, *which has been purchased by thousands of people*, **was** featured on the talk show.

"Which has been purchased by thousands of people" is a nonessential relative clause. The "diet program" is the true subject. "The diet program was featured on the talk show" is the sentence without the prepositional phrase.

- Incorrect: **Tai Chi**, *a Chinese martial art associated with many health benefits*, **are** practiced by many people seeking to alleviate stress.
- Correct: **Tai Chi**, *a Chinese martial art associated with many health benefits*, **is** practiced by many people seeking to alleviate stress.

"Tai Chi" is the singular subject, and "is" is the verb. "Benefits" is part of the nonessential appositive set off by commas.
- Incorrect: **Proper nutrition**, *along with adequate rest*, **are** needed to promote optimal muscle growth.
- Correct: **Proper nutrition**, *along with adequate rest*, **is** needed to promote optimal muscle growth.

Only "proper nutrition" is the subject. "Adequate rest" is nonessential, as it is set off by commas.

- Correct: **Proper nutrition and adequate rest are needed** to promote optimal muscle growth.

In this case, there are two subjects joined by "and," so the plural verb "are" is needed.

2) **Subject + Essential Elements + Verb**

Often, essential information is located between the subject and verb. In some cases, a participial phrase describing a noun will be present between the subject and the verb. Recall that the **present participle** ends in "-ing" and the **past participle** typically ends in "-ed," "-en," "-d," "-n," or "-t."
- Incorrect: **Employers** *overseeing a virtual workforce* **faces** unique challenges.
- Correct: **Employers** *overseeing a virtual workforce* **face** unique challenges.

The subject is "employers." "Overseeing a virtual workforce" is a participial phrase that describes the subject. The plural verb "face" is needed.

- Incorrect: The **towels** *covered in water* **is** on the chair.
- Correct: The **towels** *covered in water* **are** on the chair.

The subject is "towels." "Covered in water" is a participial phrase. The plural verb "are" is needed.

An essential relative clause contains a relative pronoun *(that, who, whom, which, whose)* or a relative adverb *(where, when, why)*. Essential clauses are NOT set off by commas because they are needed in sentences. The subject defined by an essential clause must agree with its verb.
- Incorrect: The **man** *who sold me the flowers* **were** very tall.
- Correct: The **man** *who sold me the flowers* **was** very tall.

In this case, "who sold me the flowers" defines the man. "The man" is a singular subject, so the singular verb "was" is needed.

- Incorrect: One **reason** *that ancient Greek myths are taught in schools* **are that** they convey universal themes.
- Correct: One **reason** *that ancient Greek myths are taught in schools* **is that** they convey universal themes.

"That ancient Greek myths are taught in schools" is a relative clause. The singular subject is "reason," so the singular verb "is" is needed.

Sample Question

Many people want to maintain a healthy diet while still enjoying what they eat. The growth in concern about eating healthfully among those who still crave delicious treats _____ the rise of "healthy junk food" companies, such as those making snacks resembling the taste and texture of actual "junk food."

Which choice completes the text so that it conforms to the principles of standard English?
  A) have spurred
  B) are spurring
  C) has spurred
  D) spur

The singular subject is "growth." The phrase "in concern about eating healthfully among those who still crave delicious treats" is a prepositional phrase modifying this subject. Thus, the singular verb "has spurred" is needed. **Choice C is correct.** The other choices use plural verb forms.

Drill 2: Select the choice that best completes each blank to conform to standard written English.

1. Fax machines, hardly an obsolete form of technology,____ still used today by many businesses.
   A) is
   B) are
   C) will be
   D) is being

2. The Sistine Chapel, which was reopened to the public in 1994,____ some of the world's most renowned pieces of art.
   A) host
   B) hosting
   C) have hosted
   D) hosts

3. Sections of the Appalachian Trail _____ stretches of boardwalks known as "bog bridges" on which hikers can admire the diverse terrain.
   A) includes
   B) including
   C) include
   D) which include

4. The electron microscope, which has a high-resolution power to view very small images,_____ scientific studies.
   A) have been useful in
   B) were useful in
   C) has been useful in
   D) having its usefulness regarding

5. Evidence that the Gale Crater on Mars contained water sources _____ that the planet was once habitable.
   A) suggest
   B) suggests
   C) have suggested
   D) suggesting

6. The decline in gas prices _____ expected to increase consumer discretionary spending.
   A) are
   B) is
   C) having been
   D) have been

115

7. The gallery's exhibition of artwork by local inhabitants_____ its commitment to diversity and dialogue.
   A) displays
   B) displaying
   C) display
   D) had displayed

8. The southern masked weaver, like many other birds,_____ nests by a combination of instinct and experience.
   A) learn to make
   B) learning to make
   C) learns to make
   D) learn making

9. The errors in the document _____ in other documents.
   A) are likely to be found
   B) is likely to be found
   C) are likely finding
   D) is likely finding

10. Building rapport with one's students_____ an important part of a teacher's job.
    A) are
    B) is
    C) were
    D) being

11. Agatha Christie, who wrote 66 detective novels, _____ of the most popular authors of all time.
    A) has made her one
    B) is one
    C) have been one
    D) are one

12. Every concept on the review sheets____ likely to be included on the exam.
    A) are
    B) is
    C) have been
    D) were

13. The reason that many books are popular_____ have compelling characters and engaging plots.
    A) is that they
    B) is that it
    C) are that it
    D) are that they

14. All the discussion about the need for improved materials _____ not been enough for the company to change its ways.
    A) have
    B) having
    C) has
    D) are having

15. The care the ceramics company takes in shipping its products _____ a positive reputation.
    A) has earned it
    B) has earned them
    C) have earned it
    D) have earned them

16. Each of the people on the roster, all of whom are talented athletes, _____ something valuable to the team.
    A) add
    B) adds
    C) have added
    D) adding

17. Not one person who attempted to solve the complex math problem _____ successful.
    A) have been
    B) has been
    C) having been
    D) were

18. Neither Iceland nor French Polynesia _____ mosquitoes, flies that suck blood from other animals.
    A) contain
    B) contains
    C) have contained
    D) having contained

19. There are major differences between the campaigns of the two candidates, _____ own unique message.
    A) each of which has its
    B) each has its
    C) each of which has their
    D) each of which have their

20. The paper towels used in the kitchen _____
    A) come from recycled paper, as does the napkins found on the table.
    B) comes from recycled paper, and so does the napkins found on the table.
    C) and the napkins found on the table comes from recycled paper.
    D) come from recycled paper, as do the napkins found on the table.

21. There are two options for the final project, neither of which_____ a significant time commitment.
    A) require
    B) requires
    C) requiring
    D) have required

22. Proportional representation, an electoral system in which legislative seats are awarded based on each party's share of votes received,_____ in many European countries.
    A) exist
    B) exists
    C) existing
    D) have existed

23. A fungus is an_____ for research purposes.
    A) organism from whose cells are extracted genetic material
    B) organism, from its cells genetic material is extracted
    C) organism, they extract genetic material from its cells
    D) organism from whose cells genetic material is extracted

24. The coherence and powerfulness of the pundit's editorial _____
    A) explain their appeal.
    B) explains their appeal.
    C) explain its appeal.
    D) explains its appeal.

25. That taking Vitamin C _____ by Linus Pauling.
    A) helps prevent diseases were argued
    B) helps prevent diseases was argued
    C) help prevent diseases were argued
    D) help prevent diseases was argued

26. These directors, all of whom are from the Caribbean, _____ own distinctive styles.
    A) have his or her
    B) have their
    C) has his or her
    D) has their

27. Many animals, including the black bear,_____ during the winter.
    A) hibernate
    B) hibernates
    C) hibernating
    D) has hibernated

28. According to the article, small quantities of harmless pollen _____ no damaging effects on the lungs.
    A) has
    B) have
    C) which has
    D) having

29. The bakery's active social media presence, combined with its strong reputation for delivering quality baked goods, _____ contributed to its commercial success.
    A) has
    B) have
    C) having
    D) which has

30. The customers who purchased the new laptop _____ that it works well.
    A) claim
    B) claims
    C) has claimed
    D) claiming

31. The commission investigating the claims of the manufacturers _____ some resistance.
    A) have encountered
    B) having encountered
    C) has encountered
    D) encounter

32. The zebra fish, in addition to the mouse, _____ whose genome has been completely sequenced.
    A) are animals
    B) having been an animal
    C) is an animal
    D) have been animals

33. "Unicorns" are startup companies that, based on equity funding, _____ worth over a billion dollars.
    A) is
    B) is being
    C) has been
    D) are

34. The diversity of flora and fauna at the national park _____ noted by the visitors.
    A) were
    B) was
    C) have been
    D) having been

35. What was written about the prototype for the new intervention in the company emails _____ confidential.
    A) are
    B) is
    C) being
    D) having been

36. The amount of time people _____ researching products online is significant.
    A) spends
    B) has spent
    C) spending
    D) spend

37. The people running the small gift shop in the tiny village by the river _____ friendly.
    A) is
    B) are
    C) has been
    D) being

38. The cake decorated with ornate flower designs _____ good.
    A) taste
    B) tastes
    C) tasting
    D) have tasted

39. Stenographers produce transcriptions that _____ what is said by all parties in a court of law.
    A) will have indicated
    B) indicates
    C) has indicated
    D) indicate

40. Dangerous increases in the salinity of a stream _____ the quality of drinking water obtained from it.
    A) threatens biodiversity and affects
    B) threaten biodiversity and affects
    C) threatens biodiversity and affect
    D) threaten biodiversity and affect

41. The speed, convenience, and the affordability of the car manufacturer's latest sedan _____ superior to the previous model.
    A) make them
    B) make it
    C) makes them
    D) makes it

120

42. While each of the episodes in the children's horror anthology show— which includes both dark comedic stories—_____on a unique group of characters, a few of episodes feature returning characters battling supernatural forces at different points in their lives.
   A) centers
   B) center
   C) will center
   D) are centering

Usage Unit Quiz

Communities can come together to effect meaningful environmental change despite the pressures of industrialization: when the Conejera wetlands in Bogota were under threat from urban development, environmental activists educated residents about concrete measures_____ could take to restore the wetland's natural bodies of water.

1. Which choice completes the text so that it conforms to the principles of standard English?

    A) it
    B) one
    C) they
    D) you

While the domestic canary comes in a range of colors, the feathers of _____ wild ancestors used to be rather dull. Eventually, valuing canaries for their melodic voices, humans started breeding them to have feathers of different colors.

2. Which choice completes the text so that it conforms to the principles of standard English?

    A) its
    B) their
    C) it's
    D) they're

The board game Sorry! is based on the ancient Indian board game *Pachisi*, which is played on a symmetrical cross; in Sorry!, landing one's pawn on a square occupied by another player _____ that pawn back to the start.

3. Which choice completes the text so that it conforms to the principles of standard English?

    A) send
    B) have sent
    C) are sending
    D) sends

The book *Hidden Figures* is a nonfiction text that follows the lives of Katherine Johnson, Mary Jackson, and Dorothy Vaughn, mathematicians who worked as human computers at NASA during the twentieth century. _____ work was essential to the accomplishments of NASA during the space race between the United States and the Soviet Union.

4. Which choice completes the text so that it conforms to the principles of standard English?

   A) They're
   B) Their
   C) It's
   D) Its

Sharks and remora fish share an interesting relationship. Sharks protect remora fish from predators and help them transport across the ocean, and the remora fish feed on parasites that can irritate the sharks. After sharks eat their own prey, remora fish riding on the sharks' backs detach _____ and they feed on remaining scraps.

5. Which choice completes the text so that it conforms to the principles of standard English?

   A) it,
   B) itself,
   C) them,
   D) themselves,

Colson Whitehead won his first Pulitzer Prize in 2017 for *The Underground Railroad,* a historical fiction novel that alternates perspectives between Cora, a slave who escapes from Georgia, and other characters. Though this novel gained Whitehead tremendous popularity, his writing _____ recognized before: in 2000, he won the Whiting Award, which honors emerging American writers in a variety of genres.

6. Which choice completes the text so that it conforms to the principles of standard English?

   A) were
   B) has been
   C) have been
   D) are

It has long been known that sleep can help people retain memories. In 2015, a research team led by Nicolas Dumay found evidence that _____ can also recover memories that were previously forgotten: when subjects did not initially remember information on a memory test given shortly after a study period, they were more likely to recover the memories on a subsequent test if they slept after the first test.

7. Which choice completes the text so that it conforms to the principles of standard English?

   A) it
   B) one
   C) those
   D) they

Art curator Dennys Matos, who held an art exhibition in Miami for 15 groundbreaking artists in the geometric abstraction movement, noted an interesting apparent contradiction about the artists. While they all sought to bring harmony and order to their art, in their real lives, many of them inhabited worlds that _____ rather tumultuous.

8. Which choice completes the text so that it conforms to the principles of standard English?

   A) were
   B) was
   C) has been
   D) is

Lights composed of blue wavelengths that are found in many common household devices like cell phones and computers are associated with wakefulness. Many scientists caution against using such devices at night, as _____ can disrupt normal circadian rhythms, causing problems associated with poor sleep.

9. Which choice completes the text so that it conforms to the principles of standard English?

   A) it
   B) one
   C) he or she
   D) they

Rachel Carson's *Silent Spring*, which documented the harm caused by pesticides, _____ by chemical companies but widely believed by the public, culminating in the ban of the insecticide Dichlorodiphenyltrichloroethane (DDT) in agriculture in the United States.

10. Which choice completes the text so that it conforms to the principles of standard English?

    A) were opposed
    B) was opposed
    C) have opposed
    D) are opposed

The Harlem Renaissance, a period of African American artistic revitalization in the twentieth century, saw many women host gatherings of Black intellectuals and artists. One such artist_____ Ethel Ray Nance, whose apartment became known as the "Harlem West Side Literary Salon."

11. Which choice completes the text so that it conforms to the principles of standard English?

    A) was
    B) have been
    C) are
    D) were

In the United States, hummingbirds typically migrate to the North during the spring and to the South during the winter, but the precise reasons why they migrate_____ not completely understood. Some scientists believe that hummingbirds migrate to follow flower populations, but other scientists think that hummingbirds migrate to follow insects.

12. Which choice completes the text so that it conforms to the principles of standard English?

    A) is
    B) has been
    C) are
    D) was

When studying samples of ancient DNA, scientists have to contend with issues surrounding DNA contamination by other organisms, such as bacteria. Fortunately, scientists are able to manufacture millions of strips of RNA and attach_____ to a chemical velcro—a chemical snare of sorts—that gloms onto the human DNA in samples so that it can be separated from non-human DNA.

13. Which choice completes the text so that it conforms to the principles of standard English?

    A) one
    B) that
    C) it
    D) them

Italian farmer Antonio Lancellotta has employed "agrivoltaics," a technique in which crops are grown underneath solar panels. He believes this is the solution to preserving endangered fruit threatened by climate change, including many citrons. Still, the cost, novelty, and lack of clear legislation guidance about the technique _____it from going mainstream for the time being.

14. Which choice completes the text so that it conforms to the principles of standard English?

    A) preventing
    B) has prevented
    C) have prevented
    D) would have prevented

Three striped species of zebras are the only species of the Equus genus—which includes horses and donkeys—with stripes. According to science journalist Yao-Hua Law, differences in striping patterns between species, in addition to challenges zebras face in nature,_____ clues about the functions these stripes might harbor.

15. Which choice completes the text so that it conforms to the principles of standard English?

    A) providing
    B) provide
    C) provides
    D) having provided

Graduate student Andrea Marshall discovered that a single species of mantas—a relative of stingrays—in Mozambique was actually two different species, a fact she began to suspect after noticing striking physical variations in the skin amongst the mantas she encountered in her research. That it took many years for the two species to be rightfully classified as different species _____ how much scientists have to learn about these creatures.

16. Which choice completes the text so that it conforms to the principles of standard English?

    A) highlighting
    B) highlight
    C) highlights
    D) will highlight

Cognitive science, broadly defined as the study of the mind and learning processes, has traditionally neglected the study of culture. Many a cognitive science professor_____ that cognition is an internal process tethered to biological processes, independent of cultural background. Those espousing such beliefs often focused their research on "universal" characteristics of cognition, but their sample sizes were small and not representative, making broad generalizations problematic.

17. Which choice completes the text so that it conforms to the principles of standard English?

    A) are arguing
    B) have argued
    C) has argued
    D) argue

Acclaimed Yankton Sioux artist Oscar Howe extended the boundaries of traditional Indian art. In 1958, his painting *Umine Wacipe: War and Peace Dance*— which included sharp angular shapes portraying dancers—_____ initially disqualified from a competition showcasing art by Americans Indians. His painting was deemed "not authentic" enough for incorporating European stylistic influences, despite the fact that the work also had traditional Dakota elements. Howe protested against this decision, and, as a result, the scope of artwork allowed in the competition was expanded for future years.

18. Which choice completes the text so that it conforms to the principles of standard English?

    A) has been
    B) was
    C) have been
    D) were

Vincent Van Gogh's 1888 painting *Sunflowers* portrays a mutant "double flower," which actually does exist in nature. However, what makes these mutants difficult for geneticists to study_____ that they produce less pollen than other flowers without this mutation, making it harder for the mutants to produce offspring.

19. Which choice completes the text so that it conforms to the principles of standard English?

    A) are
    B) is
    C) was
    D) were

The Epidaurus in Greece, a renowned amphitheater built in the fourth century BCE, allows performers' voices to carry over larger distances, and researchers Nico Declerq and Cindy Dekeyser finally learned the secret to the theater's mysterious acoustic properties: the filtering of low-frequency sounds by the theater's seats_____ the actors' higher-frequency voices to carry through without being compromised.

20. Which choice completes the text so that it conforms to the principles of standard English?

    A) permit
    B) permits
    C) are permitting
    D) having permitted

Unit 4: Punctuation

Lesson 10: End-of-Sentence Punctuation

There are three punctuation marks that end sentences.

1) Periods (.) end **declarative sentences,** which are sentences that state facts or opinions and **imperative sentences,** which are commands. Periods appear at the end of complete sentences.

   - Before purchasing a house, one must first make a down payment for a portion of its cost.
   - The Peace of Westphalia ended the Thirty Years' War and weakened the authority of the Holy Roman Empire.
   - Please put the dishes in the sink after you are finished eating.

2) Exclamation points convey a greater sense of excitement or urgency than periods. Exclamation points (!) are used in both **exclamatory sentences** and some **imperative sentences**.

   - That is unbelievable news!
   - Listen to your teacher!

Exclamation points are also used after interjections, non-sentence words and phrases that convey strong emotions.

   - Wow!
   - Well there!

3) Question marks (?) are used in interrogative sentences, sentences that include questions. Common words that are found in interrogative sentences include *who, whom, which, what, where, when, why,* and *how*. The question word isn't always the very first word of the sentence. Interrogative sentences can be answered with declarative sentences.

   - **Where** did Francesca come from? She came from Maine.
   - For **what** purpose have you called my office? I called your office to inform you about a new promotion.
   - To **whom** does this sweater belong? This sweater belongs to Arlene.

Helping verbs and **linking verbs** are often used at the beginning or end of interrogative sentences.
- **Should** I leave the note in your mailbox?
- You are coming to my party, **aren't** you?
- **Must** you continue to make that noise?

Do NOT use question marks after indirect questions, which are sentences that report on a question.
- I **asked** my counselor for advice.
- I **asked** her if she was feeling well.
- I **wonder** what happened at the party.

Interrogative Adverbs	Interrogative Pronouns	Linking Verbs	Helping Verbs
What	Who	Is	Will/Would
Why	Whom	Are	May/Might
When	Whose	Were	Must
Where	Which	Was	Can/Could
How			Shall/Should
			Do/Did
			Has/Have/Had

Sample Question

> _____ For one, the wings help the ostriches stabilize their bodies when they run. This ability is useful when ostriches have to make more complicated maneuvers and change directions. Furthermore, ostriches use their wings to communicate with one another.
>
> Which choice completes the text so that it conforms to the principles of standard English?
> A) If ostriches can't fly, why do they have wings?
> B) If ostriches can't fly, why do they have wings.
> C) Why do ostriches? Have wings if they can't fly?
> D) Ostriches can't fly, then why do they have wings.

The sentence after the blank provides an answer to a direct question, so an interrogative sentence with a question mark is needed. **Choice A is correct.** Choices B and D incorrectly use periods when asking direct questions. Choice C inappropriately separates a question into separate questions confusingly.

Drill 1

Part 1: Add the proper punctuation mark (period, question mark, or exclamation point) at the end of each sentence

1. What an accomplishment

2. Did the politician fully explain her opinion on the issue during the debate

3. What were the underlying causes of the Civil War

4. Lee Daniels' *Butler* is a powerful film that has been critically acclaimed

5. Quebec is Canada's largest province in area and second largest in population

6. The ambassador asked where the crisis was occurring

7. Why are Shakespeare's works taught in schools today

8. Margaret Mead wrote about the role of social convention in shaping human behavior

9. Amazing what a little practice can do

10. I humbly request that you take his advice to heart

11. I asked the historian how the ancient Egyptians built their pyramids with such precision

12. Two thumbs up

13. A wampum consists of beads made from polished shells

14. How could they believe his obvious lies

Part 2: Select the choice that best completes each sentence to conform to standard written English.

15. We asked _____
    A) can we go to the concert if we finish our project.
    B) if we can go to the concert if we finish our project.
    C) if we can go to the concert if we finish our project?
    D) we can go to the concert if we finish our project?

16. After learning extended family would be in town,_____
    A) we wondered if we should cancel the trip and reschedule for the following weekend.
    B) we wondered if we should cancel the trip and reschedule for the following weekend?
    C) we wondered should we cancel the trip and reschedule for the following weekend?
    D) we wondered should we cancel the trip and reschedule for the following weekend.

17. After guiding the students through a tour of the art exhibit, the tour guide asked them, "_____
    A) How did the art make you feel."
    B) How did the art make you feel?"
    C) If the art made you feel a certain way."
    D) If the art made you feel a certain way?"

18. _____ The team was determined to find out.
    A) What if there is a way to reverse the aging process in mice.
    B) Is there a way to reverse the aging process in mice.
    C) What if there is a way to reverse the aging process in mice?
    D) If there is a way to reverse the aging process in mice?

19. It has long been known that people can be influenced by factors outside of their conscious perception, such as background noises and sights. A group of scholars wondered if using fluffy clouds on website wallpaper_____
    A) would make customers prioritize comfort over price.
    B) it would make customers prioritize comfort over price.
    C) would it make customers prioritize comfort over price?
    D) it would make customers prioritize comfort over price?

20. Momentum can be powerful in sports._____
    A) It is uncertain if the fencing team will ever make a comeback after its underwhelming start in the tournament?
    B) It is uncertain if the fencing team will ever make a comeback after its underwhelming start in the tournament.
    C) It is uncertain will the fencing team ever make a comeback after its underwhelming start in the tournament?
    D) It is uncertain will the fencing team ever make a comeback after its underwhelming start in the tournament.

Lesson 11: Within-Sentence Punctuation

Semicolons

Semicolons (;) are generally used to provide a greater pause than a comma but a smoother transition than a period. The main function of semicolons is to connect two independent clauses that are NOT connected by coordinating conjunctions (for, and, nor, but, or, yet, so). Semicolons can, however, be used to introduce clauses containing **conjunctive adverbs.**

General Rule: If you can't replace the semicolon with a period to generate two complete sentences, the semicolon is probably unacceptable!*
- Correct: It rained on graduation **day; therefore**, the ceremony was held indoors.
- Correct: It rained on graduation **day. Therefore**, the ceremony was held indoors.

Both clauses are independent and can be separated by a semicolon. Alternatively, they can be written as two distinct sentences.

*an exception to this is when making lists, which the next lesson covers.

Common Forms of Semicolon Misuse

1) <u>**DO NOT**</u> **use semicolons to connect independent and dependent clauses.**
    - Incorrect: **Because** Zari put a lot of effort into preparing the **meal; I** could not bring myself to tell her that it did not taste good.
    - Correct: **Because** Zari put a lot of effort into preparing the **meal, I** could not bring myself to tell her that it did not taste good.

The subordinating conjunction "because" makes the first clause dependent. A comma is needed instead of a period.

2) <u>**DO NOT**</u> **use semicolons to connect independent clauses joined by a coordinating (FANBOYS) conjunction. Instead, use a comma before the coordinating conjunction.**
    - Incorrect: Dayna trained hard for the **marathon; and** she was ecstatic when she won.
    - Correct: Dayna trained hard for the **marathon, and** she was ecstatic when she won.
    - Correct: Dayna trained hard for the **marathon; she** was ecstatic when she won.

A coordinating conjunction cannot follow a semicolon when linking independent clauses.

3) <u>**DO NOT**</u> use semicolons to separate independent clauses from participial phrases (a common sentence construction seen in wrong answer choices).
    - Error: I took a boat **ride; admiring** the scenery.
    - Correct: I took a boat **ride, admiring** in the scenery

A comma should separate the independent clause from the participial phrase that follows.

Colons

Colons (:) are used to connect two related parts of a sentence. **Colons follow independent clauses** to introduce a word, list, phrase, or another full sentence that **ELABORATES** on what came before the colon. You can think of them as ending sentences that are technically grammatically complete but "leave the reader hanging" in terms of meaning.

- The holiday discounts at the local business had unfortunate consequences: long lines and reduced profit margins.

The sentence can end grammatically after "consequences," but the reader would be left wondering what the consequences were. The information after the colon resolves this mystery.

- Tatiana found her job rewarding: it allowed her to make a difference in children's lives while also honing her leadership skills.

The colon introduces the sentence clarifying why the job was rewarding.

Common Functions of Colons

1) To formally introduce a list or series following an independent clause.
    - My grocery list includes the following items: hummus, bananas, and yogurt.
    - We have many activities on our itinerary for our trip: hiking, whale watching, and rock climbing.

The colons signal lists after full sentences.

2) To introduce a word, phrase, or clause that provides an explanation, description, clarification, or amplification of the preceding independent clause. Oftentimes, a colon functions in the same way as "namely," "specifically," or "that is."
    - Some people only know Leonardo da Vinci for one thing: *The Mona Lisa*.

The colon functions similarly to the word "namely." It clarifies for what da Vinci is known.

- There was a reason class started late: the professor was stuck in traffic.

The second clause provides an explanation for the first.

- Patricia's personality contains contrasting elements: in her personal life she is mellow and reticent, but in the office, she is engaging and talkative.

The second clause clarifies in what ways Patricia's personality contains contrasting elements.

Common Forms of Colon Misuse

1) <u>**DO NOT**</u> **use a colon after a verb that cannot end a sentence (including modals like** *could, would,* **and** *should*).
   - Incorrect: My favorite subjects **are:** history, math, and Spanish.
   - Correct: My favorite subjects **are** history, math, and Spanish.
   - Incorrect: When learning a new language, you **should:** look for opportunities to speak it.
   - Correct: When learning a new language, you **should** look for opportunities to speak it.

When the last word of a **complete sentence** is a verb, a colon is acceptable.
   - Correct: Olga has been known to exaggerate: she typically embellishes the magnitude of her accomplishments.

2) <u>**DO NOT**</u> **use a colon after a preposition that introduces a prepositional phrase.**
   - Incorrect: Erin still has to purchase gifts **for:** her aunt, her sister, and her friend.
   - Correct: Erin still has to purchase gifts **for** her aunt, her sister, and her friend.

3) <u>**DO NOT**</u> **use a colon before or after words that function as colons AND that cannot end a sentence** (*such as, including, especially, namely*).
   - Incorrect: Yoga has many benefits, **including**: improved flexibility, increased strength, and improved athletic performance.
   - Correct: Yoga has many **benefits:** improved flexibility, increased strength, and improved athletic performance.
   - Correct: Yoga has many **benefits, including** improved flexibility, increased strength, and improved athletic performance.

Using both "including" AND a colon is redundant: pick one or the other.

Note that the conjunctive adverbs such as "however," "for example," "though," and "for instance" CAN precede a colon, especially when they complete an opening independent clause after a comma for dramatic effect.
   - Correct: Not all foods that contain fat are unhealthy. Take olive oil, **for instance:** while it is a monounsaturated fatty acid, it helps protect the body against several diseases and lowers overall blood cholesterol levels.
   - Correct: Lawon did not get the job he interviewed for, but the grueling interview process wasn't for nothing, **though**: he so impressed the managers that he was offered another position at the firm.

The bolded conjunctions end the independent clauses before the colons for dramatic effect. The information after the colon in each sentence is an elaboration on what came before the colon.

4) **DO NOT** use a colon before/after FANBOYS conjunctions.
   - Incorrect: The Stamp Act was perceived as **unfair for**: it raised prices without the consent of the colonists.
   - Incorrect: The Stamp Act was perceived as **unfair: for** it raised prices without the consent of the colonists.
   - Correct: The Stamp Act was perceived as **unfair:** it raised prices without the consent of the colonists.
   - Correct: The Stamp Act was perceived as **unfair, for** it raised prices without the consent of the colonists.

Either use a colon before the second independent clause that elaborates on the first independent clause or a comma before the FANBOYS conjunction "for" connecting these independent clauses.

5) **DO NOT** use a colon to signal indirect quotations (reports of what was said that don't include quotation marks).
   - Incorrect: Ahmad claimed **that:** he was taking a sabbatical.
   - Correct: Ahmad claimed **that** he was taking a sabbatical.

6) **DO NOT** use unnecessary words after the colon that are implied by the colon itself (e.g., *being that, namely, such as, specifically, particularly*) or that create confusion.
   - Incorrect: There was one **problem: being that** he misplaced his notes.
   - Correct: There was one **problem: he** misplaced his notes.

"Being that" is wordy and adds nothing of value to the sentence. The colon means "namely."

7) **DO NOT** use colons to introduce an isolated *dependent clause* unless that dependent clause is part of a full sentence or connected to a noun right before it.
   - Incorrect: Discussions for the television pilot for a children's educational engineering show were tabled: although executives loved the concept.

A dependent clause cannot follow the colon.

   - Correct: Discussions for the television pilot for a children's educational engineering show were tabled: although executives loved the concept, **the show did not perform well in focus groups.**

The bolded independent clause above makes the information after the colon a complex sentence.

   - Incorrect: The large clothing retailer adopted an innovative strategy to retain employees: which rewards employees for productivity rather than hours worked.
   - Correct: The large clothing retailer adopted an innovative strategy to retain employees: **ROWE (results-only work environment),** which rewards employees for productivity rather than hours worked.

The colon signals the elaboration on the specific strategy. Adding the name of the strategy before the relative clause that explains it corrects the error.

8) **DO NOT** use a colon to introduce a participial phrase.
   - Incorrect: The paleontologist criticized her colleague's **conclusion: claiming** it was based on statistically weak extrapolations.
   - Incorrect: The paleontologist criticized her colleague's **conclusion, claiming** it was based on statistically weak extrapolations.

A comma is needed to create a loose sentence.

Dashes

Dashes (—) are used to set off one part of a sentence from the rest of the sentence. They often take the place of commas and colons, but they have a much more dramatic effect. They are also used when other forms of punctuation are unacceptable, but a pause is needed.

Common Functions of Dashes

1) To create emphasis at the end of a complete sentence.
   - While the evidence against the defendants was substantial, the jurors reached a surprising verdict—**not guilty on all counts.**

The dash functions as a colon explaining why the verdict was surprising.

   - The class in critical reasoning teaches three core skills—**logic, informal reasoning, and the art of argumentation.**

The dash functions as a colon introducing a list.

   - I arrived—**not by plane, but by train.**

A pause is needed after "I arrived."

2) To create emphasis at the beginning of a sentence, such as to emphasize a list. An independent clause may follow the list, or the dash may interrupt the independent clause for dramatic effect.
   - **Ambition, determination, and resiliency**—these are all qualities that good sales professionals need.

3) **A pair of dashes** can highlight nonessential details in the middle of a sentence.
   - The professor teaches three "dead" languages—**Latin, ancient Greek, and Sanskrit**—to students at a university.

The list in between dashes can be removed from the sentence, and the sentence would still be complete.

4) **A pair of dashes** can be used to show a pause, break in thought, or a side comment.
   - I know—**at least I hope**—that he is being truthful.

The commentary between dashes can be removed from the sentence, and the sentence would still be complete.

A dash **CANNOT** separate a dependent clause from an independent clause that follows. A comma should separate a dependent clause from an independent clause.
- Incorrect: While I believe you are pursuing a worthwhile **endeavor**—you will face struggles along the way.
- Correct: While I believe you are pursuing a worthwhile **endeavor,** you will face struggles along the way.

Quotation marks are often used around direct quotes, titles of certain works, and individual words (e.g., to convey sarcasm or to indicate a nickname). Periods and commas generally go inside of quotation marks.
- The principal said, "Please report to the main office."

Sample Question

> The opposing processes model argues that competition itself does not have any consistent impacts on performance. Rather, the types of goals one brings to competition are important in this_____ with approach goals tend to perform better, while those with avoidance goals tend to perform worse.
>
> Which choice completes the text so that it conforms to the principles of standard English?
> A) regard; those
> B) regard: those
> C) regard, those
> D) regard those:

A colon is needed after an independent clause to signal an elaboration. In this case, the independent clause states that the goals one brings to competition are more important with regards to performance, and the information after the colon elaborates on how different types of goals (approach goals and avoidance goals) affect performance. **Choice B is correct.** Choice A is grammatically correct since a semicolon can be used to separate independent clauses, but a colon is a superior choice since the information that follows is a direct elaboration on the first independent clause. Choice C is a run-on. Choice D misplaces the colon, which must end the independent clause.

Mini Active Learning Activity

Attentional processes are often classified into two types top-down and bottom-up.

1. Where should a colon be placed in this sentence? Justify your answer.

Sabrina learned the ironic lesson that: meddling in people's lives out of a desire to help them can have unforeseen consequences that merely exacerbate their problems.

2. Explain why the colon is not appropriate here.

3. Suggest two revisions to this sentence, one of which should include a colon used properly.

Invasive species come in: many sizes and forms but have one thing in common they invade environments to which they are not native, often with devastating ecological effects.

4. Explain why the colon is not properly placed.

5. Where should the colon be moved? Justify your answer.

Tomas enjoyed his high school reunion party more than he thought: although he was initially concerned it would be awkward.

6. Explain why the colon is not appropriate here.

7. The colon should be changed to what form of punctuation? Justify your answer.

8. Suppose the writer wants to keep the colon and all the information before it the same. What is one way the writer could revise the second part of the sentence so that the sentence would be grammatically correct?

Drill 1: Select the choice that best completes each blank to conform to standard written English.

1. Mark Twain is the pen name of Samuel_____ is known for his tales taking place along the Mississippi River.
   A) Clemens, he
   B) Clemens; being
   C) Clemens; he
   D) Clemens: he

2. The need for improved infrastructure was made clear by a terrible_____ of the Tacoma Narrows Bridge.
   A) tragedy: the destruction
   B) tragedy the destruction
   C) tragedy; the destruction
   D) tragedy: being the destruction

3. _____he regretted having but one life to give for his country.
   A) Nathan Hale claimed that:
   B) Nathan Hale claimed that
   C) Nathan Hale claimed—that
   D) Nathan Hale claimed that;

4. Advocates of nuclear energy claim that it combines the environmental friendliness of solar and wind energy with the reliability of coal and_____ opponents of nuclear energy criticize its cost and safety.
   A) gas, nevertheless,
   B) gas; nevertheless,
   C) gas nevertheless
   D) gas, nevertheless

5. There are many beliefs about nutrition that have been_____ people need six to eight glasses of water a day to stay healthy, sugar causes hyperactivity in children, and low-fat versions of foods are always healthier than their counterparts with higher fat contents.
   A) challenged, all
   B) challenged: all
   C) challenged all
   D) challenged, including: all

6. The maned wolf has a unique_____ unusually long legs that help it evade predators.
   A) adaptation;
   B) adaptation; it having
   C) adaptation, it has
   D) adaptation:

7. The Statue of Liberty was made _____
   A) with: iron, copper, and concrete.
   B) with iron: as well as copper, and concrete.
   C) with iron, copper, and concrete.
   D) with; iron, copper, and concrete.

8. Relatively little is known about astatine because of its rarity and short _____ scientists have used tracer studies to make some conclusions about its chemical properties.
   A) half-life; however,
   B) half-life however
   C) half-life: however,
   D) half-life, however,

9. The launch of the product went better _____ out on the first day of sales.
   A) than expected: all the inventory was sold
   B) than expected, all the inventory was sold
   C) than expected, since all the inventory having been sold
   D) than expected; because all the inventory sold

10. Not everyone supported the _____ placed too many burdensome restrictions on trade.
    A) treaty; it
    B) treaty, it
    C) treaty it
    D) treaty— it —

11. Staff members are trained in handling radioactive _____ before they can work in the lab.
    A) materials potentially poisonous materials when people are exposed to them in high quantities
    B) materials—potentially poisonous materials when people are exposed to them in high quantities—
    C) materials; potentially poisonous materials when people are exposed to them in high quantities
    D) materials potentially poisonous materials when people are exposed to them in high quantities—

12. _____ appeared in *The Saturday Evening Post.*
    A) Norman Rockwell's art—mostly works depicting everyday life in America—
    B) Norman Rockwell's art—mostly— works depicting everyday life in America,
    C) Norman Rockwell's art—mostly works depicting everyday life in America
    D) Norman Rockwell's art: mostly works depicting everyday life in America:

13. While the 18th Amendment made the distribution of alcohol_____ it was difficult to enforce.
    A) illegal—
    B) illegal,
    C) illegal;
    D) illegal:

14. The Niña, the Pinta, and the _____ three ships were used by Christopher Columbus in his first voyage to the Americas.
    A) Santa María these
    B) Santa María; these
    C) Santa María: these
    D) Santa María—these

15. The committee consisted of a diverse group of_____ a botanist, a lobbyist, a politician, and an engineer.
    A) people;
    B) people,
    C) people, which included:
    D) people:

16. The topics covered in the psychology course included one of Leni's_____ the science of neuroplasticity.
    A) favorites; that being
    B) favorites;
    C) favorites:
    D) favorites, it is

17. When interviewing for a job, it is important that you accomplish several _____ gain the trust of the interviewer, determine if the position is the right fit for you, and communicate how your strengths will contribute to the success of the company.
    A) objectives:
    B) objectives
    C) objectives; and
    D) objectives: being that you

18. Fruit flies are ideal candidates for genetic_____ they share many genes with humans and are relatively low-maintenance.
    A) studies,
    B) studies; and
    C) studies:
    D) studies

19. _____ are the subunits of DNA and RNA.
    A) Nucleotides organic molecules that contain nitrogenous bases, phosphate groups, and sugars;
    B) Nucleotides: organic molecules that contain nitrogenous bases, phosphate groups, and sugars,
    C) Nucleotides—organic molecules that contain nitrogenous bases, phosphate groups, and sugars—
    D) Nucleotides, organic molecules that contain nitrogenous bases, phosphate groups, and sugars:

20. Because many of Zora Hurston's stories were _____ her works faded into obscurity.
    A) archived:
    B) archived—
    C) archived,
    D) archived;

21. The term "waterfowl" refers to various species of birds that live on or around water, _____ pelicans, gulls, and herons.
    A) such as:
    B) such as—
    C) such as;
    D) such as

22. According to Adam Smith, acting in one's self-interest is needed to ensure economic_____ however, some of his critics claim that there should be more of a focus on the welfare of people than on the accumulation of wealth.
    A) prosperity,
    B) prosperity
    C) prosperity;
    D) prosperity; and

23. Yao saw many_____ on lily pads along the pond.
    A) frogs dozens of them
    B) frogs, dozens of them,
    C) frogs; dozens of them
    D) frogs; dozens of them:

24. I go camping every_____ but with my friends, enjoying quality time in nature.
    A) month not by myself,
    B) month; not by myself
    C) month not by myself;
    D) month—not by myself,

143

25. Margarita implemented changes into her_____ avocado puree for butter and almond flour for wheat flour.
    A) cooking; substituting
    B) cooking; substituted
    C) cooking, substituting
    D) cooking, she substituted

26. While public relations agencies have evolved in the internet age, one thing has remained_____ need for unique content—whether online or offline—that strengthens their brands.
    A) constant: the
    B) constant—the
    C) constant; the
    D) constant, the

27. Providing tasty alternatives for consumers who are_____ the popular bakery serves cookies made with organic wheat flour and unrefined cane sugar.
    A) vegan
    B) vegan:
    C) vegan,
    D) vegan;

28. Tipping practices vary greatly by_____ in the Americas, it is customary to leave tips since tips comprise a significant portion of servers' incomes; in many European countries, tips are not expected unless the service is especially excellent since gratuity is already factored into the bill; and in many countries in East Asia, there is no strong tipping culture, and tips may even be turned down.
    A) country, so
    B) country:
    C) country, for
    D) country

29. Quick thinking, resilience, confidence, and public speaking skills—_____ from taking improvisation classes.
    A) which all benefit
    B) all benefit
    C) all benefiting
    D) that all benefit

30. Archaeologists have uncovered something_____ they found the lost underwater city of Neapolis 1,700 years after a tsunami sank it.
    A) extraordinary,
    B) extraordinary— because —
    C) extraordinary:
    D) extraordinary; being that

31. One place that people interested in the tech industry should consider working is_____ thriving environment for tech jobs.
    A) Seattle, Washington— a
    B) Seattle, Washington; a
    C) Seattle, Washington), a
    D) Seattle, Washington (a

32. The solar industry is viewed positively by many _____ a Pew Research Center survey found that 89% of U.S. adults favor expanding solar power to address both costs and environmental concerns.
    A) Americans; as
    B) Americans:
    C) Americans. As
    D) Americans,

33. By acting as natural barriers to wind and ocean_____ sand dunes offer a line of defense against coastal storms.
    A) waves;
    B) waves—
    C) waves,
    D) waves:

34. A giant lake turned_____ with microalgae that had turned red in conditions of high light intensity and salinity.
    A) blood-red, it was filled
    B) blood-red: it was filled
    C) blood-red; it was filled—
    D) blood-red. It was: filled

35. Among many consumers, there is a growing_____ business models that are environmentally sustainable.
    A) desire: for
    B) desire for:
    C) desire, for
    D) desire for

36. The athletic trainer explained a benefit of mobility_____ decreased risk of injury.
    A) drills;
    B) drills:
    C) drills
    D) drills,

37. The company's new pay policy, which increased the minimum wage to $18 an hour, was a huge_____ turnover among employees decreased markedly, saving the company millions of dollars.
    A) success: as
    B) success, as
    C) success; as
    D) success,

38. For his creative writing class, Azande_____ narrators with divergent interpretations of the same events forced readers to ponder multiple perspectives.
    A) wrote a mystery novel with a unique narrative structure, alternating
    B) wrote a mystery novel with a unique narrative structure, he alternated
    C) wrote a mystery novel with a unique narrative structure: alternating
    D) wrote: a mystery novel with a unique narrative structure, which included alternating

39. Emmanuelle Charpentier and Jennifer Doudna developed an innovation that revolutionized the field of_____ CRISPR, which is a tool that allows scientists to easily edit the genomes of many species.
    A) genomics
    B) genomics:
    C) genomics
    D) genomics

40. Basic research and applied research both use many of the same rigorous quantitative and qualitative data collection and analysis methods, but they have different focuses. Basic research is a theoretical research approach that is done primarily to advance knowledge in a specific_____ research is a practical research approach that is done primarily to solve specific problems.
    A) field; applied
    B) field: applied
    C) field, applied
    D) field—applied

Lesson 12: Items in a Series

A series is a list of three or more items. The items can include words, phrases, and clauses.

1) Use commas between items in a list or series that includes three or more items.
   - At the zoo, I saw lions, tigers, and bears.
   - Before you take a big test, make sure to get plenty of rest, eat a nutritious meal, and relax your mind.

2) **DON'T** use a comma after "and" in a list.
   - Incorrect: The flowers in the garden were red, yellow, **and,** purple.
   - Correct: The flowers in the garden were red, yellow, **and** purple.

3) **DON'T** use commas before the first item in a series when a verb precedes the first item.
   - Incorrect: Zoe **is,** smart, reliable, and honest.
   - Correct: Zoe **is** smart, reliable, and honest.

4) **DON'T** use a comma between the last adjective and the noun it describes when the series consists of adjectives.
   - Incorrect: The fair, understanding, and **respected, judge** was intolerant of unprofessional behavior in her courtroom.
   - Correct: The fair, understanding, and **respected judge** was intolerant of unprofessional behavior in her courtroom.

Semicolons

In some cases, semicolons might be necessary to separate items in a series. Use semicolons when at least one item in the series contains a comma itself.

1) Dates are separated from years and days of the week by commas.
   - Monday, June 1, 2015.

2) Commas are also used to separate cities from states and states from countries.
   - San Francisco, California.
   - Moscow, Russia.

3) Multiple dates are typically separated by semicolons when weeks or years are included.
   - The annual festivals will be held on March 8, 2024; April 7, 2025; and May 9, 2026.
   - We will meet Monday, April 8; Tuesday, April 9; and Wednesday, April 10.

4) People with formal titles that include commas are separated by semicolons.
   - The conference speakers are Ms. Nelson, School Board Trustee; Mr. Ortega, Director of Mathematics; and Ms. Quinn, President of the Parent Teacher Association.

5) Multiple geographic locations that include commas are separated by semicolons, such as cities within states and states within countries.
   - I visited London, England; Paris, France; and Tokyo, Japan.

Sample Question

> Amy Tan's popular literary works include *The Joy Luck Club*, a 1989 novel about a group of Chinese immigrant mothers and their American-born_____ a narrative essay that portrays a Christmas Eve dinner from Tan's childhood; and *The Opposite of Fate: A Book of Musings*, a memoir.
> Which choice completes the text so that it conforms to the principles of standard English?
> A) daughters, "Fish Cheeks,"
> B) daughters; "Fish Cheeks,"
> C) daughters; "Fish Cheeks"
> D) daughters, "Fish Cheeks":

A semicolon must separate the titled works, as indicated by the semicolon before "and." A comma should follow "Fish Cheeks" to introduce the phrase describing the narrative essay. **Choice B** is correct.

Drill 1: Select the choice that best completes each blank to conform to standard written English.

1. The omelet included onions,_____
   A) peppers and mushrooms.
   B) peppers, and, mushrooms.
   C) peppers, and mushrooms.
   D) peppers; and mushrooms.

2. The student _____ effective organizational habits.
   A) has excellent time management skills; a strong work ethic; and
   B) has, excellent time management skills, a strong work ethic, and
   C) has excellent time management skills, a strong work ethic, and,
   D) has excellent time management skills, a strong work ethic, and

3. The consulting firm has offices in_____
   A) Manhattan, New York, Durham, North Carolina, and Philadelphia, Pennsylvania.
   B) Manhattan, New York; Durham, North Carolina and; Philadelphia, Pennsylvania.
   C) Manhattan, New York; Durham, North Carolina; and Philadelphia, Pennsylvania.
   D) Manhattan New York; Durham North Carolina; and Philadelphia Pennsylvania.

4. Aeschylus, _____ Euripides were three of the foremost Greek playwrights.
   A) Sophocles and
   B) Sophocles, and
   C) Sophocles, and,
   D) Sophocles; and

5. Bring pencils,_____ with you to the math test.
   A) erasers, and a calculator
   B) erasers; and a calculator
   C) erasers, and, a calculator,
   D) erasers, and, a calculator

6. The bus will pass through the states of_____ California.
   A) Washington; Oregon and
   B) Washington, Oregon, and
   C) Washington, Oregon and,
   D) Washington; Oregon; and

7. The highest-grossing films of all time include_____ *The Avengers.*
   A) *Avatar, Titanic,* and
   B) *Avatar, Titanic,* and,
   C) *Avatar; Titanic;* and
   D) *Avatar; Titanic;* and,

8. Guests at the party can order one of three meals: a quesadilla with black beans, salsa, and_____ a portabella mushroom with potatoes and mixed greens.
   A) rice, a grilled chicken wrap with French fries, or
   B) rice; a grilled chicken wrap with French fries; or
   C) rice, a grilled chicken wrap with French fries, or,
   D) rice; a grilled chicken wrap with French fries or;

9. The responsibilities of architects include designing building_____ computer-aided drafting systems.
   A) plans; researching zoning laws, building codes, and city ordinances; and using
   B) plans, researching zoning laws, building codes, and city ordinances, and using
   C) plans, researching zoning laws, building codes, and city ordinances and using
   D) plans researching zoning laws building codes and city ordinances; and, using

10. Biomedical engineers are scientists who often work in_____ agencies, and private companies.
    A) academic institutions: government
    B) academic institutions, government
    C) academic institutions; government
    D) academic institutions government

11. Occupational therapists can earn a certificate in nine specialties,_____
    A) including: gerontology, mental health, pediatrics and physical rehabilitation.
    B) including— gerontology, mental health, pediatrics, and physical rehabilitation.
    C) including gerontology, mental health, pediatrics, and physical rehabilitation.
    D) including gerontology, mental health, pediatrics and physical, rehabilitation.

12. The members of George Washington's cabinet included Thomas Jefferson, Secretary of_____ Edmund Randolph, Attorney General.
    A) State, Alexander Hamilton, Secretary of the Treasury, and
    B) State, Alexander, Hamilton, Secretary, of the Treasury, and,
    C) State; Alexander Hamilton Secretary of the Treasury; and
    D) State; Alexander Hamilton, Secretary of the Treasury; and

Lesson 13: Possessive Nouns and Pronouns

Possessive forms of nouns are used to show belonging.

1) To make most singular nouns possessive, add an apostrophe (') followed by an "s." For instance, "the child's coat" means "the coat that belongs to the child."
   - The man's car is getting washed.

The car belongs to the "man."

   - The company's founder's car is getting washed.

The "founder" belongs to the "company," and the "car" belongs to the "founder."

2) To make most plural nouns possessive, simply add an apostrophe.
   - The girls' dresses are red.

Multiple girls have dresses that are red.

3) When the plural form of a verb does NOT end in an "s," put an "s" after the apostrophe.
   - The **children's** backpacks are in their lockers.
   - The **women's** clothing store is down the street.

The following are some nouns that take irregular plural forms: calf (calves), shelf (shelves), knife (knives), life (lives), wife (wives), half (halves), wolf (wolves), loaf (loaves), potato (potatoes), tomato (tomatoes), volcano (volcanoes), cactus (cacti), nucleus (nuclei), analysis (analyses), thesis (theses), crisis (crises), phenomenon (phenomena), criterion (criteria), man (men), woman (women), person (people), tooth (teeth), mouse (mice).

   - The **knives'** edges are sharp
   - Both **crises'** origins are unknown.

Possessive Recap

Type of Word	Singular Possessive Examples	Plural Possessive Examples
Word that becomes plural by adding "s" (e.g., "boys" is the plural of "boy).	The **boy's** backpack. (The backpack of the boy).	The **boys'** backpacks. (The backpacks of the boys).
Word that becomes plural by changing "y" to "-ies" (e.g., "families" is the plural of "family")	The **family's** plans (The plans of the family).	The **families'** plans (The plans of multiple families).
Plural nouns that do not end in "s" (e.g., "teeth" is the plural of "tooth")	The **tooth's** shape (The shape of one tooth).	The **teeth's** shape (The shape of multiple teeth).

4) When more than one noun is present, the meaning of the sentence changes depending on if one or both nouns are possessive. When two nouns **share ownership** of something, ONLY make the **second noun possessive**. When they **do not share ownership**, make **BOTH nouns possessive.**
   - **Saul and Evan's** report was on the Industrial Revolution.

Since both boys worked together on a single report, only the last noun should be possessive.

   - **Saul's** and **Evan's** reports were on the Industrial Revolution.

Saul and Evan worked on two different reports, so both their names require apostrophes.

5) Possessive pronouns show ownership *(mine, yours, his, hers, ours, theirs)*.
   - The game is **mine.**
   - The house on the corner is **theirs.**

6) Possessive adjectives precede nouns *(my, your, his, her, their, our, its, whose)*.
   - **Your** laptop is white.
   - I read **her** letter after it arrived in the mail.

7) Possessive adjectives and possessive nouns precede gerunds, which are nouns ending in "-ing." When "-ing" verbs function as participles (adjectives), the noun preceding the participle is NOT possessive.

   - The **children** reading the book are in the third grade.

"Reading the book" acts as a modifying phrase describing the children.

   - The **children's** reading of the book was impressive.

In this case, "reading" is a gerund (a noun that is an activity), so an apostrophe is needed.

   - The **professors** teaching biology at the institution are excellent.

"Teaching biology" is a modifying phrase describing the "professors."

   - The **professors'** teaching of biology is excellent.

Here, "teaching" functions as a noun. The teaching itself is excellent.

8) Possessive nouns should not generally precede a verb. **Know that certain words can act as both nouns and verbs depending on the context.**
   - Many people comment on the extreme heat in the town during the summer.

"Comment" is a verb meaning "say," so "people" should not be in possessive form.

   - I heard the **man** comment, "I am tired."

Verbs introduce quotes. "Comment" is a verb introducing a quote, so "man" is not in possessive form.

- I heard the **man's** comment while I was shopping.

In this case, "comment" is a noun meaning "statement," which belongs to the man.

9) Do not make the indirect object possessive when it is followed by an direct object. Recall that an indirect object is the recipient of the direct object, the object on which the verb acts.
   - Common Error: Arunita gave the **kids' snacks** during the train ride to the city.
   - Correct: Arunita gave the **kids snacks** during the train ride to the city.

"Snacks" is the direct object, and "kids" is the indirect object, so no apostrophes are needed. "Kids' snacks" means "snacks of the kids." Note that the first (incorrect) version of the sentence nonsensically means "Arunita gave the *snacks of the kids* during the train ride to the city."

Sample Question

> Many marine mammals rely heavily on echolocation, a process by which they use sound waves to locate objects and gain information about their surroundings. By emitting sound waves and interpreting their reverberations off of objects, marine mammals can get a sense of these_____ Thus, echolocation essentially functions as a means by which these animals "see the world."
>
> Which choice completes the text so that it conforms to the principles of standard English?
>   A) object's shapes and positions.
>   B) objects shapes and positions.
>   C) objects' shapes and positions.
>   D) objects' shapes' and positions.

The shapes and positions belong to multiple objects. Thus, only "objects" should take the possessive form. It should be in the plural possessive form, as choice C shows. **Choice C is correct.** Choice A incorrectly suggests the shapes and positions belong to one object. Choice B fails to make "objects" possessive. Choice D illogically suggests something belongs to "shapes."

Mini Active Learning Activity

Answer the questions about each sentence.

The <u>teachers'</u> grade book was on her desk.

1. Why is the underlined portion incorrect?

2. What should the underlined portion say?

<u>Meteorologist's</u> forecasts are often very accurate, though these forecasts are less accurate for days farther into the future.

3. Why is the underlined portion incorrect?

4. What should the underlined portion say?

Larissa's and Cael's <u>projects'</u> each impressed the judges, and they both earned top marks.

5. Why is the underlined portion incorrect?

6. What should the underlined portion say?

Student A: The professor gave her **students'** many chances to succeed, such as low-stakes quizzes and extra credit opportunities.

Student B: The professor gave her **students** many chances to succeed, such as low-stakes quizzes and extra credit opportunities.

7. Which student wrote the sentence correctly? Justify your answer.

Sentence 1: **Fei and Eli's** research examined the impact of social media on sports marketing.

Sentence 2: **Fei's and Eli's** research examined the impact of social media on sports marketing.

8. What is the difference between each sentence's meaning?

Drill 1: Select the choice that best completes each blank to conform to standard written English.

1. Francis Marion, an American Revolutionary soldier known as the "Swamp Fox" due to his unconventional war tactics, grew up on his_____ plantation and worked as a farmer.
   A) families'
   B) families
   C) family's
   D) family

2. The candidate who supported ordinary workers was known as the "_____ candidate."
   A) peoples'
   B) people's
   C) peoples
   D) person'

3. The various_____ between nation states have been instrumental in maintaining the balance of power in the region.
   A) alliance's
   B) alliances
   C) alliances'
   D) alliance

4. The musical_____ latest song was an instant success, earning the ensemble a substantial amount of popularity.
   A) groups'
   B) groups
   C) group's
   D) group

5. _____collaborative research on the structure of DNA earned them a Nobel Prize.
   A) Watson and Crick's
   B) Watson's and Crick's
   C) Watson's and Crick
   D) Watson and Cricks'

6. Lola and Cabrina were elated that their project won first prize, as evidenced by the _____when they were given their award.
   A) girl's reactions
   B) girls' reactions'
   C) girls' reactions
   D) girls reactions'

7. Many of F. Scott _____ such as "The Curious Case of Benjamin Button," are set in the Jazz Age.
   A) Fitzgerald stories,
   B) Fitzgerald's stories,
   C) Fitzgerald's story's,
   D) Fitzgerald's' stories',

8. The professor sent all of his students a survey at the end of the semester, and he adjusted future iterations of the course based on his_____ feedback.
   A) student's
   B) student's is
   C) students'
   D) students

9. Shinichi_____ of teaching the violin, which is based on the principles of language acquisition, is popular in many schools throughout the world.
   A) Suzukis method
   B) Suzuki's method
   C) Suzuki's method's
   D) Suzukis' method'

10. Nina_____ during the Civil Rights Movement reflected her opposition to the subjugation of minorities.
    A) Simone's impassioned musical performances
    B) Simone's impassioned musical's performances
    C) Simones' impassioned musical performances
    D) Simone's impassioned musical performances'

11. _____is mild and dry during the summer but extremely cold during the winter.
    A) Crater Lake weather
    B) Crater Lake weather's
    C) Crater Lake's weather
    D) Crater Lake's weathers

12. _____separate projects helped advance our knowledge of electricity.
    A) Michael Faraday and Nikola Tesla's
    B) Michael Faraday's and Nikola Tesla
    C) Michael Faradays' and Nikolas Tesla
    D) Michael Faraday's and Nikola Tesla's

13. _____ the highest free-standing mountain in the world and is home to three volcanic cones.
    A) Tanzania's Mount Kilimanjaro's is
    B) Tanzanias' Mount Kilimanjaro's is
    C) Tanzania Mount Kilimanjaro's is
    D) Tanzania's Mount Kilimanjaro is

14. The_____ team won five consecutive games.
    A) men's basketball's
    B) men's basketball
    C) men' basketball
    D) mens' basketball

15. _____is a Lhasa Apso.
    A) Alistair's mother's cousin's dog
    B) Alistair's mother's cousin's dog's
    C) Alistair's mother cousin's dog
    D) Alistair's mother cousin dog

16. I did not appreciate ____ questioning of my authority.
    A) you
    B) your
    C) you're
    D) yours

17. While the councilwoman tried to deny being at fault, the responsibility for ensuring that the procedures were followed was _____
    A) her.
    B) she.
    C) her's.
    D) hers.

18. _____ protesting ultimately did a lot to raise awareness for the issues plaguing the city.
    A) Ourselves
    B) We
    C) Our
    D) Ours

19. Many_____ chemistry find the subject demanding but rewarding.
    A) students studying
    B) student study
    C) student's studying
    D) students' studying's

20. Citizens can take actions to protect their national_____ and their resources.
    A) park's
    B) parks
    C) parks;
    D) parks'

21. I appreciate the way the_____ coach their teammates.
    A) leader's
    B) leaders'
    C) leaders
    D) leader's'

22. I did not agree with the_____ and he had no evidence to support his assertions.
    A) speaker's claim,
    B) speaker's claim's,
    C) speakers claim,
    D) speaker claim,

23. I heard the _____ "My work is intended to spark dialogue."
    A) author's claim
    B) authors' claim,
    C) author's claiming,
    D) author claim,

24. The nutritionist explained _____ to me.
    A) waters health benefits
    B) waters' health benefits
    C) water's health benefits
    D) water's health benefit's

25. The_____ walking through the park enjoyed the summer weather.
    A) children's
    B) children
    C) child's
    D) childrens'

26. The_____ that relieve pain are called endorphins.
    A) brains' neurotransmitters'
    B) brain's neurotransmitters
    C) brains neurotransmitters
    D) brain's neurotransmitter's

27. After a major public scandal involving a troublesome employee, the _____ practices cohere with its purported mission earned him plaudits from the media.
    A) executive's thoughtful efforts to make his company's
    B) executives' thoughtful efforts to make his company's
    C) executives thoughtful efforts to make his company's
    D) executive's thoughtful efforts to make his companies'

28. The incubator in the youth department of the library held three _____
    A) chicken eggs'.
    B) chicken's eggs.
    C) chickens eggs.
    D) chicken eggs.

Lesson 14: Restrictive and Nonrestrictive Punctuation

Restrictive elements (essential elements) are needed to preserve the meaning of a sentence, and they are **not set off by commas, dashes, or parentheses.** They often serve to define the subject.

- Restrictive: Only people **who are residents of the town** can enter the beach without paying a fee.

Without the bolded clause, the sentence would improperly suggest that all people can enter the beach without paying a fee.

Restrictive Examples
- The trophy **that I own** sits on my shelf.
- The experts **whose ideas were cited in the paper** are credible.
- I remember the time **when we went snorkeling.**

Nonrestrictive elements (nonessential elements) are supplemental words, phrases, and clauses that are set off from the rest of the sentence by commas, dashes, or parentheses.

- Nonrestrictive: My friend, **who recently bought a new dishwasher**, is relieved to no longer have to wash dishes by hand.

It is clear that the speaker's friend is the subject. The sentence is understandable without the bolded clause.

Nonrestrictive Examples
- My brother, **known for his stories of his travels across the globe,** invited me to go on vacation with him.
- The cathedral, **which was built during medieval times,** exemplifies Gothic architecture.
- I learned about the news from the announcement, **which was made on the loudspeaker.**
- Since Mrs. Malaprop, **who was a character in an English play by Richard Brinsley Sheridan,** frequently misused words with similar sounds, a comic jumbling of words is referred to as a malapropism.

The bolded clauses provide supplemental information that can be deleted from the sentences.

Relative Clause Tips

Relative clauses are clauses beginning with relative pronouns (*who, whom, which, that*) or relative adverbs (*where, when, why*).

1) "That" is always restrictive and is virtually never preceded by a comma unless one is needed for other reasons (e.g., to set off a nonessential phrase before the relative clause).
   - Incorrect: I listened to the song on the radio, **that my favorite country singer wrote.**
   - Correct: I listened to the song on the radio **that my favorite country singer wrote**.

The restrictive clause clarifies to which song the speaker is referring.

2) "Which" is *usually* nonrestrictive.
   - Correct: The song, **which I listened to on the radio,** was written by the country singer.

3) When a relative clause with "that" is interrupted by nonrestrictive elements, add a comma AFTER "that."
   - Sugar is a substance that, **when consumed in large amounts,** is harmful.

The restrictive clause "that is harmful" is interrupted by the bolded nonrestrictive clause.

Appositive Tips

An appositive is a noun or phrase that renames or provides additional information about a noun.

1) Appositives that can be easily removed from sentences are generally nonrestrictive.
   - My calculus class, **the hardest class offered in the math department,** ends next Tuesday.
   - The replica, **an accurate representation of the ship,** is made of wood.
   - The United States' first president, **George Washington,** gave a famous farewell address.
   - George Washington, **President of the United States,** gave a famous farewell address.

The sentences above make sense when the bolded appositives are ignored. When the commas are removed, the sentences read awkwardly and do not have the necessary pauses.

2) Lengthy phrases that require pauses are generally nonrestrictive.
   - My friend Jayce, **a natural prankster who appreciates a good joke,** tricked our teacher.

The bolded phrase can be removed from the sentence.

3) Many appositives and definitions (including definitions of verbs and adjectives)— especially those preceded by *or, also known as, named,* or *called*— are nonrestrictive.
   - Godfrey has an alpha, **or dominant,** personality type.
   - Organic compounds, **also known as carbon-based compounds,** exist in living organisms.

In each example, the bolded appositive renames the noun before the comma ("alpha" and "organic compounds").

4) If a sentence is no longer grammatical when the appositive is removed, the appositive is always restrictive.
   - Incorrect: Councilwoman, **Marisol Jones,** is at the convention.
   - Correct: Councilwoman **Marisol Jones** is at the convention.

The sentence is not logical when the bolded appositive is ignored ("Councilwoman is at the convention" does not make sense). The name is needed for the sentence to make sense, so "Marisol Jones" is restrictive (essential).

5) If a sentence is grammatical when an appositive is ignored, there is sometimes an option to make the appositive restrictive. An appositive can be made restrictive when it is very short (such as a name) and clarifies confusion about the identity of the noun.
   - Nonrestrictive: My cousin, Dylan, lives in San Diego.
   - Restrictive: My cousin Dylan lives in San Diego.

In the first sentence, "Dylan" is a nonrestrictive appositive. The sentence makes sense without the name, and one can assume that the speaker has only one cousin, which is why the name is supplemental information. In the second sentence, it can be assumed that the speaker has more than one cousin. "Dylan" is essential because it clarifies to which cousin the speaker is referring.

6) States following names of cities and countries following names of states/cities are nonrestrictive.
   - While vacationing in Ghent, **Belgium**, I saw the Belfry of Ghent, a large bell tower.
   - Washington, **D.C.**, is where the Supreme Court listens to oral arguments.

Titles with Names in More Depth

When a name follows a title, such as a professional title, the name will generally either be set off by a pair of commas (more rarely dashes) on *both sides* of the name OR by no punctuation at all. The general rule is that if a name is needed, *do not use commas.* If the name is optional, set it off by commas (or dashes).

1) **Check to see if the sentence even makes sense when the name is deleted. If the sentence sounds off without the name, then the name is essential. NO COMMAS are needed. Consider the sentence below.**
   - Correct: Engineering major **Dora Smith** entered a robotics competition and won first prize.

If we get rid of the name, we are left with the sentence below.
   - Incorrect: Engineering major entered a robotics competition and won first prize.

The sentence no longer makes sense without the name, so the name is essential. No punctuation must be added to the original sentence.

2) **If the name is optional grammatically, you generally should set if off by commas. You are especially likely to need commas when an article precedes the title (*the, a, an*).**
   - Correct: An engineering major, **Dora Smith,** entered a robotics competition and won first prize.

Notice we can rewrite the sentence below without the name, so commas are needed.
   - Correct: An engineering major entered a robotics competition and won first prize.

3) **When a title follows the name, the title is generally optional.**
   - Sammy Jones, **Professor of European History**, recently earned tenure.

The title is a nonessential appositive, so it is set off by commas.

Titles with Multiple People

When a title refers to more than one person, the sentence will often be grammatically correct when the names are ignored. To better determine if the names are essential, pretend the sentence is only about one person.
- Correct: Researchers **James Watson and Francis Crick** received a Nobel Prize for their discovery of the structure of DNA.
- Correct: Researchers received a Nobel Prize for their discovery of the structure of DNA.

The first sentence is grammatically correct when the names are ignored, as the second sentence shows. However, this is not the case in the singular version of the sentence, as shown below.
- Correct: Researcher **James Watson** received a Nobel Prize for his discovery of the structure of DNA.
- Incorrect: Researcher received a Nobel Prize for his discovery of the structure of DNA.

Because the name is needed in the singular version of the sentence, this shows that the names in the plural version are important enough to not be set off by commas.

Dashes and Parentheses

1) To add more emphasis to nonessential information, consider using dashes instead of commas.

- My grandma—**who just turned 80 years old**—ran in a marathon.

The writer wants to emphasize the grandmother's age for dramatic effect.

2) The dash is often preferable to the comma when setting off a series.
- When I went to the aquarium, I observed my favorite animals—**whales, dolphins, and otters**—playfully swimming in the water.

If commas were used instead of dashes, the structure of the sentence would be confusing.

DO NOT use a dash with a comma to set off nonessential elements in the middle of a sentence. Pick one punctuation mark to be consistent.
- Incorrect: Dr. Clark—**a professor of paleontology,** delivered a fantastic lecture.
- Correct: Dr. Clark—**a professor of paleontology**—delivered a fantastic lecture.
- Correct: Dr. Clark**, a professor of paleontology,** delivered a fantastic lecture.

To take away emphasis from nonessential information, consider using **parentheses.** Information inside parentheses can be in the form of an independent clause.
- The dog **(a Pomeranian)** is running through the field.

The breed of the dog is treated almost as an afterthought.

Parenthetical elements interrupt the flow of a sentence without distorting its meaning. They are nonrestrictive.

Common Parenthetical Expressions

as a matter of fact	in fact
by the way	in the meantime
for example/for instance	needless to say
incidentally	no doubt
however	though

- It is, **in fact,** a very common practice.
- It seems, **however,** that you do not follow the rules.

Note: Parenthetical conjunctive adverbs should be set off by commas, NOT dashes!
- Incorrect: The subjects—**meanwhile**—remained oblivious to the true purpose of the study.
- Correct: The subjects, **meanwhile,** remained oblivious to the true purpose of the study.

Oftentimes, a subject and a verb act as a parenthetical clause. Generally, the parenthetical clause serves to interrupt a sentence for the purpose of indicating a subject's thoughts, feelings, findings, or commentary.
- The memo, **he noticed**, was filled with inaccuracies.
- The house, **she discovered**, lacked running water.
- The play, **Rafa observed**, was subversive in its themes.

Sample Question

> Bong_____ of the critically acclaimed movie *Parasite*, is one of the most successful South Korean directors, known for his films with sudden tone shifts and slapstick humor. *Parasite* became the first non-English movie to win the Academy Award for Best Picture.
> Which choice completes the text so that it conforms to the principles of standard English?
>   A) Joon-ho the director
>   B) Joon-ho, the director,
>   C) Joon-ho, the director
>   D) Joon-ho— the director

"The director of the critically acclaimed movie *Parasite*" acts as a nonessential appositive between commas that renames Bong Joon-ho. The sentence is complete, and its meaning is clear when this phrase is removed. **Choice C is correct.** Choice A incorrectly suggests the appositive is restrictive. Choice B confusingly sets off "the director" by commas within the appositive. Choice D incorrectly uses a dash at the beginning of the appositive when a comma is already at the end of it (after *Parasite*), resulting in inconsistent punctuation.

Mini Active Learning Activity

Add missing punctuation to each sentence.

1. The Davy lamp—which was named after its inventor Humphrey Davy—consisted of a wick lamp that had a flame enclosed inside a mesh screen.

2. It is dishonorable to slander, or defame, other people's characters.

3. With its body in a crouched position and its tail tucked between its legs, the younger wolf, displaying telltale signs of submission, showed the more dominant wolf it did not mean to challenge its authority; rather, it just wanted to play.

4. In 1981, Jimmy Carter awarded the Presidential Medal of Freedom to journalist Walter Cronkite, one of the most trusted voices in news.

5. Sans-culottes, literally meaning "those without breeches," were common people during the French Revolution, many of whom were urban laborers who became militant partisans.

Drill 1: Select the choice that best completes each blank to conform to standard written English.

1. My_____ wonderful adventure.
   A) trip needless to say was a
   B) trip needless, to say was a,
   C) trip, needless to say, was a
   D) trip, needless to say was a

2. Jai alai_____ bounced off a wall at high speeds.
   A) is a sport, that involves a ball being,
   B) is a sport that, involves a ball being
   C) is a sport that involves, a ball being
   D) is a sport that involves a ball being

3. _____earned a hefty commission for his work.
   A) My brother, Esteban who is a great salesman,
   B) My brother Esteban who, is a great salesman,
   C) My brother Esteban, who is a great salesman,
   D) My brother Esteban who is, a great salesman,

4. Only a_____ can become a Foreign Service Officer.
   A) person who successfully completes a background check
   B) person, who successfully completes a background check
   C) person, who successfully, completes a background check
   D) person, who successfully completes a background check,

5. Social_____ is frequently used by businesses to attract new clients and strengthen their brand recognition.
   A) media which has become popular in recent years,
   B) media, which has become popular in recent years
   C) media, which has become popular in recent years,
   D) media which has become popular in recent years

6. _____is frequently taught in high schools for its timeless themes.
   A) *1984*, a dystopian tale by George Orwell,
   B) *1984* a dystopian tale by George Orwell
   C) *1984,* a dystopian tale by George Orwell
   D) *1984* a dystopian tale by George Orwell,

7. The three central crops of various Native American_____ were often planted close together by companion planting.
   A) groups: corn, beans, and squash,
   B) groups—corn, beans, and squash—
   C) groups, corn, beans, and squash,
   D) groups: corn, beans, and squash—

8. The dogs_____ in Ivan Pavlov's experiments developed a conditioned response to the sound of a bell, as they learned to associate it with feeding time.
   A) that, were used
   B) that, were used,
   C) that were, used
   D) that were used

9. Stockholm,_____ the Nobel Prizes are awarded every year.
   A) Sweden is the city where
   B) Sweden, is the city, where,
   C) Sweden, is the city where
   D) Sweden is the city, where

10. Using eggs, toast, cinnamon, and milk, Blanche made French_____
    A) toast which is her favorite breakfast food.
    B) toast, which is her favorite breakfast food.
    C) toast which is, her favorite breakfast food.
    D) toast which is her (favorite breakfast food).

11. _____the few female pharaohs in ancient Egypt, ruled Egypt for less than three years.
    A) Nitocris, one of
    B) Nitocris one, of
    C) Nitocris one of
    D) Nitocris is one of

12. Thomas Jefferson's mansion at_____ appears on the back of the nickel.
    A) Monticello, (Jefferson designed it himself)
    B) Monticello (Jefferson designed it himself)
    C) Monticello—designed by Jefferson, himself
    D) Monticello, designed, by Jefferson himself

13. *Star Trek* was a television series of the_____ used futuristic storylines to indirectly comment on contemporary social issues.
    A) 1960s, that
    B) 1960s that,
    C) 1960s; that
    D) 1960s that

14. Harriet Tubman was an active proponent,_____ of women's suffrage, and she worked alongside advocates such as Susan B. Anthony to advance the cause.
    A) or supporter
    B) or supporter—
    C) or supporter,
    D) or, supporter

15. Microsoft_____ established the Bill and Melinda Gates Foundation to advance philanthropic pursuits.
    A) founder, Bill Gates,
    B) founder Bill Gates
    C) founder Bill Gates,
    D) founder: Bill Gates,

16. New York's 99th _____ popular for reaching across party lines.
    A) mayor, Fiorello La Guardia, was
    B) mayor—Fiorello La Guardia, was
    C) mayor Fiorello La Guardia was,
    D) mayor: Fiorello La Guardia, was

17. An Aeolian_____ was performed by the students in the music theory class.
    A) scale, also known as a natural minor scale
    B) scale also known as a natural minor scale
    C) scale and also known as, a natural minor scale,
    D) scale, also known as a natural minor scale,

18. Only_____ can become professors at most universities.
    A) people, who have obtained doctorate degrees,
    B) people who have obtained doctorate degrees
    C) people (who have obtained doctorate degrees)
    D) people who have obtained doctorate degrees,

19. The philosopher's_____ is a legendary substance said to transform ordinary metals into gold.
    A) stone, also known as the stone of the philosophers
    B) stone—also known as the stone of the philosophers,
    C) stone also known as the stone of the philosophers:
    D) stone, also known as the stone of the philosophers,

20. *The Grapes of Wrath* is a _____ addition to winning a Pulitzer Prize, has been adapted into a movie that was critically acclaimed.
    A) book that, in
    B) book that in
    C) book, that in
    D) book that in,

21. Hector's science_____ was rather unoriginal.
    A) project though very thorough
    B) project: though very thorough
    C) project, though very thorough,
    D) project—though very thorough,

22. Many_____ face challenges of balancing quality and growth.
    A) small businesses, millions of them across the United States—
    B) small businesses, millions of them across the United States,
    C) small businesses—millions of them across the United States,
    D) small businesses: millions of them across the United States,

23. Isaac_____ an influential figure in the Scientific Revolution.
    A) Newton, a physicist from the United Kingdom was,
    B) Newton, a physicist, from the United Kingdom was
    C) Newton, a physicist from the United Kingdom, was
    D) Newton a physicist, from the United Kingdom was

24. The string orchestra performed the first song of Grieg's Holberg _____ at the concert.
    A) Suite; the prelude
    B) Suite the prelude
    C) Suite, the prelude
    D) Suite, the prelude,

25. The Eiffel_____ is a lattice tower in Paris.
    A) Tower, named after engineer, Alexandre Gustave Eiffel,
    B) Tower named after engineer, Alexander Gustave Eiffel,
    C) Tower, named after engineer Alexander Gustave Eiffel,
    D) Tower named after engineer Alexander Gustave Eiffel,

26. Cinderella is a fairy tale_____ has an evil stepmother.
    A) character who, in many versions of the story,
    B) character who in many versions of the story,
    C) character who, in many versions of the story
    D) character, who in many versions of the story,

27. When the_____ to improve health standards for pesticide use in banana production, was developed, environmental activists were pleased.
    A) project which, was designed
    B) project, designed
    C) project designing it
    D) project, it was designed,

28. When my_____ immigrants, showed me photographs from their childhoods, I decided to take a trip to visit their native country.
    A) grandparents who are both
    B) grandparents, they are both
    C) grandparents, both
    D) grandparents— who are both

29. The blue_____ for its fast running speed—is threatened by both predation and human factors.
   A) wildebeest which, is known
   B) wildebeest, known
   C) wildebeest, known—
   D) wildebeest—known

30. In addition to being a teacher, Mary Harris_____ was a tireless labor activist.
   A) Jones dubbed "Mother Jones" by the American Railway Union
   B) Jones— dubbed "Mother Jones" by the American Railway Union—
   C) Jones— dubbed "Mother Jones"— by the American Railway Union
   D) Jones, dubbed "Mother Jones," by the American Railway Union

31. Due to the gubernatorial candidate's acceptance of donations from interest groups, voters are concerned that the politician will be_____ the whims of her donors.
   A) beholden; or indebted to
   B) beholden, or indebted to—
   C) beholden, or, indebted to,
   D) beholden, or indebted, to

32. Collective bargaining— a process of negotiation between employers and employees over salaries and working_____ was not protected by legislation in the United States until the 20th century.
   A) conditions,
   B) conditions:
   C) conditions—
   D) conditions;

33. The painter originally commissioned to paint a wall in Rockefeller_____was asked to stop painting before he completed his work due to its controversial anti-capitalist nature.
   A) Center, mural artist, Diego Rivera,
   B) Center, mural artist Diego Rivera,
   C) Center mural artist, Diego Rivera,
   D) Center mural artist Diego Rivera,

34. The literature professor's main area of_____ is the travelog as a unique art form.
   A) interest, he says
   B) interest he says
   C) interest, he says,
   D) interest he says,

35. Memorizing new _____ is easier when one has some background knowledge on the subject.
    A) facts, some psychologists argue,
    B) facts some, psychologists argue
    C) facts some psychologists argue,
    D) facts some psychologists, argue

36. If companies pay dividends to shareholders, some experts _____ investors will be more likely to purchase stocks.
    A) contend then
    B) contend; then
    C) contend. Then
    D) contend, then

37. Beneficial insect release—a common method used to limit the number of nefarious pests— is effective to an _____ it is most effective when the pest densities are low or medium.
    A) extent,
    B) extent, but
    C) extent, however,
    D) extent; though

38. A common myth is that it takes 25 years before one will see a return on investment for using solar panels. Depending on a variety of factors, such as the amount of the initial _____ one may see a return in investment almost immediately.
    A) investment;
    B) investment
    C) investment,
    D) investment—

39. Hospitals, community health clinics, and urgent care _____ employ physician assistants.
    A) centers among other places
    B) centers among, other places,
    C) centers, among other places,
    D) centers among other places,

40. Because of her skills and experience, Nancy commands a _____ above the salaries of her peers.
    A) salary that is. Well
    B) salary. That is well
    C) salary that is well
    D) salary, that is well

41. Employees will often address conflicts with their employers via litigation or arbitration (both are methods of settling_____ depending on the terms of the employee contract.
    A) disputes,
    B) disputes)
    C) disputes;
    D) disputes—

42. Many advertisers pulled funding for the cable pundit's television_____ at least out of a desire to avoid being boycotted by the public— after she made offensive remarks.
    A) show if not out of moral concerns,
    B) show. If not out of moral concerns,
    C) show—if not out of moral concerns,
    D) show— if not out of moral concerns—

43. Madeline_____ was Secretary of State in the 1990s.
    A) Albright a professor of, international relations at Georgetown University,
    B) Albright a professor of international relations, at Georgetown University,
    C) Albright, a professor, of international relations at Georgetown University
    D) Albright, a professor of international relations at Georgetown University,

44. The lobby of the normally drab hotel was_____ for the holiday season.
    A) decorated, with colorful lights,
    B) decorated, with colorful lights
    C) decorated with colorful lights,
    D) decorated with colorful lights

45. Many_____ affect public health.
    A) factors, such as the availability of medical resources and environmental conditions
    B) factors such as the availability of medical resources and environmental conditions
    C) factors such as the availability of medical resources and environmental conditions,
    D) factors, such as the availability of medical resources and environmental conditions,

46. Many people recognized that the story circulating on social media was clearly a work of satire, but_____ unable to discriminate between fact and fiction, believed that the story was true.
    A) some who were
    B) some,
    C) some, they were
    D) some

47. In addition to being_____ physicians are in high demand.
    A) well-compensated, earning a median base salary of $180,000
    B) well-compensated (earning a median base salary of $180,000),
    C) well-compensated: earning a median base salary of $180,000,
    D) well-compensated— earning a median base salary of $180,000,

48. Lydian coins, which were struck around_____ were the first known examples of coins made of precious metals.
   A) 640 BCE by King Alyattes of Lydia,
   B) 640 BCE by King Alyattes of Lydia
   C) 640 BCE, by King Alyattes, of Lydia,
   D) 640 BCE, by King Alyattes of Lydia

49. Nonpartisan_____ the Center for Media and Democracy seek to promote transparency in news reporting so that the public can engage in informed debates about issues.
   A) organizations such as:
   B) organizations: such as
   C) organizations, such as
   D) organizations such as

50. As more workers face increasing demands in their daily lives,_____ arrangements in which workers work full-time hours in less than five days per week— have become more popular.
   A) compressed workweeks,
   B) compressed workweeks—
   C) compressed workweeks;
   D) compressed workweeks:

51. A study _____ led to the discovery of an Earth-sized exoplanet that seems to be filled with volcanoes.
   E) by astronomers, Merrin Peterson and Björn Bennek,
   F) by astronomers, Merrin Peterson and Björn Bennek
   G) by astronomers Merrin Peterson and Björn Bennek,
   H) by astronomers Merrin Peterson and Björn Bennek

52. Doctor Adil _____ is a leading scholar in environmental and conservation issues.
   E) Najam, President of the World Wildlife Fund (WWF),
   F) Najam President of the World Wildlife Fund, (WWF),
   G) Najam, President of the World Wildlife Fund, (WWF),
   H) Najam President of the World Wildlife Fund (WWF),

53. Car ownership used to be high in the large city. After improvements in public _____ more residents have opted to forgo cars and commute on buses and trains.
   A) transportation however
   B) transportation, however
   C) transportation, however,
   D) transportation—however—

Lesson 15: Unnecessary Punctuation

When commas are added to sentences at incorrect places, sentences become unclear and/or ungrammatical.

DO use commas

1) After an introductory phrase or clause that is separate from the main subject and verb.
   - A staunch advocate of voting rights for women, Elizabeth Cady Stanton was one of the first women to launch organized women's suffrage movements in the United States.

2) When separating two independent clauses with a coordinating conjunction.
   - Archaeologists believe that Machu Picchu was used as a Royal Estate, and it is Peru's most famous tourist attraction.

3) When an independent clause follows a dependent clause.
   - Because many people refuse to believe that they are wrong, they tend to pay attention to information that confirms rather than contradicts their existing attitudes.

4) To set off parenthetical or nonrestrictive elements of a sentence.
   - The television show, which has been on the air for eleven years, tapes its last episode tomorrow.

5) Between coordinate adjectives (adjectives that separately modify a noun and whose order can be reversed without affecting the meaning of the sentence).
   - It was an interesting, thought-provoking, and energetic presentation.

6) To separate items in a series.
   - I like to read mystery books, autobiographies, and fantasy novels.

7) Between dates and years and between weekdays and months.
   - The Declaration of Independence was adopted on July 4, 1776.
   - My appointment is Monday, January 8th.

8) Between cities and states (and again after the state when the state is not the last word) and between states/cities and countries (and again after the country when the country is not the last word).
   - The meeting will be held in Albany, New York, next week.
   - Madrid, Spain, has a population of almost 3.2 million people.

9) Before direct quotations (colons are generally used for long quotes).
   - He said, "Nice to meet you."
   - George Bernard Shaw made a famous statement: "A little learning is a dangerous thing; drink deep, or taste not the Pierian spring: there shallow draughts intoxicate the brain, and drinking largely sobers us again."

DON'T use commas

1) To separate compound subjects or objects.
   - Incorrect: **Meriwether Lewis, and William Clark** were the first Americans to explore the western portion of the United States.
   - Correct: **Meriwether Lewis and William Clark** were the first Americans to explore the western portion of the United States.

   - Incorrect: He is respected for his **kindness, and thoughtfulness.**
   - Correct: He is respected for his **kindness and thoughtfulness.**

2) To separate elements connected by coordinating conjunctions that are NOT independent clauses.
   - Incorrect: I read the **book, and** watched the movie.
   - Correct: I read the **book and** watched the movie.

   - Incorrect: It is a **simple, but effective** solution.
   - Correct: It is a **simple but effective** solution.

3) Between a subject or subject clause and its verb.
   - Incorrect: **She, told** stories around the campfire.
   - Correct: **She told** stories around the campfire.

   - Incorrect: The **reason that I didn't believe him, was** the lack of evidence.
   - Correct: The **reason that I didn't believe him was** the lack of evidence.

4) Between a verb and its object (a noun or pronoun receiving the action of the verb).
   - Incorrect: He was **given, a** warning for his behavior, which was disruptive to the learning process.
   - Correct: He was **given a** warning for his behavior, which was disruptive to the learning process.

5) Before an intensive pronoun (pronoun ending in "self").
   - Incorrect: I'm not sure of the **answer, myself.**
   - Correct: I'm not sure of the **answer myself.**

6) Between an adjective and the noun it modifies.
   - Incorrect: The **blue, sweater** is in the drawer.
   - Correct: The **blue sweater** is in the drawer.

7) In comparisons before and after "than."
   - Incorrect: There is **more, than** enough time to prepare.
   - Incorrect: There is **more than,** enough time to prepare.
   - Correct: There is **more than** enough time to prepare.

8) Between an adverb and the word (adjective, verb, or another adverb) it modifies.
   - Incorrect: I am **very, sorry.**
   - Correct: I am **very sorry.**

9) Between a preposition and its object.
   - Incorrect: Give the **note to, your** cousin.
   - Correct: Give the **note to your** cousin.

10) Before a preposition (unless the preposition is part of a nonessential phrase).
    - Incorrect: The **lack, of evidence** is alarming.
    - Correct: The **lack of evidence is** alarming.

11) Immediately after the words "such as," "although," and "like."
    - Incorrect: **Although,** I was upset, my anger subsided with time.
    - Correct: **Although** I was upset, my anger subsided with time.

    - Incorrect: There are many benefits associated with taking online classes, **such as,** lower costs and greater convenience.
    - Correct: There are many benefits associated with taking online classes, **such as** lower costs and greater convenience.

12) After a coordinating (FANBOYS) conjunction.
    - Incorrect: I was tired **so,** I took a nap.
    - Correct: I was tired**, so** I took a nap.

13) Before an open parenthesis.
    - Incorrect: The restaurant served funnel cake, **churros, (fried dough pastries)**, and flan.
    - Correct: The restaurant served funnel cake, **churros (fried dough pastries)**, and flan.

14) Before a technical term, nickname, or unusually used term set off by quotes (unless a comma is needed regardless of the presence of quotation marks, such as when the quoted term begins a nonessential phrase in the middle of a sentence).
    - Incorrect: Henry Clay was known **as, "The Great Compromiser."**
    - Correct: Henry Clay was known **as "The Great Compromiser."**

15) Before most quotes that are integrated within the syntax of a sentence.
    - I questioned if his mean comments were "just in jest."
    - She insisted that "we work harder."

16) Between cumulative adjectives (adjectives that build on one another and need to be placed in a certain order to modify a noun).
    - Incorrect: The **dark, blue, woolen** sweater was in the store.
    - Correct: The **dark blue woolen** sweater was in the store.

It would not make sense to say "a woolen, blue, dark sweater."

Cumulative adjectives typically appear in the following order.

Article/Possessive	the, a, an, Michael's, Peggy's
Quantity	three, many, few
Opinion/Evaluation	kind, smart, talented
Size	big, large, small, tiny
Physical Quality	rough, skinny, cluttered
Shape	long, short, square
Age	old, young, new
Color	red, orange, green
Nationality/Religion	Bolivian, French, Italian, Japanese, Jewish, Catholic, Hindu, Muslim
Material	wooden, metal, concrete
Type	multi-purpose, T-shaped
Purpose	mixing (e.g., mixing bowl), walking (e.g., walking stick)

- I bought a **beautiful blue French** car for my birthday.
- There is a **large white detergent** bottle under the sink.
- There are some **small antique cooking pots** on the stove.

17) Before a "that" clause (clause beginning with "that" following a noun, adjective, or verb).
- Incorrect: The metanalysis **indicates, that** peer cues influence unhealthful adolescent behaviors.
- Correct: The metanalysis **indicates that** peer cues influence unhealthful adolescent behaviors.

18) There is generally no comma before the term "because" unless one is needed to avoid confusion.
- Incorrect: Sales have **increased, because** the product has been improved.
- Correct: Sales have **increased because** the product has been improved.

Sample Question

> Associate Research Professor Gunther Kletetschka at the UAF Geophysical_____ that plasma created at the moment of impact was partially responsible for a meteorite's minimal magnetism.
> Which choice completes the text so that it conforms to the principles of standard English?
> A) Institute, revealed
> B) Institute: revealed
> C) Institute revealed
> D) Institute; revealed

No punctuation should separate the subject (the professor) from the verb ("revealed"). **Choice C is correct.**

Mini Active Learning Activity

Explain why the underlined portion in each sentence is incorrect (a sentence or phrase is enough).

1. An advantage of knowing computer programming languages <u>is, that</u> employers are often willing to pay a premium for workers who are competent at coding.

2. In the once bustling industrial city of Lowell, Massachusetts, after their demands for labor condition reforms were not met, factory workers known as the "<u>Lowell mill girls," quit</u> their factory jobs at the mills in search of better opportunities.

3. Machine learning algorithms <u>build models,</u> and make predictions based on data.

4. The <u>swift athletic</u> runner shocked nobody by setting a new world record.

5. With the rise of streaming services like Spotify, music is <u>more accessible, than</u> ever before.

6. A newly <u>renovated, studio</u> apartment along Lake Michigan sold at a discounted price.

7. Concern over even in an <u>appearance, of impropriety</u> led the company to bar hiring certain qualified individuals who may possess a conflict of interest.

8. Many actors struggled to master transition from theater to <u>silent, films</u> in the early twentieth century.

Drill 1: Select the choice that best completes each blank to conform to standard written English.

1. *War and Peace* is an epic novel by Leo Tolstoy that is widely considered one of the most_____
   A) important, works of, world literature.
   B) important works of, world literature.
   C) important, works of world literature.
   D) important works of world literature.

2. The Tennessee Valley Authority was created by the federal government to_____ of the areas near the Tennessee River.
   A) promote, the economic development
   B) promote the economic development
   C) promote the economic development,
   D) promote, the economic development,

3. One of the most celebrated actresses in Hollywood,_____
   A) Meryl Streep has received many, prestigious awards for her various, performances.
   B) Meryl Streep has received many prestigious awards for her various, performances.
   C) Meryl Streep has received many, prestigious awards for her various performances.
   D) Meryl Streep has received many prestigious awards for her various performances.

4. The North Atlantic Treaty_____ the latter is no longer in existence.
   A) Organization and the Warsaw Pact both formed during the Cold War, though
   B) Organization, and the Warsaw Pact both formed during the Cold War, though
   C) Organization, and the Warsaw Pact both formed during the Cold War though
   D) Organization and the Warsaw Pact, both formed during the Cold War, though

5. Caligula was a ruler of the Roman Empire who_____
   A) appointed, his horse to, the Senate.
   B) appointed his horse to, the Senate.
   C) appointed, his horse to the Senate.
   D) appointed his horse to the Senate.

6. Many companies hire_____
   A) professional, consultants to evaluate the effectiveness of, their business practices.
   B) professional consultants, to evaluate the effectiveness of their business practices.
   C) professional, consultants to, evaluate the effectiveness of their business practices.
   D) professional consultants to evaluate the effectiveness of their business practices.

7. Rococo_____
   A) art, popular during the eighteenth century, was known for its elaborate detail, and serpentine designs.
   B) art popular during the eighteenth century was known for its elaborate detail, and serpentine designs.
   C) art, popular during the eighteenth century, was known for its elaborate detail and serpentine designs.
   D) art, popular during the eighteenth century was known for its elaborate detail and serpentine designs.

8. _____ acted as a mentor to the young businessman, who opened up his own bakery.
   A) Mitsuki, a skilled entrepreneur, herself,
   B) Mitsuki, a skilled entrepreneur herself,
   C) Mitsuki a skilled entrepreneur herself
   D) Mitsuki, a skilled, entrepreneur herself,

9. Members of the "beat" movement_____ traditional middle-class values.
   A) of, the 1950s rejected,
   B) of, the 1950s rejected
   C) of the 1950s, rejected,
   D) of the 1950s rejected

10. _____ is known for his award-winning films that explore gritty themes.
    A) Director, Lee Daniels
    B) Director, Lee Daniels,
    C) Director Lee Daniels
    D) Director Lee Daniels,

11. Both Radio City Music_____ are popular music venues in Manhattan.
    A) Hall, and Carnegie Hall
    B) Hall and Carnegie Hall
    C) Hall and Carnegie Hall,
    D) Hall, and Carnegie Hall,

12. The assistant made a_____ forgivable error in the company email.
    A) significant, but
    B) significant but
    C) significant; but
    D) significant but,

13. The Yalta_____ Franklin Delano Roosevelt, Winston Churchill, and Joseph Stalin.
    A) Agreement, was an agreement made at the end of World War II between
    B) Agreement, was an agreement made at, the end of World War II between,
    C) Agreement was an agreement made at the end of World War II between:
    D) Agreement was an agreement made at the end of World War II between

14. The ability to work effectively with team_____ needed in the healthcare industry.
    A) members, is
    B) members is
    C) members; is
    D) members, it is

15. Known for his unique_____ Franklin Lloyd Wright created buildings that blended in with their surroundings.
    A) architectural techniques,
    B) architectural, techniques
    C) architectural techniques
    D) architectural techniques:

16. The artist made a variety of pieces of_____ acrylic paintings, ice sculptors, and cartoon sketches.
    A) artwork, such as,
    B) artwork, such as
    C) artwork such as:
    D) artwork, such as:

17. The_____was served at the block party in the quiet suburban community.
    A) delicious, chocolate, cake
    B) delicious chocolate, cake
    C) delicious, chocolate cake
    D) delicious chocolate cake

18. The_____ teacher was respected by her students.
    A) caring, approachable, and intelligent
    B) caring approachable and intelligent
    C) caring approachable and intelligent,
    D) caring, approachable, and intelligent,

19. While the idea_____ is not practical.
    A) itself, is creative, it
    B) itself, is creative it
    C) itself is creative, it
    D) itself is creative, it,

20. Some artists are now able to make pottery out of metals from used smartphones, a development_____
    A) hailed by architects, and environmentalists.
    B) hailed, by architects and environmentalists.
    C) hailed by, architects and, environmentalists.
    D) hailed by architects and environmentalists.

21. While making a career change can be scary, for the motivated, resilient,_____ the rewards of making such a transition can prove significant.
    A) and persistent person though,
    B) and, persistent person, though;
    C) and persistent person, though,
    D) and persistent person, though

22. As a French political leader during the 20th _____ helped produce the Treaty of Versailles in the aftermath of World War I.
    A) century, and George Clemenceau,
    B) century, George Clemenceau
    C) century, George Clemenceau,
    D) century; and George Clemenceau

23. _____ serve his community by starting a business.
    A) Quincy, always the opportunist, decided that he could make money, and
    B) Quincy, always the opportunist, decided that he could make money and
    C) Quincy, always the opportunist decided that he could make money and,
    D) Quincy always the opportunist, decided that he could make money and

24. One of the finest examples of Mughal_____ preeminence.
    A) architecture, the Taj Mahal is, a symbol of cultural
    B) architecture the Taj Mahal is a symbol of cultural
    C) architecture, the Taj is a, symbol of cultural,
    D) architecture, the Taj Mahal is a symbol of cultural

25. Equipment such as_____ conditioning units can produce noise pollution.
    A) blenders, washing, machines, and air
    B) blenders, washing machines, and, air
    C) blenders, washing machines, and air
    D) blenders, washing machines, and air,

26. _____ is home to a famous opera house, which is known for its modern expressionist design.
    A) Sydney, Australia,
    B) Sydney Australia
    C) Sydney, Australia
    D) Sydney Australia,

27. If customers voice concerns about the product, _____ make improvements to it.
    A) and the firm will,
    B) and the firm will
    C) the firm will,
    D) the firm will

28. The French_____ is lower than that of a trumpet.
    A) horn's, mellow sound,
    B) horn's, mellow sound
    C) horn's mellow sound,
    D) horn's mellow sound

29. Many political scientists disparagingly use the_____ "banana state" to suggest that a country has an unstable government.
    A) term:
    B) term
    C) term,
    D) term;

30. Hopi katsina_____ are works of art that are often given to children as educational tools.
    A) dolls, (carved representations of spiritual messengers),
    B) dolls, (carved representations of spiritual messengers)
    C) dolls (carved representations of spiritual messengers)
    D) dolls, carved representations of spiritual messengers

31. Ideas or behaviors that spread throughout a culture are_____
    A) called, "memes."
    B) called "memes."
    C) called: "memes."
    D) called ("memes").

32. California is sometimes referred to_____ because of its agricultural businesses in table and wine grapes.
    A) as, "The Grape State,"
    B) as, "The Grape State"
    C) as "The Grape State,"
    D) as "The Grape State"

33. _____in *The Philadelphia Story* earned him an Oscar.
    A) Actor, James Stewart's performance
    B) Actor James Stewart's performance,
    C) Actor James Stewart's performance
    D) Actor, James Stewart's performance,

34. A line from Shakespeare's "Hamlet" was_____ "To be, or not to be? That is the question."
    A) quoted: in an article,
    B) quoted in an article:
    C) quoted, in an article,
    D) quoted in an article

35. When caring for deciduous trees, one must _____ all damaged and diseased branches are removed.
    A) ensure, that
    B) ensure that
    C) ensure that—
    D) ensure— that

36. The governor regarded the uptick in peaceful protests against his polices as little_____ for his administration.
    A) more than a minor annoyance
    B) more, than a minor annoyance,
    C) more, than a minor, annoyance,
    D) more than a, minor, annoyance

37. The author noted that the protagonist of her novel frequently_____ "to protect her secrets."
    A) lied:
    B) lied
    C) lied,
    D) lied in order,

38. Welsh monks began to collect Welsh tales_____ when they realized much of their country's literary heritage was being lost.
    A) sometime, around 1300
    B) sometime, around 1300:
    C) sometime, around 1300
    D) sometime around 1300

39. What makes Homer's *Iliad* so_____ is its profound ability to occupy the Western imagination.
    A) special:
    B) special
    C) special,
    D) special;

40. Becca's_____ made her stand out amongst her classmates.
    A) highly, stylized, purple-toned hair
    B) highly stylized, purple-toned hair
    C) highly stylized, purple-toned, hair
    D) highly stylized purple-toned, hair

41. The law office hired an interior design firm____ "had been highly recommended" by a client.
    A) that—
    B) that,
    C) that:
    D) that

184

42. The white chicken chili was_____ for additional flavor.
    A) topped with cilantro
    B) topped (with cilantro)
    C) topped with cilantro—
    D) topped with, cilantro,

43. Methane pollution can be_____ and businesses— such as major grocery stores— separate trash from organic waste.
    A) reduced if more individuals,
    B) reduced, if more individuals,
    C) reduced if more individuals
    D) reduced; if more individuals

44. When looking for new housing, you must_____ which options are desirable given your goals and affordable given your monthly budget.
    A) identify,
    B) identify
    C) identify;
    D) identify:

45. After a major scandal,_____ "Mayor to Step Down."
    A) the headline of the local newspaper declared
    B) the headline of the local newspaper declared,
    C) the headline, of the local newspaper, declared
    D) the headline, of the local newspaper declared,

46. While the professor's method of teaching is_____ it has yielded impressive learning outcomes in her students.
    A) unorthodox, and controversial,
    B) unorthodox, and controversial
    C) unorthodox and controversial,
    D) unorthodox and controversial

47. Many of Abraham Lincoln's most famous sayings shed insight into his personal_____ have been driven many times upon my knees by the overwhelming conviction that I had nowhere else to go. My own wisdom and that of all about me seemed insufficient for that day."
    A) struggles: "I
    B) struggles— "I
    C) struggles; I
    D) struggles, "I

48. The man was so stoic despite his boss's persistent_____ "He looked like a statue."
    A) insults, that one coworker commented,
    B) insults that one coworker commented,
    C) insults, that one coworker commented
    D) insults that one coworker commented

49. Television_____ are often popular, while those with more convoluted stories tend to attract smaller but more ardent fanbases.
    A) shows that are engaging and easy to follow
    B) shows, that are engaging and easy to follow,
    C) shows that are engaging, and easy to follow
    D) shows— that are engaging— and easy to follow

50. The wedding planner who was featured in a magazine article went back to doing what she does_____ brides and grooms to help them plan their perfect day.
    A) best— "engaging,"
    B) best: "engaging"
    C) best, "engaging,"
    D) best; "engaging"

51. The intelligence analyst of the small island nation_____ there was not enough evidence to justify the prime minister's fear of an invasion from neighboring territories.
    A) argued: that
    B) argued, that
    C) argued that:
    D) argued that

52. The athlete said he needed help____ "managing [his] stress and taking [his] mistakes in stride."
    A) with
    B) with,
    C) with:
    D) with;

53. Sustained disinformation campaigns on social_____ widespread misunderstandings.
    A) media can lead to:
    B) media, can lead to,
    C) media can lead to
    D) media can lead: to

54. Dittmar Park, New York,_____ one of the oldest collections of Victorian homes in the state.
    A) is home: to
    B) is home to
    C) is home, to
    D) is home to,

Punctuation Unit Quiz

Many works by Belgian sculptor Arte Quinze explore themes_____ social interactions, which he accomplishes in part by creating huge sculptures in public places that include bridges, roofs, and canopies under which people can engage in vigorous dialogue.

1. Which choice completes the text so that it conforms to the principles of standard English?

    A) of—
    B) of;
    C) of,
    D) of

Arcesilaus was an ancient Greek philosopher who was the founder of Skepticism, a school of thought concerned with the reality of knowing. He argued for "the suspension of _____ that humans have limited abilities to understand reality.

2. Which choice completes the text so that it conforms to the principles of standard English?

    A) truth"; claiming
    B) truth," claiming
    C) truth." Claiming
    D) truth": claiming

In 2017, Yale University launched the art exhibition *Artists in Exile: Expressions of Loss and Hope*, which spanned the works of over 40 artists from a period of 200 years: the exhibition told_____ from a variety of eras and geographic areas.

3. Which choice completes the text so that it conforms to the principles of standard English?

    A) stories' of exile
    B) story's of exile's
    C) stories of exile
    D) stories of exile'

After performing in a string of romantic comedies for many years, Jennifer Lopez transitioned to a more serious dramatic role in 2019's *Hustlers*, a film that_____ "brassy and invigorating."

4. Which choice completes the text so that it conforms to the principles of standard English?

   A) reviewer, Justin Chang, calls
   B) reviewer Justin Chang calls
   C) reviewer Justin Chang calls,
   D) reviewer Justin Chang calls,

Psychologists who research creativity have postulated why many people who get work done at coffee shops are more productive at _____ in the office, formal agendas and limited variety in visual stimuli often stifle creativity, while the informal ambience and variation in visual stimuli at coffee shops boost creativity.

5. Which choice completes the text so that it conforms to the principles of standard English?

   A) tasks
   B) tasks,
   C) tasks:
   D) tasks while

Previous studies have shown that bees can be trained to learn to perform cognitive tasks, such as counting and navigating environments, but many of these tasks resemble natural behaviors bees already perform in the wild. If bees were trained to learn a complex task such as playing a version of football, _____ Researcher Clint Perry was determined to find out.

6. Which choice completes the text so that it conforms to the principles of standard English?

   A) they could learn:
   B) they could learn?
   C) could they learn.
   D) could they learn?

Lignin, a polymer found in plant cell walls, provides plants with rigidity and structural support. In an important 2022 study, _____ showed that, at the cellular level, enzymes called LACCASEs adjust their lignin chemistry in order to resist environmental stressors.

7. Which choice completes the text so that it conforms to the principles of standard English?

   A) plant physiologist, Edouard Pesque
   B) plant physiologist Edouard Pesque,
   C) plant physiologist, Edouard Pesque,
   D) plant physiologist Edouard Pesque

Yellowstone National Park in the Northwest and Yosemite National Park in the Sierra Nevada mountains are just two of many national parks in the United States dedicated to preserving diverse _____ providing visitors with educational opportunities about natural habitats; and promoting recreation and healthy living.

8. Which choice completes the text so that it conforms to the principles of standard English?

   A) resources, both flora and fauna;
   B) resources, both flora and fauna,
   C) resources both flora and fauna;
   D) resources; both flora and fauna;

Academy Award winner Anna May Wong was a cultural icon and the first Asian American actress to gain international acclaim for appearing in over 60 movies, but her journey was not without its _____ grew frustrated with regularly being hired to play villains, at one point moving to Europe, where she had more opportunities to play leads.

9. Which choice completes the text so that it conforms to the principles of standard English?

   A) struggles, however, she
   B) struggles however she
   C) struggles, however; she
   D) struggles; however she

An experiment in the world's largest particle physics laboratory at the University of Colorado Boulder may have stumbled upon a new insight that has implications for understanding how human activities that release iodine impact the atmosphere. The researchers were able to determine a mechanism by which a gas form of _____ forms, thus providing crucial insights into atmospheric particle formation.

10. Which choice completes the text so that it conforms to the principles of Standard English?

    A) iodine, iodic oxide
    B) iodine iodic oxide
    C) iodine, iodic oxide,
    D) iodine iodic oxide,

Astronomer Annie Jump Cannon was originally hired by Edward Charles Pickering to work at the Harvard College Observatory to perform calculations and analyze photographs of stars, but she did more than the tedious work she was hired _____ she created the spectral classification system for classifying stars, a system still used today.

11. Which choice completes the text so that it conforms to the principles of standard English?

    A) to do: though
    B) to do; though
    C) to do, though:
    D) to do, though,

The platypus—a unique creature that is furry like a mammal but can lay eggs like a bird—has long puzzled scientists. But the study of the _____ gives researchers unique information that can help them understand how humans evolved and that can provide important insights for medical advances.

12. Which choice completes the text so that it conforms to the principles of standard English?

    A) platypuses unique genome
    B) platypus's unique genome
    C) platypus's unique genome's
    D) platypus's unique genomes'

Professor Anish Krishman notes that author Gabriel Garcia Marquez, when crafting his fictional works, employed magical realism—a genre that includes fantastic elements intertwined within otherwise realistic situations— as an instrument of exploring political tensions. His seminal novel *One Hundred Years of Solitude,* for example, portrays a banana plague that conveys his concern over environmental exploitation, while his novel _____ presents a veiled critique against dictatorships with the story of an eternal dictator who has ruled for three centuries, something only possible in the world of magic.

13. Which choice completes the text so that it conforms to the principles of standard English?

    A) *Autumn of the Patriarch;*
    B) *Autumn of the Patriarch—*
    C) *Autumn of the Patriarch,*
    D) *Autumn of the Patriarch*

Bichloride compounds, compounds that contain chlorine and another element, can be highly unstable. A team of researchers found a way to stabilize one of these unruly compounds, _____ a development that, according to lead researcher David Lacy, "opens the floodgates to a whole new area of research."

14. Which choice completes the text so that it conforms to the principles of Standard English?

    A) manganese trichloride ($MnCl_3$),
    B) manganese trichloride, ($MnCl_3$)
    C) manganese trichloride ($MnCl_3$)
    D) manganese trichloride, ($MnCl_3$),

The First Peoples Fund was established in 1995 to provide various programs to support Native American artists and entrepreneurs. It established a youth development initiative, Dances with_____ Rolling Rez Arts, in 2016; and the Oglala Lakota Artspace, in 2021.

15. Which choice completes the text so that it conforms to the principles of Standard English?

    A) Words™; in 2014, a mobile arts space;
    B) Words™, in 2014, a mobile arts space,
    C) Words™, in 2014; a mobile arts space,
    D) Words™; in 2014, a mobile arts space,

Susan B. Anthony was one of the foremost suffragists of her generation. She fought _____ to champion the rights of disenfranchised populations; in 1872, she was arrested after casting her vote in the 1872 Presidential election, leading to her conviction for voting illegally.

16. Which choice completes the text so that it conforms to the principles of Standard English?

    A) vociferously, sometimes illegally
    B) vociferously—sometimes— illegally
    C) vociferously — sometimes illegally—
    D) vociferously sometimes illegally

Dionaea muscipula, more commonly known as the Venus flytrap, consumes prey that comes across its leaves. Yet the process of closing its trap is energy-intensive and time-consuming, so the plant will only close its trap for prey large enough in size to be worth its time. Dieter Hodick and Andreas Sievers proposed that touching a trigger hair on a Venus flytrap's lobes produces an electric action potential that induces calcium channels to open. They postulated that a rapid influx of calcium ions will signal the flytrap to close its _____ a prey of sufficient size lands on its surface.

17. Which choice completes the text so that it conforms to the principles of Standard English?

    A) trap whenever
    B) trap; whenever
    C) trap, whenever
    D) trap: whenever

Though most literary scholars regard Samuel Beckett as a modernist literary figure, Samuel Beckett's relationship with modernism has always been strained, perhaps even more so than James Joyce's. Though Beckett was undoubtedly influenced by authors writing in the modernist tradition, some critics _____ his works defy categorization.

18. Which choice completes the text so that it conforms to the principles of Standard English?

    A) contend, that
    B) contend that:
    C) contend—
    D) contend that

Researchers at Nanyang Technological University in Singapore discovered a new way to harness and store wind power as electricity. Powered with _____ two meters per second, the wind harvester is a low-cost device that may revolutionize the renewable energy industry.

19. Which choice completes the text so that it conforms to the principles of Standard English?

A) energy generated by wind at velocities as low as
B) energy, generated by wind, at velocities as low as
C) energy generated by wind, at velocities, as low as
D) energy generated by wind at velocities as low as,

For many years, art experts debated which version of the painting *St. John* by Michelangelo Merisi da Caravaggio was authentic, the one housed in the Doria Pamphilj Gallery in Rome or the one in the Capitoline Museum in Rome. The mystery was resolved when X-ray technology detected a ghostly image in the Capitoline version—in this case the image of an arm that had the image of a ram's horn painted _____ that suggested the painting was authentic: a forger copying the original painting's outline would not bother painting a horn over an arm.

20. Which choice completes the text so that it conforms to the principles of Standard English?

A) over it
B) over it;
C) over it,
D) over it—

Raw water is not always safe for drinking. Scientists often use the _____ to raise the pH of water: the increased alkalinity of the water kills harmful microorganisms.

21. Which choice completes the text so that it conforms to the principles of Standard English?

A) compound, calcium oxide,
B) compound calcium oxide
C) compound, calcium oxide
D) compound calcium oxide,

Unit 5: Expression

Lesson 16: Transitions

A sentence can be grammatically correct without being logical. A logical sentence is one that makes sense. Recall from lesson 3 that conjunctions within sentences must show the correct relationship (contrast, comparison, cause and effect, sequence, etc.) in context.

- Illogical: Missy studied hard for the test, **but** she got a perfect score.

If Missy studied hard, one would expect her to do well on the test. The coordinating conjunction "but" illogically suggests a contrasting relationship. In this case, "and" or "so" would be more logical.

In the context of a text, transition words can be used to effectively link ideas within sentences, between sentences, at the beginning of paragraphs, and at the end of paragraphs.

Recap of Some Common Transitions (see Lesson 3 for more comprehensive lists)

Alternative	alternatively, instead, on the other hand
Compare	as, like, likewise, similarly
Contrast	although, by contrast, but, conversely, even though, in contrast to, nevertheless, nonetheless, on the other hand
Addition	also, and, aside from, in addition, furthermore, moreover, what's more, firstly, secondly, lastly
Time	as, at last, finally, first, initially, next, previously, subsequently, then, traditionally, ultimately
Cause	as, because, due to the fact, for, since
Dismissal/Digression	at any rate, in any case, in any event
Effect	consequently, hence, therefore, thus, to these ends
Example	for example, for instance
Emphasis	indeed, in fact
Clarity	in other words, that is, specifically
Concession	admittedly, granted, of course
Conclusion	in conclusion, in summary, then
Definition	as such, in broad terms
Detail	particularly, specifically

Sample Question

> Native American author, artist, and illustrator Shonto Begay celebrates traditional Navajo culture in his works, but this practice does not indicate a lack of concern for portraying contemporary Navajo life; his painting *Grandmother's Love Cup*,_____ features a woman dressed in traditional Navajo garb in a contemporary kitchen that prominently features a cup with a mass produced design, thus reflecting more modern values of consumerism and manufactured commercialism. In fact, the majority of Begay's paintings portray modern Navajos in everyday situations.
>
> Which choice completes the text with the most logical transition?
> A) though,
> B) for instance,
> C) secondly,
> D) in other words,

The first sentence claims Begay is <u>not</u> unconcerned about portraying contemporary (modern) Navajo life in his works despite his celebrating of traditional Navajo culture, meaning he *is* concerned about portraying it. The information after the semicolon introduces a painting that provides support for this claim. **Choice B is correct** because it uses an example transition to signal a discussion of one specific painting: this example supports the broader point made earlier in the sentence (it is a painting that blends aspects of both traditional Navajo culture and modern life, showing his concern with portraying contemporary Navajo life). Choice A incorrectly suggests a contrast relationship between the detail about the painting and the point made before the semicolon. Choice B uses an illogical continuation transition (there is no second point being made: the information after the semicolon illustrates the claim made before it). Choice D is incorrect because the second sentence does not restate the previous one in different words; rather, it gives an example to illustrate the idea.

Drill 1: Select the choice that provides the most logical transition.

1. The psychology program offers a course in the psychology of thinking. _____ "thinking" can be described as the manipulation of mental representations of information.
   A) In broad terms,
   B) Also,
   C) Nevertheless,
   D) Consequently,

2. When exercising, you should work at an intensity that is high enough to challenge you. _____ you do not want to over-exert yourself and risk injury.
   A) In addition,
   B) For example,
   C) However,
   D) Furthermore,

3. When applying to be a consultant at certain firms, you must first take part in a behavioral interview where you discuss your past accomplishments. _____ you must participate in a case interview where you are asked to apply your problem-solving skills to a business situation. Finally, you must pass a written exam.
   A) Next,
   B) Conversely,
   C) Indeed,
   D) Granted,

4. Rudyard Kipling was an English author lauded for his children's stories, such as *The Jungle Book*. _____ he was celebrated for his poetry.
   A) In fact,
   B) Moreover,
   C) Consequently,
   D) For instance,

5. A healthy corporate culture is crucial to both large and small businesses alike. _____ businesses with such cultures are more likely to retain employees and motivate workers to produce quality products and services.
   A) Still,
   B) Even so,
   C) Indeed,
   D) Next,

6. Thomas Jefferson believed that the cornerstone of the American economy should be agriculture. _____ Alexander Hamilton believed that industrialization was needed for the economic development of the nation.
   A) Conversely,
   B) Still,
   C) Finally,
   D) Furthermore,

7. Distillation is the process of separating the components of a liquid by boiling it and then condensing the resulting vapors. Distillation is used in many processes. _____ distillation is used to purify water.
   A) Secondly,
   B) Consequently,
   C) For instance,
   D) Additionally,

8. A Mach number is the speed of an object as a multiple of the speed of sound. _____ an object traveling at twice the speed of sound travels at a speed of Mach 2.
   A) Furthermore,
   B) Finally,
   C) For example,
   D) Moreover,

9. The Green Revolution during the late 1960s was associated with a series of initiatives that increased the production of cereals worldwide. _____ over a billion people were saved from starvation.
   A) For example,
   B) Last,
   C) Consequently,
   D) Also,

10. The maximum distance that light in space can travel in one year is a light year. The nearest star to the Earth (other than the sun) is about four light years away. _____ the light we see in the sky from this star actually left the star four years ago.
    A) For instance,
    B) Therefore,
    C) Nevertheless,
    D) In addition,

11. During the Renaissance, perspective was a technique by which painters added a sense of depth to their art. _____ chiaroscuro was another technique by which artists made paintings appear three-dimensional.
    A) Instead,
    B) As a result,
    C) Likewise,
    D) Indeed,

12. Consumer attention has been shifting from television to the internet. _____ television advertisements are less effective at attracting potential consumers than they once were.
    A) Nevertheless,
    B) Thus,
    C) For example,
    D) Then,

13. The best-preserved building in ancient Rome is the Pantheon. Its precise function is not known._____ the decorations in the building suggest that it was a temple.
    A) However,
    B) Therefore,
    C) For example,
    D) Finally,

14. There are many reasons to consume kale, which has become an increasingly popular green vegetable. Kale is a great source of Vitamin C. _____ kale has properties that help reduce cholesterol levels.
    A) However,
    B) Also,
    C) Thus,
    D) For instance,

15. Neil deGrasse Tyson showed a clear interest in science at a young age. _____ he purchased a telescope when he was in middle school with money he earned walking dogs.
    A) Similarly,
    B) Likewise,
    C) However,
    D) In fact,

16. Studying abroad provides students with the opportunity to hone their foreign language skills, thus making them more desirable to certain employers. It also affords them the opportunity to become immersed in a new culture and grow more self-reliant. For both practical and personal reasons,_____ studying abroad is a worthwhile endeavor.
    A) however,
    B) nonetheless,
    C) then,
    D) in any case,

17. Many of the athletic coach's new students had never participated in organized sports before. _____ many of them were eager to learn the skills he taught them.
    A) In fact,
    B) Instead,
    C) Still,
    D) Otherwise,

18. The continental drift theory was not always as widely accepted as it is today. _____ the theory was seen as implausible to many geologists.
    A) However,
    B) Initially,
    C) Furthermore,
    D) Thus,

19. The blogger argued that simply giving employees raises is not enough to motivate them to be more productive in the long run. _____ inspiring employees, giving them autonomy, and treating them with respect are actions more likely to motivate them to do their best work.
    A) On the other hand,
    B) Likewise,
    C) Consequently,
    D) Moreover,

20. Direct to garment printing technology allows for the printing of textiles with specialized ink jet technology and occurs without direct hand contact. _____ this technique lowers printing costs and allows for precise imaging.
    A) Still,
    B) In effect,
    C) Nevertheless,
    D) For instance,

21. Strikes hamper the ability of managers to control the way their businesses operate. _____ strikes limit managerial authority.
    A) For example,
    B) Thus,
    C) Nonetheless,
    D) In other words,

22. Young athletes can benefit greatly from physical therapy. For one, physical therapy can increase muscle strength and flexibility, which are assets both on the field and in daily life. Physical therapy can also improve blood circulation, resulting in higher oxygen levels in the body so that athletes can perform more effectively. _____ physical therapy is "therapeutic" for the mind and can build focus and motivation in individuals.
    A) In short,
    B) What's more,
    C) For example,
    D) In other words,

23. The candidate for governor is relying on a strategy that involves galvanizing first-time voters. _____ her campaign is reaching out to such voters both door-to-door and via social media.
    A) In addition,
    B) By the same token,
    C) To this end,
    D) In brief,

Lesson 17: Rhetorical Synthesis

Rhetorical synthesis questions (or "notes questions") are some of the most intimidating questions on the new SAT. These questions will provide you with a bulleted list of points on a topic and ask you to select a sentence that achieves a certain goal. Common types of goals might be creating sentences that do the following:

1) Highlight a difference between two things.
2) Highlight a similarity between two things.
3) Introduce a literary work or work of art and its creator to an audience unfamiliar with the creator.
4) Introduce a book on a topic to an audience who *is* familiar with the topic.
5) Present the aim (purpose) of a research study.
6) Present the findings (results) of a research study.
7) Present the methodology (research techniques) employed in a study.

The good news is, while these questions often look time-consuming on the surface, they are actually rather quick to answer in most cases. More often than not, you do not even need to read the bullet points all that carefully. The question itself often gives away what the right answer must be. The wrong choices will typically include true details that simply fail to meet the goals of the original question. Let's look at some model questions.

Sample Question

> While researching a topic, a student takes the following notes.
>
> - Sucre is the capital of Bolivia.
> - The population of Bolivia is 360,544.
> - Sucre contains 3.0% of Bolivia's population.
> - Tbilisi is the capital of Georgia.
> - The population of Georgia is 1,201,769.
> - Tbilisi contains 32.0% of Georgia's population.
>
> The student wants to provide information about the relative sizes of the two countries' capitals. Which choice most effectively uses relevant information from the notes to accomplish this goal?
>
> A) Sucre is the capital of Bolivia, yet it only contains 3.0% of Bolivia's population.
> B) Tbilisi, the capital of Georgia, contains 1,201,769 people and contains 32.0% of its population.
> C) Not only is Georgia's capital Tbilisi (with a population of 1,201,769) larger in population than Bolivia's capital of Sucre (with a population of 360,544), but Georgia's capital's population also accounts for a greater percentage of its overall population.
> D) While 32.0% of Georgia's population lives in its capital, only 3.0% of Bolivia's does.

The correct answer must give information about the **sizes** of **both** nations' capitals. Only Choice C does this, so **Choice C is correct.** Choices A and D give no information about the population sizes. Choice B only gives population size data for Georgia. **Even without the bulleted list, we can see that only Choice C addressed the goal of the student, which was to compare population sizes.**

Let's look at one example that is slightly more advanced.

Sample Question

> While researching a topic, a student takes the following notes.
> - David Drake was an enslaved potter who lived in Edgefield, South Carolina, in the nineteenth century.
> - He was known as "Dave the Potter."
> - After the Civil War, Drake became a free man.
> - Drake made over 40,000 pieces of pottery over his lifetime, some of which sell for as much as $50,000 today.
> - The Metropolitan Museum of Art features some of his works in its American Wing collection.
> - One prominent work, *Storage jar*, is a monumental storage jar with a capacity of 25 gallons, made of alkaline-glazed stoneware and containing several written inscriptions.
>
> The student wants to provide a description of the jar to someone unfamiliar with David Drake. Which choice most effectively uses relevant information from the notes to accomplish this goal?
> - A) David Drake, also known as "Dave the Potter," was a slave from South Carolina, gaining freedom at the conclusion of the Civil War.
> - B) You can see one of David Drake's works, *Storage jar*, at the Metropolitan Museum of Art.
> - C) A huge alkaline-glazed piece of stoneware with a storage capacity of 25 gallons, *Storage jar* was created by potter David Drake, a former slave from South Carolina who became free after the Civil War and who made over 40,000 pieces of pottery during his lifetime.
> - D) *Storage jar* is a large jar with a capacity of 25 gallons, made of alkaline-glazed stoneware and containing several written inscriptions.

Only Choice C provides details that describe the sculpture *and* biographical details about Drake. **Choice C is correct.** Choice A only meets one goal: it introduces David Potter. However, it fails to introduce the work *Storage jar*. Choice D has the opposite problem. It describes *Storage jar*, but it fails to introduce David Potter. Choice B is the second best choice, but it is still very weak. While it does mention both David Drake and *Storage jar*, it gives no significant details about them that effectively orient the reader. For example, it casually refers to Drake as if the audience already knows who he is.

Drill 1: Select the choice that best answers each question.

While researching a topic, a student takes the following notes.

- The construction of the Panama Canal began in 1881.
- The United States took over its construction from 1904 to 1914.
- The canal is 51 miles long.
- The canal runs due South from its entrance at Colón on the Atlantic side to the Bay of Panama on the Pacific side.
- It was the first trans-isthmian canal funded by the United States that linked the Atlantic to the Pacific, allowing the United States to trade more cheaply and efficiently.
- The Panama Canal became a symbol of U.S. technological prowess.

1. The student wants to emphasize the distance covered by the canal. Which choice most effectively uses relevant information from the notes to accomplish this goal?

    A) The Panama Canal represented a remarkable technological achievement for the United States, making trade more efficient.
    B) The construction of the Panama Canal was a long process, starting in 1881 and ending in 1914.
    C) The Panama Canal was the first trans-isthmian canal funded by the United States.
    D) Over 51 miles long, the Panama Canal links the Atlantic to the Pacific, extending from Colón to the Bay of Panama.

While researching a topic, a student takes the following notes.

- Stephen King is an American science fiction author.
- *The Skeleton Crew* was published in 1985.
- It contains 22 short stories that depict characters in supernatural situations.
- *Nightmares and Dreamscapes* was published in 1993.
- It contains 24 short stories that depict characters in supernatural situations.

2. The student wants to emphasize a similarity between King's books. Which choice most effectively uses relevant information from the notes to accomplish this goal?

    A) *The Skeleton Crew* was published in 1985, while *Nightmares and Dreamscapes* was published in 1993.
    B) Stephen King is a science fiction author who frequently publishes works that depict supernatural phenomena.
    C) *The Skeleton Crew* (published in 1985) and *Nightmares and Dreamscapes* (published in 1993) are short story collections by Stephen King that depict characters in supernatural situations.
    D) *Nightmares and Dreamscapes* is a supernatural short story collection by Stephen King, which has more stories in it than *The Skeleton Crew* has.

While researching a topic, a student takes the following notes.

- The Trans-Siberian Express is the longest train journey in the world.
- The journey begins in Moscow and ends in Vladivostok.
- The journey is 5,722 miles long.
- The California Zephyr is a train trip in North America.
- The journey begins in Chicago and ends in San Francisco.
- The journey is 2,348 miles long.

3. The student wants to compare the lengths of two rail journeys. Which choice most effectively uses relevant information from the notes to accomplish this goal?

   A) The Trans-Siberian Express is 5,722 miles long, which is more than twice as long as the California Zephyr, which is 2,348 miles long.
   B) While the Trans-Siberian Express begins in Moscow, the California Zephyr begins in North America.
   C) Both the Tran-Siberian Express, which is in Europe and Asia, and the California Zephyr, which is in North America, are railway journeys.
   D) One of North America's railway routes is the California Zephyr, which extends from Chicago to San Francisco.

While researching a topic, a student takes the following notes.

- There are 20,000 bee species globally, about 4,000 of which are from the United States.
- From 2006-2015, 25% fewer bee species have been found than were found before 1990.
- Neonicotinoid pesticides, which are used by farmers to treat crops, are highly toxic to bees and have stressed their populations, killing bees and altering their behaviors.
- Bees pollinate 300 million flowers a day, and 75% of crops depend on pollinators.
- The World Bee Project leverages AI technology to monitor bee populations and protect their numbers.

4. The student wants to emphasize a factor that is causing decreasing biodiversity for bees. Which choice most effectively uses relevant information from the notes to accomplish this goal?

   A) There are 20,000 bee species, but, in relation to their numbers in 1990, their numbers declined by 25% from 2006 to 2015.
   B) Neonicotinoid pesticides used in agricultural processes, which are toxic to bees, have contributed to declining bee numbers.
   C) The World Bee Project is dedicated to recovering the population of bees, organisms essential to pollination.
   D) The majority of crops, about 75%, are dependent on the activity of bees, who pollinate 300 million flowers a day.

While researching a topic, a student takes the following notes.

- Ester Hernandez is a multidisciplinary visual artist who depicts Latina and Native women through prints, pastels, and installations.
- In 1988, she launched a solo exhibition, *The Defiant Eye,* in San Francisco, California.
- In 2008, her screen print *Sun Raid* was added to the Smithsonian American Art Museum.
- In 2012, she was commissioned as a bilingual illustrator for *Have You Seen Marie?*
- Hernandez lives in the California Bay Area.

5. The student wants to introduce the artist's 2008 screen print. Which choice most effectively uses relevant information from the notes to accomplish this goal?

   A) Ester Hernandez is a true multidisciplinary artist who makes use of a variety of mediums.
   B) Before making *Sun Raid* and illustrating *Have You Seen Marie?*, Hernandez launched her solo exhibition *The Defiant Eye* in San Francisco, California.
   C) Added to the Smithsonian American Art Museum in 2008, the screen print *Sun Raid* was made by multidisciplinary visual artist Ester Hernandez.
   D) Ester Hernandez depicts Latina and Native women in her various art projects, which include prints, pastels, and installations.

While researching a topic, a student takes the following notes.

- The National Museum in New Delhi, India, is one of the largest museums in India.
- It was established in 1949 with a goal of preserving India's history.
- Its manuscript collection contains over 14,000 works in various languages and dialects representing different provinces and schools.
- The manuscripts cover the period of the 7th century to the 20th century.
- The manuscripts have been subject to critical studies by scholars in the arts and a variety of fields.
- The manuscripts are on a variety of materials, such as paper, cloth, wood, and metal.

6. The student wants to explain how the National Museum preserves India's history. Which choice most effectively uses relevant information from the notes to accomplish this goal?

   A) The National Museum brings together resources from various provinces and schools in India, including resources made of paper, cloth, wood, and metal.
   B) Founded in 1949, the National Museum includes written artifacts in a variety of mediums.
   C) The manuscript collection in the National Museum is studied by scholars.
   D) Including over 14,000 thousand works in diverse languages and dialects that cover a period of over 1,300 years, the National Museum's manuscript collection showcases important writings from India's history in a variety of mediums.

While researching a topic, a student takes the following notes.

- Viet Thanh Nguyen was awarded the Pulitzer Prize for Fiction in 2016.
- Nguyen was born in Vietnam and now lives and works as a professor in California.
- Nguyen's most recent novel, *The Committed*, has earned critical and popular acclaim.
- *The Committed* is a historical fiction novel set during the Vietnam War in both Los Angeles, California, and Vietnam.

7. The student wants to introduce *The Committed* to an audience unfamiliar with the novel and its author. Which choice most effectively uses relevant information from the notes to accomplish this goal?

   A) *The Committed* is a historical fiction novel set during the Vietnam War in both Los Angeles and Vietnam, Viet Thanh Nguyen's homeland.
   B) Viet Thanh Nguyen was awarded the Pulitzer Prize for Fiction in 2016, and he now works as a professor in Los Angeles, California.
   C) Critically and popularly acclaimed novel *The Committed* is a historical fiction novel set during the Vietnam War, written by Pulitzer Prize winner Viet Thanh Nguyen.
   D) Viet Thanh Nguyen, who wrote *The Committed,* was born in Vietnam and lives in California.

While researching a topic, a student takes the following notes.

- Lithium-ion batteries provide large supplies of electricity in short intervals and are thus the dominant source of energy reserves.
- Lithium-ion batteries can be flammable, are expensive, and do not last long.
- The process of extracting lithium to make batteries pollutes the environment.
- Sand batteries have a low cost, as sand is easy to obtain because of its abundance.
- The storage capacity of sand batteries is 1,000 times cheaper than that of lithium-ion batteries, and sand can stay hot for long periods of time.
- Sand batteries provide one promising high-power, high-capacity alternative to lithium-ion batteries.

8. The student wants to explain one advantage of sand batteries. Which choice most effectively uses relevant information from the notes to accomplish this goal?

A) The sand for sand batteries, which is highly abundant, can be accessed in a way that does not pollute the environment as extracting lithium for lithium-ion batteries does.
B) In spite of its cost, lithium-ion batteries remain the leading source of energy reserves.
C) Lithium-ion batteries are currently the most popular method of energy storage, but sand batteries have been proposed as a viable alternative.
D) Though they have different storage capacities and prices, both sand batteries and lithium-ion batteries can be used to store energy.

While researching a topic, a student takes the following notes.

- The triceratops was a plant-eating horned dinosaur that lived 66 to 69 million years ago.
- A fossil of a triceratops named "Big John" is one of the largest triceratops fossils ever found, and its skull is over 5 feet long.
- A gash in Big John's neck frill had a size and shape suggesting it was caused by another triceratops's horn.
- In 2022, a research team led by Ruggero D'Anastasio did a chemical analysis of the bones and found sulfur associated with the healing phases of bone trauma.
- The team speculated that the triceratops died of an infection from its wound months after an attack by another triceratops.

9. The student wants to present the study and its findings. Which choice most effectively uses relevant information from the notes to accomplish this goal?

    A) In 2022, Ruggero D'Anastasio's research team was interested in learning about the triceratops Big John.
    B) The neck frill of a triceratops was the focus of Ruggero D'Anastasio's research team's study.
    C) In a 2022 study, Ruggero D'Anastasio and colleagues employed chemical techniques to study the skull of a triceratops.
    D) In a 2022 study, Ruggero D'Anastasio and his team chemically analyzed a wound on a triceratops skull and concluded that it likely died as a result of an infection resulting from an attack by another triceratops.

While researching a topic, a student takes the following notes.

- The pinweed is an invasive species that has been replacing the native heronbill in the Sonoran Desert.
- Biologist Sarah Kimball investigated whether rainfall conditions impacted the pinweed's ability to grow at a faster than the heronbill.
- She found that during a season with average rainfall (2007-2008), both species grew at about the same rate.
- During a season with higher than average rainfall (2004-2005), the pinweed grew at a faster rate.
- During both seasons, the pinweed was better at conserving water than was the heronbill.
- Kimball concluded that abundant rainfall and superior water conservation account for the pinweed's ability to outcompete the heronbill.

10. The student wants to emphasize the aim of a research study. Which choice most effectively uses relevant information from the notes to accomplish this goal?

    A) Because of a study done by Sarah Kimball, it is now known that rainfall abundance allows the pinweed to outcompete the native heronbill in the Sonoran Desert.
    B) Sarah Kimball set out to determine if there was a relationship between rainfall conditions and the rate at which the pinweed grows relative to the rate at which the heronbill grows in the Sonoran Desert.
    C) Sarah Kimball analyzed the growth of both the pinweed and the heronbill in the Sonoran Desert during two growing seasons.
    D) Because of Sarah Kimball's research, we now know that the pinweed is better at retaining water than is the heronbill, regardless if a season has more rainfall than usual.

While researching a topic, a student takes the following notes.

- The Selma march to Montgomery of 1965 was a march for civil rights to protest racist policies.
- Martin Luther King Junior was a prominent advocate for advancing racial equality through civil protests.
- Amelia Boynton Robinson became active in the women's suffrage movement early in life and used her position in the Dallas County Voters League to register Black voters.
- Martin Luther King Junior became a prominent face of the Selma march who led nonviolent demonstrations to the capitol in Montgomery, Alabama, drawing attention to the need for the Voting Rights Act.
- Boynton Robinson worked behind the scenes to get Martin Luther King Junior to come to Selma by urging him to visit in a letter, and she volunteered her home for strategy meetings and organizing events.

11. The student wants to compare the roles that two activists played in the Selma march. Which choice most effectively uses relevant information from the notes to accomplish this goal?

A) While Martin Luther King Junior played a more obvious role as a leader of the Selma march, Boynton Robinson helped ensure his participation and put in important background work planning this historic event.
B) Martin Luther King Junior and Boynton Robinson contributed to the Selma march in different ways; King drew attention to the need for the Voting Rights Act, and Robinson was active in the women's suffrage movement in her early career.
C) The Selma march revealed deep racial inequities that prompted the passage of the Voting Rights Act.
D) Boynton Robinson and Martin Luther King Junior both were passionate about civil rights, as shown by Robinson's history of activism registering Black voters, prompting their involvement in the Selma march.

While researching a topic, a student takes the following notes.

- Robert Rauschenberg was a twentieth-century American artist.
- He invented the word "combine" to describe hybrid artwork that included elements of both painting and sculpture.
- His combine paintings integrated three-dimensional objects into paintings with the purposes of challenging the viewers, invading their space, and making them ponder a puzzle.
- His combine *Monogram* depicted an angora goat whose midsection is in a car tire.
- His combine *Canyon* included a taxidermized bald eagle, a pillow, a mirror, and other materials.

12. The student wants to provide an explanation of the term "combine" and an example of it. Which choice most effectively uses relevant information from the notes to accomplish this goal?

    A) The term "combine" was coined by artist Robert Rauschenberg, which refers to artwork that combines elements of sculptures and painting.
    B) Robert Rauschenberg used the term "combine" to describe his artwork that blended painting and sculpture: its integration of three-dimensional objects invaded viewers' space and prompted them to think.
    C) Robert Rauschenberg coined the term "combine" to describe hybrid artwork that included elements of both painting and sculpture, such as *Canyon,* which featured a taxidermized bald eagle among other objects.
    D) *Monogram* and *Canyon* are notable examples of "combines," a term Robert Rauschenberg coined to describe some of his artwork.

While researching a topic, a student takes the following notes.

- Harriet Tubman was one of the most famous conductors of the Underground Railroad, a secret network that provided aid to people escaping slavery.
- Tubman earned the nickname "Moses" for helping so many enslaved people escape.
- Tubman worked in a variety of roles during the Civil War: she worked as a cook, nurse, and spy.
- Tubman was the only woman to lead a military operation during the Civil War, resulting in the emancipation of hundreds of slaves.
- During her life, Tubman was a tireless advocate of abolitionism, suffrage, and human rights.

13. The student wants to emphasize the uniqueness of Tubman's contributions. Which choice most effectively uses relevant information from the notes to accomplish this goal?

    A) During the Civil War, Harriet Tubman, nicknamed "Moses," did important human rights work.
    B) Harriet Tubman, a notable conductor of the Underground Railroad, was the only woman who led a military action during the Civil War, and hundreds of slaves were liberated as a result.
    C) Harriet Tubman was a champion of abolitionism, suffrage, and human rights.
    D) During the Civil War, Harriet Tubman worked in a variety of jobs to support the war effort while also acting as a conductor on the Underground Railroad.

While researching a topic, a student takes the following notes.

- Some research has suggested peer tutoring has the potential to improve learning outcomes.
- Seth Alexander and colleagues conducted a study to find out what tutors and learners found most helpful in peer tutoring sessions.
- They surveyed 56 learners and 20 tutors at a peer tutoring program at a college in an undergraduate medical program.
- The researchers found that both tutors and learners had high agreement that practice questions and reteaching foundational concepts were important to quality tutoring sessions.

14. The student wants to emphasize the study's methodology. Which choice most effectively uses relevant information from the notes to accomplish this goal?

    A) The opinions of tutors and learners about peer tutoring programs can be found among those who participated in a peer tutoring program in medical education at a university, as researchers led by Seth Alexander found.
    B) To determine tutor and learner opinions about conditions that make peer tutoring most effective, Seth Alexander and colleagues surveyed learners and tutors who were participants in a peer tutoring program in medical education at a university.
    C) Because peer tutoring has been shown to have educational benefits, a research team led by Seth Alexander decided to learn more about what makes for an effective tutoring session.
    D) Tutors and learners alike who participated in a peer tutoring program at a college agreed that practice problems and review of foundational concepts were important components to quality tutoring sessions.

Expression Unit Quiz

Researchers studying the sounds produced by walruses' clapping found that walruses in their tanks clap very hard;_____ the water between their flippers vaporizes into a cloud of bubbles that collapse onto themselves to produce a loud sound.

1. Which choice completes the text with the most logical transition?

    A) by the same token,
    B) conversely,
    C) consequently,
    D) to these ends,

Sleep deprivation is a common issue affecting many people. _____ it has been thought that humans today get less sleep than did people in preindustrial times. However, recent research suggests that humans from preindustrial hunter and gatherer societies got less sleep than previously thought.

2. Which choice completes the text with the most logical transition?

    A) Secondly,
    B) Likewise,
    C) Traditionally,
    D) As a result,

While open office designs seem to promote openness and cohesion among workers, some researchers say they may do more harm than good. For example, many workers in open office settings experience unhappiness caused by a lack of privacy normally afforded to them in more traditional workspaces._____ workers in open office settings report being subject to more distractions that hamper their productivity.

3. Which choice completes the text with the most logical transition?

    A) However,
    B) In other words,
    C) Thus,
    D) What's more,

Artists prior to the Renaissance did not generally focus on presenting subjects realistically. For example, they often used rigid lines that made their subjects appear flat. _____ Renaissance artists made use of light, shadows, and perspective to give their art the appearance of depth.

4. Which choice completes the text with the most logical transition?

    A) Similarly,
    B) Consequently,
    C) Conversely,
    D) Still,

While paintings and sculptures are traditionally considered distinct art forms, many modern artists are breaking down the boundaries between two and three dimensions. Dianna Molzan, _____ creates hybrid paintings that use traditional paint tools on three-dimensional surfaces, generating the impression that she is painting through them.

5. Which choice completes the text with the most logical transition?

    A) for example,
    B) however,
    C) secondly,
    D) however,

In the past, if scientists wanted to rearrange dinosaur bones to learn how they fit together, their efforts were limited in part by the weight of the bones. _____ with digital technologies, scientists can rearrange the bones virtually, creating elegant 3-D scale models.

6. Which choice completes the text with the most logical transition?

    A) Currently,
    B) Similarly,
    C) As a result,
    D) Moreover,

Baby hares are born looking like their parents, with hair, open eyes, and an ability to hop independently. Baby rabbits, _____ are hairless, blind, and dependent on their mothers for care. Perhaps this explains why hares are less sociable than rabbits, as they are able to be more independent from a younger age.

7. Which choice completes the text with the most logical transition?

    A) in other words,
    B) by contrast,
    C) similarly,
    D) accordingly,

Zebras in a herd look remarkably similar to one another, which creates a disorienting optical illusion for predators hunting them, thus aiding zebras in survival. This beneficial trait for zebras is frustrating for human researchers,_____ who want to monitor zebra populations and avoid counting the same zebra twice in their studies.

8. Which choice completes the text with the most logical transition?

    A) for instance,
    B) likewise,
    C) therefore,
    D) though,

While graduates from Ph.D. programs have traditionally aspired to obtain careers in academia, Michael Roach and Henry Sauermann found evidence of shifting attitudes among Ph.D. students and graduates. _____ more and more students lose interest in academic careers upon starting their Ph.D. programs, with 15% of students having no interest in working as academics even upon starting their programs.

9. Which choice completes the text with the most logical transition?

    A) Still,
    B) Increasingly,
    C) Likewise,
    D) For this reason,

The praying mantis is a unique insect known for its prominent long legs and triangular head attached to a long neck. Unlike most insect species, the praying mantis can rotate its head a full 180 degrees. _____ it is a formidable predator, as it can look out for prey without ever moving the rest of its body, allowing it to launch surprise attacks.

10. Which choice completes the text with the most logical transition?

    A) Consequently,
    B) What's more,
    C) For example,
    D) Similarly,

There are many benefits to working from home for employees and employers alike, including increased flexibility and reduced overhead expenses. Some jobs require employees to show up in person in order to serve customers. _____ businesses that are able to utilize remote workers should consider doing so.

11. Which choice completes the text with the most logical transition?

    A) As a result,
    B) Still,
    C) Conversely,
    D) In other words,

Mass and weight are often confused with one another, but they are different scientific concepts. Mass is the amount of matter in an object and is unchanged regardless of where the object is. _____ weight is the measure of gravity on an object and varies by location (for instance, an object on Mars would have a different weight than it does on the moon).

12. Which choice completes the text with the most logical transition?

    A) Thus,
    B) Regardless
    C) On the contrary,
    D) In short,

Small businesses often see public support balloon when they face direct threats from large competitors, a study by Neeru Paharia and colleagues shows. When a large ice cream chain moved within steps of a small ice cream shop in Newton, Massachusetts, customers stood by the smaller shop, forcing the chain to shut down. _____ when a Starbucks moved near a small coffee chain in Los Angeles, California, customers supported the smaller chain, and its sales shot up.

13. Which choice completes the text with the most logical transition?

    A) Similarly,
    B) For example,
    C) Therefore,
    D) In conclusion,

While researching a topic, a student takes the following notes.

- Emily Brontë published the novel *Wuthering Heights* in 1847, a work of Gothic fiction.
- She published the book under the pen name Ellis Bell.
- Many scholars have speculated that her novel may have actually been written by her brother Branwell, who had previously written some poems and an unfinished novel.
- Irene Cooper Willis claimed in an interview in 1867 that a timid woman like Emily could not have written such a coarse novel.
- In 2020, researchers Rachel McCarthy and James O'Sullivan employed stylometry, a computer-aided technique that shows how likely it is an author wrote a text, and found that it was very statistically unlikely Branwell contributed to the text of *Wuthering Heights*.
- The researchers argued that Emily is the true author of *Wuthering Heights*.

14. The student wants to make a general point about a methodology used by literary researchers. Which choice most effectively uses relevant information from the notes to accomplish this goal?

    A) Based on stylometry, McCarthy and O'Sullivan concluded that Emily Brontë is the true author of *Wuthering Heights*.
    B) As a computer-aided technique shows, Branwell Brontë very likely did not write the text of *Wuthering Heights*.
    C) When making evaluations about the disputed authorship of novels, researchers often employ statistical analyses.
    D) Although the content of *Wuthering Heights* seemed unlikely to have come from a person with Emily Brontë's personality, she nonetheless is the most likely author.

While researching a topic, a student takes the following notes.

- The moon has generally been thought to be dry.
- A 1994 flyby mission of the Clementine spacecraft found evidence suggestive of potential water and ice on the moon.
- Erik Hauri and colleagues analyzed lunar beads collected from previous lunar missions with an ion microprobe, a highly sensitive research tool, for evidence of water.
- In 2011, the team found a significant amount of water inside the beads.
- The team estimated that the water content on the moon's magma may have originally been upwards of 750 parts per million.

15. The student wants to emphasize the aim of a research study. Which choice most effectively uses relevant information from the notes to accomplish this goal?

    A) Before 2011, some evidence existed that the moon was not completely arid.
    B) Erik Hauri and colleagues used a highly sensitive research tool, an ion microprobe, to analyze lunar samples.
    C) Erick Hauri and colleagues set out to determine if the moon has ever harbored water particles.
    D) Erick Hauri and colleagues estimated that water content on the moon's magma may have originally been upwards of 750 parts per million.

While researching a topic, a student takes the following notes.

- Geese are known to fly for hundreds of miles over the Himalayas to migrate from Mongolia to India or Tibet for the winter.
- The flying strategy geese employ has not been well understood.
- Scientists generally assumed geese flew at high altitudes.
- A team of researchers led by Charles Bishop implanted trackers on geese that measured their altitude, heart rate, and other measures.
- The team found that the geese actually flew in a trajectory resembling that of a roller coaster, regularly descending to lower altitudes.
- The team concluded that a likely reason the birds descended was to conserve energy, as the low density at higher altitudes requires birds to expend more energy.

16. The student wants to present the aim of a research study and its methodology. Which choice most effectively uses relevant information from the notes to accomplish this goal?

    A) Contrary to expectations, a team of researchers found that geese descend to lower altitudes during their migrations.
    B) Seeking to understand the flying strategy of migrating geese, Charles Bishop and colleagues implanted trackers to measure their altitudes throughout their journeys.
    C) The air at higher altitudes is more dense than that at lower altitudes, so geese migrating over the Himalayas frequently fly at lower altitudes to conserve energy.
    D) Charles Bishop and colleagues analyzed how the flying strategy of migrating geese over the Himalayas related to the energy demands of their migrations.

While researching a topic, a student takes the following notes.

- European rabbit populations declined in rural areas but thrived in cities, which raised the question of how urbanity (how city-like a location is) affects rabbits' social organization and burrow structures.
- A team of researchers led by Madlen Ziege investigated how urbanity affects burrow sizes and spacing.
- The team found 191 burrows in Frankfurt at nine city parks, four suburban parks, and three rural sites.
- The team found that high urbanity was correlated with burrows that were smaller and simpler.
- Because cities are warmer than the countryside, city rabbits might not require as many rabbits to keep warm.
- Cities also have more abundant resources, so there may be less need for rabbits to form large groups due to no shortage of food.

17. The student wants to emphasize the aim of the research study. Which choice most effectively uses relevant information from the notes to accomplish this goal?

   A) European rabbits in cities tend to form smaller and simpler burrows than those in the countryside.
   B) As Madlen Ziege and colleagues found, European rabbits in the city might be able to maintain smaller burrows than their rural counterparts because of differences in resource abundance and temperature.
   C) Researchers analyzed over 191 rabbit burrows at locations of differing urbanities to analyze patterns.
   D) Researchers wanted to know how urbanity affected European rabbits' burrow organization since these rabbits' populations were thriving in the cities and declining in the countryside.

While researching a topic, a student takes the following notes.

- Wall Street is an eight-block long street in Manhattan, New York.
- It is the center of financial markets in the United States.
- In 2012, anthropologist Melissa Fisher published *Wall Street Women*.
- The book charts the careers of the first generation of women who established themselves with careers on Wall Street.
- One topic the book explores is the women's impressions of changes in Wall Street's cultural climate.

18. The student wants to introduce Melissa Fisher's book to an audience that is already familiar with Wall Street. Which choice most effectively uses relevant information from the notes to accomplish this goal?

    A) Melissa Fisher's book *Wall Street Women* explores the experiences of the first generation of women who worked as professionals on Wall Street.
    B) Wall Street, referred to in the title of Melissa Fisher's book, acts as the center of financial markets in the United States.
    C) Perceptions of the changing cultural climate of Wall Street is one topic explored in Melissa Fisher's book.
    D) *Wall Street Women* highlights the experience of women working on Wall Street, an eight-block street in Manhattan, New York.

While researching a topic, a student takes the following notes.

- The Olmec Civilization resided in what is now modern-day Mexico from 1200 to 400 BCE.
- This civilization is considered one of the foremost Mesoamerican civilizations, and it is famous for its vibrant cities, elaborate art, and ceremonial architecture.
- Alfonso Caso was one historian who argued that the Olmec Civilization first developed many cultural practices and artifacts that were seen in other Mesoamerican civilizations.
- This theory is called mother culture theory, or *cultura madre*.
- Some evidence for this theory comes from the fact that other Mesoamerican cultures borrowed the Olmecs' calendar system and ball games.

19. The student wants to introduce mother culture theory to an audience unfamiliar with the Olmecs. Which choice most effectively uses relevant information from the notes to accomplish this goal?

A) Historian Alfonso Caso believed the Olmecs were very influential on other Mesoamerican civilizations.
B) The mother culture theory is supported by evidence that other Mesoamerican civilizations adopted the Olmec calendar system and ball games.
C) Mother culture theory argues that the Olmecs, a civilization occupying modern-day Mexico from 1200 to 400 BCE, was the first to develop many cultural practices adopted throughout Mesoamerica.
D) The Olmec civilization, which was located in modern-day Mexico and notable for its thriving cultural practices and artifacts, was influential in a number of important ways.

While researching a topic, a student takes the following notes.

- The Ojibwe people are a group of Indigenous people from parts of what is now southern Canada and the northern United States.
- Winona LaDuke is an economist, environmentalist, and writer whose father was from the Ojibwe White Earth Reservation in Minnesota.
- She worked as a principal at a high school on White Earth after graduating Harvard University in 1982.
- At Harvard, she joined a group advocating for the rights of Indigenous people.
- In 1989, she founded the White Earth Land Recovery Project (WELRP) to recover land for Indigenous people and promote environmental sustainability.
- WELRP works to revive traditional farming practices of Indigenous people, such as wild rice cultivation.

20. The student wants to emphasize the duration and purpose of LaDuke's activism. Which choice most effectively uses relevant information from the notes to accomplish this goal?

   A) Winona LaDuke, who has advocated for Indigenous issues since her time as a student at Harvard University, later founded the WELRP in 1989 to recover land for Indigenous people and revive their traditional practices.
   B) Winona LaDuke, who is Obijwe, works to protect the interests of Indigenous people and promote environmentally sustainable practices.
   C) Winona LaDuke has worked to promote the interests of Indigenous people, as shown by her role as principal at an Ojibwe high school.
   D) Located in Canada and the northern United States, the Obijiwe nation has many traditional agricultural practices that Winona LaDuke has worked to revive.

Answer Key

Key

Lesson 1: Basic Parts of Speech

Drill 1

1. **B.** The adjective "advanced" modifies the noun "words."
2. **D.** The adverb "thoroughly" modifies the adjective "impressed."
3. **C.** "Is" acts as a helping verb in the verb phrase "is falling."
4. **C.** "About economic policy" is a prepositional phrase that modifies "the discussion."
5. **B.** "They" is a personal pronoun.
6. **C.** "Six" modifies the noun "rings."
7. **D.** "Himself" is an intensive pronoun.
8. **B.** "Introduce" is an action verb.
9. **A.** "Smoke" is a substance, so it is a noun.
10. **A.** "Underneath" is a preposition of location.
11. **A.** "Bond" is an abstract idea, so it is a noun.
12. **B.** "Extremely" is an adverb that modifies the other adverb "quickly."
13. **B.** "To" is a preposition of location.
14. **B.** The participial phrase with the participle "working" describes "Delia."
15. **C.** The appositive phrase describes the "dog."
16. **A.** The phrase begins with the preposition "for" and modifies "need."
17. **D.** "Heat of evaporation" renames "heat of vaporization."
18. **B.** The adverb "quite" describes the adjective "concerned."
19. **D.** "Anything" is an indefinite pronoun.
20. **B.** The participial phrase with the participle "renowned" describes the Leaning Tower of Pisa.
21. **A.** "Complain" is the present tense of the regular verb "complain" when the subject is "they."
22. **D.** "Talks" is the present tense of the regular verb "talk" when the subject is singular and in the third person.
23. **C.** "Has begun" is the present perfect tense of the irregular verb "begin."
24. **D.** "Have examined" is the present perfect tense of "examine."
25. **B.** The irregular verb "be" becomes "are" when "you" is the subject in the present tense.
26. **C.** "Had broken" is the past perfect tense of the irregular verb "break."
27. **A.** "Have swum" is the present perfect tense of the irregular verb "swim."
28. **B.** "Was" is the past tense of "be" when the subject is singular and in the third person.
29. **D.** "Have done" is the present perfect tense of the irregular verb "do."
30. **C.** "Have gone" is the present perfect tense of the irregular verb "go."
31. **D.** "Have driven" is the present perfect tense of the irregular verb "drive." "Have not" is used in the present perfect tense.
32. **B.** "Had run" is the past perfect tense of the irregular verb "run."

Lesson 2: Sentence Structure

Drill 1
1. **Dependent.** The sentence is an adverb clause expressing causation.
2. **Independent.** The sentence has a subject and a verb, and it expresses a complete thought.
3. **Independent.** The sentence has a subject and a verb, and it expresses a complete thought.
4. **Dependent.** "That" functions as "the fact that," producing a noun clause.
5. **Dependent.** The sentence is a noun clause.
6. **Dependent.** The sentence is a relative clause with a relative pronoun.
7. **Dependent.** The sentence is a relative clause with a relative pronoun.
8. **Independent.** The sentence has a subject and a verb, and it expresses a complete thought.
9. **Dependent.** The sentence is an adverb clause expressing a purpose.
10. **Dependent.** The sentence is an adverb clause expressing a time relationship.
11. **Dependent.** The sentence is a relative clause with an adverb.
12. **Independent.** The sentence has a subject and a verb, and it expresses a complete thought.
13. **Dependent.** The sentence is an adverb clause expressing a condition.
14. **Dependent.** The sentence is a noun clause.
15. **Independent.** The sentence has a subject and a verb, and it expresses a complete thought.
16. **Dependent.** The sentence is a relative clause with a relative pronoun.
17. **Dependent.** The sentence is an adverb clause expressing a time relationship.
18. **Independent.** The sentence has a subject and a verb, and it expresses a complete thought.
19. **Independent.** The sentence has a subject and a verb, and it expresses a complete thought.
20. **Dependent.** The sentence is an adverb clause expressing a condition.
21. **Complex.** The sentence contains a dependent clause beginning with "while" followed by an independent clause after the comma.
22. **Compound.** The sentence has two independent clauses connected by the conjunction "and."
23. **Compound.** The sentence has two independent clauses connected by the conjunction "but."
24. **Simple.** The sentence has one independent clause.
25. **Complex.** The sentence contains a dependent clause beginning with "although" followed by an independent clause after the comma.
26. **Complex.** The sentence contains an independent clause followed by the dependent clause beginning with "until."
27. **Compound.** The sentence has two independent clauses connected by the conjunction "so"
28. **Complex.** The sentence contains a dependent clause beginning with "unless" followed by an independent clause after the comma.
29. **Simple.** The sentence has one independent clause after a participial phrase.
30. **Complex.** The sentence contains an independent clause followed by the dependent clause beginning with "as."

Lesson 3: Coordination and Subordination

Drill 1
1. **A.** "And" shows the proper addition relationship that illustrates what venture capitalists do.
2. **C.** "Neither…nor" is a word pair.
3. **B.** "Either…or" is a word pair.
4. **B.** "So" is needed to show that Kristina rested as a result of her headache.
5. **C.** "Nor" shows that neither option was acceptable to Ben. The "did he" construction requires "nor" rather than "and."
6. **D.** A contrast conjunction is needed to illustrate the differences between the claims made by the professor and the critics.
7. **D.** "For" is needed to show why Cleo bought a new house.
8. **B.** "So" is needed to show that Sandy volunteered at the soup kitchen as a result of her needing to fulfill service hours.
9. **A.** A contrast conjunction shows the difference between what the professor did well (he explained the concepts clearly) and did not do well (he did not engage the students).
10. **B.** "Both…and" is a word pair.

Drill 2
1. **B.** A contrast between people's beliefs about the koala's classification and its actual classification is needed.
2. **D.** A contrast transition is needed to show that even though it was snowing, the weather was not severe enough to close school.
3. **B.** The cause and effect transition is needed to emphasize the reason Tony was chosen.
4. **D.** An example transition is needed to give an example of a bird that attacks humans.
5. **C.** A transition showing the sequence of Dickens's actions is needed.
6. **D.** A transition showing clarity is needed. The second clause explains what you need to do to perfect your craft.
7. **B.** A contrast transition is needed to show the difference between strict and broad constructionists.
8. **C.** An emphasis transition is needed to stress how e-learning has become popular.
9. **A.** A contrast transition that highlights a surprising outcome is needed. Even though the scientist experienced ridicule, he continued to advocate his views.
10. **B.** "However" interrupts the sentence to show the contrast relationship between the benefits of the program and the need to consult a doctor before starting it.

Drill 3
1. **B.** A contrast conjunction is needed to show the contrast between the speaker disagreeing with some suggestions and finding some advice helpful.
2. **A.** "When" shows the proper time/sequence relationship.
3. **A.** A contrast conjunction shows the difference between the experience being frustrating and teaching the speaker valuable lessons.
4. **D.** "As long as" shows the proper condition relationship for accompaniment to the museum.
5. **A.** "Because" clarifies why the symphony was named "Choral Symphony."
6. **A.** "Until…that" is a word pair.
7. **B.** "Not so much…as" is a word pair.
8. **C.** "As…as" is a word pair.
9. **D.** "Such…that" is a word pair.
10. **A.** "Although" shows the correct contrast relationship between the types of works Picasso painted.

Drill 4

1. **B.** "Not only…but also" is a word pair.
2. **B.** "Not only…but also" is a word pair.
3. **C.** "Given that" shows a condition that clarifies why it is not surprising that the other doctors seek the physician's advice.
4. **C.** "At once…and" is a word pair.
5. **C.** "Just as…so" is a word pair.
6. **D.** "For" shows the proper cause relationship to indicate why the Luddites opposed the machinery.
7. **A.** "Between…and" is a word pair.
8. **C.** "Since" illustrates the correct cause and effect relationship. Due to the ant's ability to glide (cause), it avoids being crushed (effect).
9. **C.** The song exemplifies how the singer voiced political beliefs.
10. **D.** "While" shows that two events happened simultaneously. Pablo Neruda became famous and was a teenager at the same time.
11. **A.** If the condition is met (passing the exam), the desired result (passing the class) still might not occur.
12. **D.** "Despite" is needed because in spite of the executive's efforts, the company struggles.
13. **B.** "Whereby" means "by means of which" or "through which" and shows the correct relationship between a process (aerobic respiration) and the results of that process (obtaining energy).
14. **A.** "Notwithstanding" means "in spite of" and shows that Esufunle's work does not prevent him from making time for his family.
15. **C.** "Thus" shows the proper cause and effect relationship (the tree prevented the speaker from seeing what happened).
16. **B.** "Therefore" shows the proper cause and effect relationship (the fans were surprised at the actor's success in a dramatic role since she is known for her comedies).
17. **D.** A contrast transition is needed to show that Shannon ignored her family's advice.
18. **B.** "So much…that" is a word pair.

Lesson 4: Sentence Boundaries

Drill 1
1. **C.** The main verb "forms" is needed to avoid a fragment.
2. **C.** The subject "she" is needed in the sentence to avoid a fragment. The main verb is "made."
3. **B.** The main verb "travel" is needed to avoid a fragment.
4. **C.** The main verb "encourages" is needed to avoid a fragment. "To use" is an infinitive that pairs with the main verb.
5. **B.** The main verb "has" is needed to avoid a fragment.
6. **B.** The main verb "are" makes the sentence complete, and "where" sets off the relative clause.
7. **D.** The main verb "concluded" is needed to avoid a fragment.
8. **A.** The main verb "incorporate" is needed to avoid a fragment.
9. **C.** "A team of astronomers" is an appropriate subject that clarifies who discovered the planet and is needed to avoid a fragment.
10. **B.** Choice B adds the appropriate contrast transition and creates an independent clause with the main verb "can perform."
11. **C.** The subject is "doctors," and the main verb is "recommend."
12. **C.** "Will give" is the only choice that is a main verb, avoiding a fragment.
13. **D.** The word "is" must be added before "named" to create a main verb.
14. **D.** When the nonessential information ("already available in the United States") is removed from the sentence in D, the resulting sentence is complete, with "contribute" being the main verb.
15. **B.** "Served" is the only choice that is a main verb, avoiding a fragment.
16. **B.** "A crowd of people " is the main subject, and "usually waits" is the main verb.
17. **D.** "Offer" is the only choice that is a main verb, avoiding a fragment.
18. **C.** When the nonessential appositive between the commas is removed from the sentence, the resulting sentence must be complete. "Teaches" functions as the main verb.
19. **C.** "Was" can function as a main verb to create an independent clause after the introductory phrase before the comma.
20. **D.** "Ranged" is the only choice that is a main verb, avoiding a fragment.
21. **D.** D creates an independent clause by avoiding a subordinating conjunction, allowing "turns" to function as a main verb.
22. **D.** D correctly uses the main verb "is" to create a predicate for the subject.
23. **A.** When the nonessential clause between commas is ignored, the sentence is complete, with "dressed" acting as a main verb.
24. **B.** When the nonessential appositive defining the subfield is ignored, the sentence is complete, with "include" acting as a main verb.
25. **A.** A creates an independent clause after the opening phrases, with "its body" acting as the subject and "can maintain" as the main verb phrase.
26. **B.** B creates a complex sentence, a dependent clause beginning with "although" separated from an independent clause by a comma.
27. **B.** B creates a complex sentence, a dependent clause beginning with "because" separated from an independent clause by a comma.
28. **D.** D creates a complex sentence, a dependent clause beginning with "because" separated from an independent clause by a comma.
29. **C.** The sentence must be complete when the nonessential phrase is ignored. The main verb "is" is needed so that an appositive follows an independent clause.
30. **D.** An independent clause is needed after the first independent clause since the clauses are connected by the coordinating (FANBOYS) conjunction "but" after a comma. Choice D makes the second clause independent while using the proper word pair ("until...that").

31. **D.** "Is" acts as a main verb for the subject clause "that Revanth is an excellent writer" (meaning the "the fact that Revanth is an excellent writer").
32. **B.** A comma should connect the independent clause to the appositive phrase beginning with "a practice" that follows.
33. **D.** The sentence must be complete when the parenthetical information ("as a result") is ignored. "Left" can act as a second main verb in the past tense. The other choices create fragments.
34. **B.** The sentence must be complete when the parenthetical information between commas is ignored. "Was" acts as a main verb for the subject "neurotoxin."
35. **C.** Because there is a comma before the coordinating conjunction "but," a full sentence must follow this word. "She" is a main subject and "decided" is a main verb, with "upon noticing her students' issues playing certain difficult musical passages" acting as an opening phrase to the second clause.
36. **D.** The compound verb phrases forming the predicate should be connected by "and" ("rang" and "signaled" are the main verbs).
37. **B.** The object should be the noun "deductions" to complete the predicate logically.

Mini Active Learning Activity
1. The sentence is a run-on. Specifically, it contains a comma splice.
2. The smoothest revision would be to add a coordinating conjunction after the comma to correct the run-on. Below are some possible suggestions.
    - People from all over the state lined up hours in advance for the opening of the new water **park, and they** were not disappointed.
    - People from all over the state lined up hours in advance for the opening of the new water **park; they** were not disappointed.
    - People from all over the state lined up hours in advance for the opening of the new water **park. They** were not disappointed.
3. The sentence inappropriately uses a semicolon to connect an independent clause to a phrase.
4. The simplest revision is to change the semicolon to a comma. Below are potential revisions.
    - When a polar vortex is strong and healthy, cold air is kept farther north. When the Arctic polar vortex weakens, part of this low-pressure system can break **off, causing** temperatures to plummet as far south as Florida.
    - When a polar vortex is strong and healthy, cold air is kept farther north. When the Arctic polar vortex weakens, part of this low-pressure system can break **off, thus causing** temperatures to plummet as far south as Florida.
    - When a polar vortex is strong and healthy, cold air is kept farther north. When the Arctic polar vortex weakens, part of this low-pressure system can **break off, an event which causes** temperatures to plummet as far south as Florida.
    - When a polar vortex is strong and healthy, cold air is kept farther north. When the Arctic polar vortex weakens, part of this low-pressure system can break **off. This** can cause temperatures to plummet as far south as Florida.
5. The sentence is a run-on. Specifically, it contains a comma splice.
6. Separating the clauses into two sentences, changing the comma to a semicolon, or adding a coordinating conjunction after the comma would be the most logical revisions. Below are some possible suggestions.
    - Some of the students presented prototypes for educational interventions grounded in emotion **research, but** others proposed areas for future research in the field, highlighting gaps in the literature.
    - Some of the students presented prototypes for educational interventions grounded in emotion **research, and** others proposed areas for future research in the field, highlighting gaps in the literature.

- Some of the students presented prototypes for educational interventions grounded in emotion **research. Others** proposed areas for future research in the field, highlighting gaps in the literature.
- Some of the students presented prototypes for educational interventions grounded in emotion **research; others** proposed areas for future research in the field, highlighting gaps in the literature.
- **While** some of the students presented prototypes for educational interventions grounded in emotion research, others proposed areas for future research in the field, highlighting gaps in the literature.

7. The underlined portion uses a semicolon before a coordinating conjunction introducing a second independent clause.
8. The simplest revision is changing the semicolon to a comma, though creating a relative clause beginning with "who" would arguably produce the smoothest flow. Below are possible revisions.
    - Economic growth, an integral feature of the global economy, has long fascinated **scholars, and they** have proposed many theories for this phenomenon.
    - Economic growth, an integral feature of the global economy, has long fascinated **scholars, who** have proposed many theories for this phenomenon.
    - Economic growth, an integral feature of the global economy, has long fascinated **scholars; they** have proposed many theories for this phenomenon.
    - Economic growth, an integral feature of the global economy, has long fascinated **scholars. They** have proposed many theories for this phenomenon.
9. **No**. Sentence 1 is a run-on. Specifically, it contains a comma splice. The conjunctive adverb "in fact" introduces a second independent clause, so a comma before it is inappropriate.
10. **Yes**. The conjunctive adverb "in fact" acts as an interrupter between commas. When it is ignored, the sentence is complete.
11. The comma before "in fact" should be changed to a semicolon in Sentence 1 to correct the run-on. The result is two independent clauses separated by a semicolon.
12. The sentence connects a dependent clause beginning with "although" to an independent clause by a comma and the coordinating conjunction "yet." A comma + a coordinating conjunction should be used to connect two independent clauses. "Although" and "yet" are also redundant in terms of meaning ("yet" is implied by "although").
13. The simplest revision is to delete "yet" so that a comma separates the dependent clause from the independent clause that follows. Alternatively, delete "although" so that the coordinating conjunction "yet" links the two independent clauses separated by a comma. Possible revisions are shown below.
    - Although Lila's ideas about how to run her company were met with skepticism by her **naysayers, she** proved them wrong when her unorthodox ideas increased her profits.
    - **Lila's** ideas about how to run her company were met with skepticism by her naysayers, **yet** she proved them wrong when her unorthodox ideas increased her profits.
    - **Lila's** ideas about how to run her company were met with skepticism by her **naysayers. However**, she proved them wrong when her unorthodox ideas increased her profits.
    - **Lila's ideas** about how to run her company were met with skepticism by her **naysayers. She** proved them wrong when her unorthodox ideas increased her profits.
    - **Lila's** ideas about how to run her company were met with skepticism by her **naysayers; she** proved them wrong when her unorthodox ideas increased her profits.
    - **Lila's** ideas about how to run her company were met with skepticism by her **naysayers; however, she** proved them wrong when her unorthodox ideas increased her profits.

Drill 2
1. **B.** A semicolon should precede "however" to avoid a comma splice and link the independent clauses.
2. **D.** Adding "of which" after "each" makes the second clause dependent, avoiding a comma splice.
3. **D.** A semicolon should separate the independent clauses.
4. **B.** The coordinating conjunction "but" after a comma creates a complete sentence and clarifies the contrast relationship between the two parts of the sentence.
5. **D.** The subordinating conjunction "because" makes the sentence complete and clarifies the cause and effect relationship between the dependent and independent clauses.
6. **C.** When the nonessential clause between commas is ignored, the sentence is complete in C, with "abdicated" acting as a main verb.
7. **C.** A comma should separate the independent clause from the phrase that follows.
8. **C.** A modifying phrase can be separated by an independent clause by a comma to avoid a comma splice.
9. **B.** An independent clause cannot be set off by commas between the elements comprising another independent clause. "Who" is needed to create a nonessential relative clause.
10. **C.** Adding the subordinating conjunction "because" makes the second clause dependent, creating a complex sentence.
11. **C.** An independent clause should follow the comma separating it from the opening modifying phrase. "Are becoming" is a main verb
12. **D.** Choice D connects an independent clause to a dependent clause defining "a trait" with a comma.
13. **C.** The first sentence contains an independent clause. The second contains a dependent clause separated from an independent clause by a comma.
14. **C.** Choice C interrupts the independent clause with a nonessential appositive between commas.
15. **B.** The complete sentences should be separated by periods. The second sentence contains a prepositional phrase followed by an independent clause.
16. **C.** A comma links the participial phrase to an independent clause.
17. **B.** B creates a loose sentence that contains an independent clause separated from a participial phrase by a comma.
18. **C.** C uses a comma to separate an independent clause from an appositive phrase modifying the book.
19. **D.** D uses a comma to separate an independent clause from an appositive phrase modifying the film.
20. **C.** "Of which" is needed to avoid a run-on, making the second clause after the comma dependent (following an opening independent clause).
21. **B.** "And" connects the two verb phrases, creating a complete sentence.
22. **A.** "Traveling in packs" is a phrase describing the subject "lions," and "are" is a main verb.
23. **C.** The relative pronoun "which" creates a dependent clause after the independent clause so that a comma can separate them.
24. **C.** A period should separate the complete sentences.
25. **C.** The participle is needed to make the phrase in the middle of the sentence between commas nonessential, thus avoiding a run-on.
26. **B.** B appropriately adds a comma after the first independent clause, connecting it to a participial phrase beginning with "believing."
27. **C.** C appropriately avoids a run-on by connecting the independent clause to a participial phrase beginning with "showing" with a comma.
28. **B.** The contrast coordinating conjunction "but" should follow the comma in order to connect the two independent clauses.
29. **D.** Adding "of whom" to "both" makes the second clause dependent, avoiding a run-on. Since people are being discussed, "whom" should be used instead of "which."
30. **C.** C appropriately connects the independent clause to an appositive beginning with "a form" that follows a comma.
31. **C.** A comma can separate an independent clause from a participial phrase beginning with "hoping," creating a loose sentence.

32. **B.** B avoids a run-on by connecting the independent clause to a participial phrase beginning with "meaning" with a comma.
33. **D.** A comma should introduce the dependent clause beginning with "where." "She hoped" should not be set off by commas since it is essential information.
34. **C.** A semicolon is inappropriate since the second clause is not independent. A comma can separate an independent clause from a phrase, as in C.
35. **D.** A comma can separate the independent clause from the dependent clause beginning with "while" that follows to avoid a run-on.
36. **B.** The dependent clause has a compound predicate with two verbs connected by "and" that provide benefits of the program. A comma should introduce the independent clause that completes the contrast, highlighting a potential negative aspect of it.
37. **B.** "And" can be used to set off the information between commas as nonessential information. When it is ignored, the result is a complex sentence. The other choices result in comma splices since they each use a conjunctive adverb instead of a coordinating conjunction between independent clauses.
38. **B.** The supplementary adverb "however" ends the first clause for dramatic effect. A semicolon should separate this clause from the second independent clause.
39. **C.** Ignore the nonessential phrase between commas. "And" appropriately connects the components of the compound predicate (each action done by the subject, the students).

Lesson 5: Modifiers

Mini Active Learning Activity
1. The bolded phrase is supposed to describe **the company**, but as it is written now, it seems to be describing **consumers.**
2. "The company" must be the first word after the comma. A possible revision is shown below.
    - Having ascertained that the skincare product did not violate any existing patent protections, the company determined the best way in which to market it to consumers.
3. The bolded phrase is supposed to describe **many colleges and universities,** but as it is written now, it seems to be describing **the students.**
4. "Many colleges and universities" should follow the comma. A possible revision is shown below.
    - Recognizing the importance of having a student body from diverse communities, many colleges and universities have made recruitment efforts to students in remote communities.
5. The bolded phrase is supposed to describe **Vera Rubin,** but as it is written now, it seems to be describing **the conclusion.**
6. "Vera Rubin" should follow the comma. A possible revision is shown below.
    - Noticing that stars in the Andromeda galaxy were moving in unexpected ways, Vera Rubin concluded that "dark matter" must exist in the universe.
7. Since Ronald Reagan follows the comma, the modifying phrase should describe him. As the sentence is written now, it seems to describe the people who know Ronald Reagan rather than Ronald Reagan himself.
8. The underlined portion should be changed to a word like "known" to correct the dangling modifier. The introductory phrase should describe Reagan.

Drill 1
1. **C.** The modifying phrase describes Elizabeth, the word that should follow the comma.
2. **D.** The modifying phrase describes the old cabin, the word that should follow the comma.
3. **A.** The modifying phrase describes Joseph Strauss, the word that should follow the comma.
4. **C.** The modifying phrase describes Marco Polo, the word that should follow the comma.
5. **D.** The modifying phrase describes the legislature, the word that should follow the comma.
6. **D.** "Knowing him" seems to describe the people who know Tim. The past participle "known" logically modifies Tim, the noun following the modifying phrase.
7. **D.** The modifying phrase describes the Palace of Parliament, the word that should follow the comma.
8. **A.** The modifying phrase describes Greece, the word that should follow the comma.
9. **B.** The modifying phrase describes the abacus, the word that should follow the comma.
10. **B.** The modifying phrase "having been chosen to speak at the conference" correctly describes Jacqueline, the noun following the comma.
11. **C.** The modifying phrase describes the company's environment, the word that should follow the comma.
12. **C.** The modifying phrase describes Sigmund Freud, the word that should follow the comma. The relative pronoun "which" refers to psychoanalysis, so this pronoun should follow that word.
13. **B.** The modifying phrase describes the Children's House, the word that should follow the comma.
14. **B.** The modifying phrase describes "you," the word that should follow the comma.
15. **C.** The modifying phrase describes the company, the word that should follow the comma.
16. **C.** "Designed to improve people's posture" clearly describes the biofeedback devices, the word after the comma.
17. **B.** "Who" refers to today's lecturer, not today, so it should follow the "lecturer."
18. **D.** The participial phrase beginning with "blending" that describes the chameleon should follow the independent clause to avoid a run-on.

19. **C.** The participle "using" is needed to describe the washing machine and avoid a run-on.
20. **B.** "Which" is the relative pronoun that refers to the beak.
21. **B.** B connects an independent clause to a past participial phrase describing the mammals by a comma, avoiding a run-on.
22. **C.** C separates an independent clause from a present participial phrase describing the methods by a comma. Note that B could confusingly suggest the listed methods are artifacts since "which" follows "artifacts," so is C is the stronger choice (though an argument can be made that B is technically acceptable)
23. **B.** The participial phrase "renowned for its hanging gardens" refers to Babylon. It should follow the independent clause by a comma to avoid a run-on.
24. **C.** The modifying phrase describes the field of "strategy management," the word that should follow the comma
25. **C.** "Ever since it had been introduced" avoids a dangling modifier by clearly referring to cinnamon, the word after the comma.
26. **B.** A phrase must follow the independent clause after the comma to avoid a run-on. B creates a participial phrase that appropriately modifies the group of flowers.
27. **D.** "Where" modifies "the Apollo Theater," which should precede "where" to avoid a modifying error.

Lesson 6: Verbs

Drill 1
1. **A.** The present tense is needed because the number of hours people currently spend listening is lower than it was in the past.
2. **A.** The past tense is needed since the time period of the sentence is the 1300s.
3. **D.** The future perfect is needed because an action will be completed before another in the future (the project will be completed before the arrival).
4. **B.** The past tense is needed because the time period is 4,000 years ago.
5. **D.** The present perfect is needed since the action (the bell ringing at 7:55) began in the past and is continuing in the present. "Ring" is an irregular verb that changes to "rung" in the perfect tenses.
6. **B.** The present perfect is needed because the Dutch ovens were first built in the past, but they are still used today.
7. **B.** The past perfect is needed because it describes an action that happened before another action in the past (Carrie Nation was an advocate before she appeared on vaudeville).
8. **C.** The past perfect is needed because it describes an action that happened before another in the past (the claims were disproved before the error was acknowledged).
9. **A.** The present perfect can be used to describe an action that is completed before another in the future. People cannot register until they have paid.
10. **C.** The future tense is needed, as indicated by "next month."
11. **B.** The past tense is needed because the time period that the action occurred in was the 1970s.
12. **A.** The present tense is needed because "can do" implies that there are things one can do in the present.
13. **C.** "Would rent" shows that the action was repeated in the past.
14. **B.** The present perfect is needed because the number of people who report working from home began increasing in the past and continues to increase.
15. **C.** The past perfect is needed to describe an action that happened before another (the wound was treated before the antibiotic was given) and avoid a dangling modifier.
16. **D.** The past tense verb "settled" is consistent with the past tense verb "produced."
17. **C.** The sentence takes place in the past, so "would" is appropriate.
18. **B.** The past tense is needed. It describes a reaction in the past (the fans being concerned) to an event that happened in the past (the host quitting). The word "would" also suggests that the action happened in the past.
19. **B.** The past tense verb "piled" is consistent with the past tense verb "produced."
20. **A.** The word "would" suggests that the past tense is needed.
21. **B.** The present tense is needed due to the word "argues." Other methods currently give steak a less rich flavor.
22. **C.** The past perfect is used to describe an action that was completed before another (the suspect denied his involvement before he admitted his guilt).
23. **B.** The sentence takes place in the present tense. The issues discussed remain relevant in modern times.
24. **B.** The present tense of "do" must recur throughout the sentence.
25. **D.** The modal verb "would" is needed since the sentence expresses the future from the perspective of the past.
26. **B.** The past tense is needed to describe Sharonda's former beliefs, which persisted up to the moment she caught her friend in a lie, as indicated by "until." A would have been correct had "before" been used instead of "until" (meaning she stopped seeing him as trustworthy before the time she caught him a lie).
27. **C.** The present perfect tense is needed because the action began in the past and is ongoing (the company started priding itself during its founding and still prides itself now).

28. **B.** The infinitive "to build" connects the independent clause to the dependent clause that follows, showing the appropriate cause and effect relationship.

Structure Unit Quiz

1. **A.** A correctly uses a main present tense verb that indicates the threats facing polar bears still exist.
2. **B.** B correctly uses a relative clause beginning with "that" to define the field of neuromarketing, completing the predicate beginning with the subject "neuromarketing" and the verb "is."
3. **C.** Only C avoids a fragment with a main present tense verb "contend."
4. **C.** A semicolon should separate the two parts of the sentence that themselves can stand alone as full sentences. "Rather" acts as a conjunctive adverb starting a second independent clause contrasting with an idea in the first independent clause.
5. **C.** The introductory participial phrase describes the French armies, which should follow the comma to avoid a dangling modifier error.
6. **B.** The present tense is needed to show how Enheduanna is viewed today.
7. **B.** A semicolon should separate the full sentences.
8. **A.** A avoids the dangling modifier. The opening participial phrase describes von Ahn, who should follow the comma.
9. **D.** D correctly uses a coordinating (FANBOYS) conjunction "but" after a comma to link the independent clauses, avoiding a run-on.
10. **C.** C avoids the dangling modifier. The opening participial phrase describes Simone, who should follow the comma.
11. **D.** D correctly uses a participial phrase after the comma following the independent clause, creating a loose sentence.
12. **B.** B correctly uses a period to separate two complete sentences.
13. **C.** The past tense should be used with "would," which shows the future from the perspective of the past.
14. **B.** The past perfect tense is needed when describing an action completed before another time period in the past.
15. **B.** A comma should connect the independent clause to the phrase that follows.
16. **B.** A semicolon should separate the complete sentences. Note that the second clause includes the main verb ("was") before its subject ("a translucent quartz gemstone").
17. **B.** The opening phrase describes the salt batteries, which should follow the comma to avoid a dangling modifier. The dependent clause beginning with "as" (meaning "because") follows the independent clause, showing a cause and effect relationship.
18. **B.** B correctly separates participial phrase from an opening independent clause by a comma, creating a loose sentence.
19. **D.** The opening participial phrase describes Carver, who should follow the comma to avoid a dangling modifier.
20. **C.** A comma is needed to separate the independent clause from the dependent clause beginning with a contrast transition that follows.
21. **B.** The two complete sentences should be separated by a period. Although a semicolon can be placed before "while," no comma should follow this subordinate conjunction.
22. **C.** A comma should separate the complete sentence from the participial phrase beginning with "producing," creating a loose sentence.
23. **C.** A period should be used to separate the complete sentences.

Lesson 7: Possessive Determiners

Drill 1
1. **A.** "It is" is appropriate in context.
2. **B.** The possessive determiner "your" is needed since the ideas belong to the pronoun "you."
3. **D.** The possessive determiner "whose" is needed since the advice belongs to someone unknown.
4. **A.** The existential "there" is needed.
5. **A.** "Who is" is appropriate in context.
6. **B.** The possessive determiner "your" is needed since the record belongs to the pronoun "you."
7. **C.** The adverb of location "there" is needed.
8. **B.** The singular possessive determiner "its" is needed since the culture belongs to the singular noun "town."
9. **A.** A possessive determiner is needed since the arguments belong to someone or multiple people. Only "their" is a possessive determiner.
10. **B.** "You are" is appropriate in context.
11. **C.** The singular possessive determiner is needed since the "wood" belongs to the singular noun "tree" (the Silver Maple).
12. **D.** In context, the existential "there" is needed.
13. **B** The possessive determiner "your" is needed since the thesis belongs to the pronoun "you."
14. **A.** "They are" is appropriate in context.
15. **C.** The plural possessive determiner "their" is needed since the "bungalows" belong to the plural noun "hotels."
16. **C.** The singular possessive determiner "its" is needed since the "capacity" belongs to the singular noun "company."
17. **D.** The plural possessive determiner "their" is needed since the "appeal" belongs to the plural noun "solar panels."
18. **A.** The plural possessive determiner "their" is needed since the "effectiveness" belongs to the plural noun "herbicides."
19. **B.** The existential "there" is needed.
20. **A.** The singular possessive determiner "its" is needed since the "services" belong to the singular noun "organization."

Lesson 8: Pronouns
Mini Active Learning Activity
1. **Luxury vacations.** These are what are too expensive for many people.
2. **Them.** A plural objective pronoun is needed.
3. **Zebras.** Zebras are the owners of the stripes.
4. **Them.** A plural objective pronoun is needed.
5. **Louisa May Alcott and other female authors.** All of the female authors listed are the owners of the books.
6. **Their.** A plural possessive determiner is needed.
7. **Smartphone.** The sentence refers to the invention of the smartphone.
8. **Its.** A singular possessive determiner is needed.
9. **Venus flytrap.** The Venus flytrap is the owner of the positions.
10. **Its.** A singular possessive determiner is needed.
11. **Observers.** These people would remember the moment.
12. **They.** A plural subjective pronoun is needed.

Drill 1
1. **A.** The pronoun "them" refers to "kidneys."
2. **C.** The plural possessive determiner "their" is needed because it shows that the neural pathways belong to the plural noun "the brains of toddlers."
3. **B.** The singular possessive determiner "its" is needed because it shows that the appearance belongs to the singular noun "Empire State Building."
4. **B.** The singular possessive determiner "its" is required because of the presence of "each." Each anthology story acts as its own singular owner.
5. **A.** The singular possessive determiner "its" is required because it shows that the blooms belong to the singular noun "Empress Tree. "
6. **B.** The plural indefinite pronoun "some" is required because it refers to "math and science."
7. **A.** The singular possessive determiner "its" is required because it shows that the streets belong to the singular noun "town."
8. **D.** The singular possessive determiner "its" is required because it shows that the tail belongs to the singular noun "gecko."
9. **C.** "They" refers to the plural noun "examples." The plural possessive determiner "their" shows that the function belongs to the plural noun "examples." The main verb for the plural subject is "are."
10. **D.** The presence of "each" requires the singular possessive determiner "his." The owner is "each [one] of their sons" (a singular noun).
11. **B.** "It" is required because it refers to the singular noun "cable company."
12. **C.** "His" is required because it refers to the speech belonging to Lincoln, a singular noun.
13. **C.** "Each" (meaning "each restaurant," a singular noun) requires the singular possessive determiner "its" and the singular noun "cuisine."
14. **C.** "They" refers to the plural noun "works."
15. **A.** "They" refers to the plural noun "textbooks."
16. **D.** The singular possessive determiner "its" is required because it shows that the civic duty belongs to the singular collective noun "jury."
17. **B.** "They" refers to the plural noun "peregrine falcons."
18. **C.** "Themselves" refers to the plural "mentors." The reflexive form is needed since mentors are both the subjects and recipients of the action.
19. **A.** The plural possessive determiner "their" is required to show that the ways of coping belong to the plural noun "individuals."
20. **C.** The plural pronoun "those" refers to plants that are far away in location.
21. **D.** The modifying phrase should describe cost-plus pricing. D creates a participial phrase that accomplishes this goal.

Lesson 9: Subject Verb Agreement

Drill 1
1. **Is.** The singular subject is "radiocarbon dating," so the singular verb "is" is needed.
2. **Were.** The plural subject is "fairy tales," so the plural verb "were" is needed.
3. **Are.** The subjects are "aqueous solutions and precipitates," so the plural verb "are" is needed.
4. **Neutralizes.** The conjunction "or" connects the singular subjects "acid" and "base." The singular verb "neutralizes" is needed.
5. **Is.** "Each" requires the use of the singular verb "is."
6. **Have.** "A number of" requires the plural verb "have."
7. **Depends.** When "whether" is used as part of a subject, a singular verb (in this case, "depends") is needed.
8. **Is.** The gerund phrase "planting flowers" is a singular subject, so the singular verb "is" is needed.
9. **Has.** "The number of" requires the singular verb "has."
10. **Are.** The "there are" construction is needed since it is followed by "reasons."
11. **Helps.** A singular verb (in this case, "helps') is needed when "that" functions as "the fact that."
12. **Are.** The plural subject "many applications" requires "there are."
13. **Were.** The plural verb "were" is needed because there are two subjects ("flour and sugar").
14. **Has.** "Many a" requires the singular verb "has."
15. **Sings.** "Along with" requires the singular verb "sings" since the subject before this phrase ("Joaquin") is singular.
16. **Have.** "Few" is plural, so the plural verb "have" is needed.
17. **Was.** The singular subject "cinema" requires the singular verb "was."
18. **Contain.** The plural verb "contain" is needed because the subject "all of the books" is plural.
19. **Looks.** "Each" requires a singular verb (in this case, "looks").
20. **Plays.** "Neither" requires a singular verb when separating singular nouns.
21. **Are.** The plural verb "are" is needed because the subject "doors" is plural. The verb follows the prepositional phrase "across the hall."
22. **Is.** The gerund phrase "making napping a part of corporate culture" is a singular subject, so the singular verb "is" is needed.

Mini Active Learning Activity
For 1-6, the prepositional phrases are **bolded**, as these phrases begin with prepositions to provide more details about the nouns preceding them
1. Beatriz loves spending days **on the lake** kayaking and paddle boarding **with her family**.
2. Critics said that the lead actor's performance **in the production of** *Hamlet* deserved an award.
3. The cake **with the cherry on top** is your sister's.
4. Return the toys **to their drawers** when you are done playing.
5. A hole **in the pipe** was responsible **for the leak**.
6. College student development theory is a body **of scholarship** that seeks to explain ways students learn, grow, and develop so that professionals **in higher education** can serve students' needs.
7. **In many states.** This phrase modifies "voter turnout."
8. **Voter turnout (singular).** This is what hovers.
9. **No change is needed.** The singular subject and singular verb agree.
10. **Of the first events.** This phrase modifies "one."
11. **One (singular).** The remarks represented one of the events.
12. **Was.** A singular verb is needed to agree with the singular subject.
13. **Of new jobs.** The phrase describes the proliferation.
14. **Proliferation (singular).** This is what gave residents hope.
15. **No change is needed.** The singular subject and singular verb agree.
16. **Of 3D printing.** The phrase modifies "uses."

17. **Uses (plural).** The uses have expanded.
18. **Have.** A plural verb is needed to agree with the plural subject.
19. **In the farmer's vegetable garden.** This phrase modifies "rows."
20. **Rows (plural).** The rows provided conditions conducive to growing lettuce.
21. **No change is needed.** The plural subject and plural verb agree.

Drill 2
1. **B.** The plural subject is "fax machines," so the plural verb "are" is needed. The nonessential clause between the commas should be ignored, so "technology" is not the subject.
2. **D.** The singular subject is the "Sistine Chapel," so the singular verb "hosts" is needed. The nonessential clause between the commas should be ignored, so "1994" is not the subject. The sentence takes place in the present.
3. **C.** The plural subject is "sections," so the plural verb "include" is needed. The prepositional phrase "of the Appalachian Trail" should be ignored, so "the Appalachian Trail" is not the subject.
4. **C.** The singular subject is "electron microscope," so the singular verb "has" is needed. The nonessential clause between the commas should be ignored, so "images" is not the subject.
5. **B.** The singular subject is "evidence," so the singular verb "suggests" is needed. The relative clause ("those…sources") should be ignored, so "sources" is not the subject.
6. **B.** The singular subject is "decline," so the singular verb "is" is needed. The prepositional phrase "in gas prices" should be ignored, so "prices" is not the subject.
7. **A.** The singular subject is "exhibition," so the singular verb "displays" is needed. The prepositional phrase ("of…inhabitants") should be ignored, so "inhabitants" is not the subject.
8. **C.** The singular subject is "southern masked weaver," so the singular verb "learns" is needed. "Like other birds" is nonessential, so "birds" is not the subject.
9. **A.** The plural subject is "errors," so the plural verb "are" is needed. In order for the sentence to be complete, it must say "are likely to be found." The prepositional phrase "in the document" should be ignored, so "document" is not the subject.
10. **B.** The singular gerund phrase subject "building rapport" requires the singular verb "is."
11. **B.** The singular subject is "Agatha Christie," so the singular verb "is" is needed. "Agatha Christie has made her one of the most popular authors of all time" (the sentence that results from removing the nonessential clause) is not logical.
12. **B.** The singular subject is "every concept," so the singular verb "is" is needed. "Review sheets" is not the subject because it is part of the prepositional phrase ("on…review sheets").
13. **A.** The singular subject is "reason," so the singular verb "is" is needed. "Books" is not the subject because it is part of the essential clause ("that…books"). The pronoun "they" replaces "books."
14. **C.** The singular subject is "all the discussion," so the singular verb "has" is needed. "Materials" is not the subject because it is part of the prepositional phrase ("about…materials").
15. **A.** The singular subject is "care," so the singular verb "has" is needed. The singular noun "company" requires the singular pronoun "it." "Products" is not the subject because it is part of the prepositional phrase ("in…products").
16. **B.** The singular verb "adds" is needed because the singular subject is "each." The nonessential clause should be ignored, so "athletes" is not the subject.
17. **B.** "One" is a singular subject, so the singular verb "has" is needed.
18. **B.** The singular verb "contains" is needed because when "neither" is present, the verb must agree with the second noun. "French Polynesia" is singular.
19. **A.** The singular subject "each" requires the singular verb "has" and the singular determiner "its." "Of which" is needed to prevent a comma splice.
20. **D.** The plural subject "paper towels" requires the plural verb "come," and the other plural subject "napkins" requires the plural verb "do."
21. **B.** "Neither of which" is a singular subject, so the singular verb "requires" is the correct verb.

22. **B.** The singular subject is "proportional representation," so the singular verb "exists" is needed. The nonessential appositive between the commas should be ignored.
23. **D.** The singular subject "genetic material" follows the prepositional phrase "from whose cells" and requires the singular verb "is."
24. **C.** The two subjects ("coherence and powerfulness") require the plural verb "explain." The singular owner "editorial" requires the singular possessive determiner "its." "Editorial" is not the subject of the verb because it is part of a prepositional phrase ("of the editorial").
25. **B.** "Taking Vitamin C" is the singular gerund phrase subject that agrees with the singular verb "helps." "That" (meaning "the fact that") requires the singular verb "was argued."
26. **B.** Because the plural subject is "directors," the plural verb "have" and the plural determiner "their" are needed. "The Caribbean" is part of the nonessential clause.
27. **A.** "Animals" is the plural subject, so the plural verb "hibernate" is needed. "Black bear" is part of the nonessential phrase.
28. **B.** The plural subject is "quantities," so the plural verb "have" is needed. "Pollen" is part of the prepositional phrase beginning with "of."
29. **A.** The singular subject is "social media presence," so the singular verb "has" is needed following the nonessential phrase between the commas.
30. **A.** The plural subject is "customers," so the plural verb "claim" is needed. The relative clause ("who…laptop") describes the customers.
31. **C.** The singular subject is "commission," so the singular verb "has encountered" is needed. The participial phrase ("investigating...manufacturers") describes the commission.
32. **C.** The singular subject is "zebra fish," so the singular verb "is" is needed. "Mouse" is part of the nonessential phrase between the commas.
33. **D.** The plural subject is "unicorns," so the plural verb "are" is needed. "Funding" is part of the nonessential phrase between the commas.
34. **B.** The singular subject is "diversity," so the singular verb "was" is needed. The prepositional phrase ("of…park") should be ignored.
35. **B.** The subject clause beginning with "what" is singular, so the singular verb "is" is needed.
36. **D.** The plural subject "people" requires the plural verb "spend."
37. **B.** The plural subject "people" requires the plural verb "are." The participial phrase between the subject and the verb should be ignored.
38. **B.** The singular subject "cake" requires the singular verb "tastes." The participial phrase between the subject and the verb should be ignored.
39. **D.** The plural subject "transcriptions" within the relative clause beginning with "that" requires the plural verb "indicate."
40. **D.** The plural subject "increases" requires the plural verbs "threaten" and "affect."
41. **B.** The plural subjects ("speed, convenience, and affordability") require the plural verb "make." The singular "it" refers to the singular noun "sedan."
42. **A.** The singular subject "each" requires the singular verb "centers."

Usage Unit Quiz

1. **C.** "They" refers to the "residents."
2. **A.** The singular possessive determiner is needed since the feathers belong to "it" (the canary).
3. **D.** The singular subject "landing" requires the singular verb "sends."
4. **B.** The plural possessive determiner "their" is needed since the work belonged to the "Hidden Figures."
5. **D.** The plural reflexive pronoun "themselves" agrees with "they" and conveys that the remora are being detached.
6. **B.** A singular verb is needed to correspond to the singular subject "his writing."
7. **A.** The singular pronoun "it" refers to "sleep."
8. **A.** The plural verb "were" is needed since the plural subject is "worlds."
9. **D.** The plural pronoun "they" refers to "devices."
10. **B.** The singular subject "*Silent Spring*" requires the singular verb "was opposed."
11. **A.** The singular subject "Ethel Ray Nance" requires the singular verb "was."
12. **C.** The plural subject is "reasons," so the plural verb "are" is required.
13. **D.** "Them" refers to the "strips."
14. **C.** The plural subjects "the cost, novelty, and lack of clear legislation guidance" require the plural subject "have prevented."
15. **B.** The plural subject "differences" requires the plural verb "provide."
16. **C.** The singular subject "that" (meaning "the fact that") requires the singular verb "highlights."
17. **C.** The subject "many a cognitive science professor" is singular, so the singular verb "has argued" is needed.
18. **B.** The "painting" is the singular subject and the sentence takes place in the past, so "was" is needed.
19. **B.** The singular subject is "what" and the sentence takes place in the present, so "is" is needed.
20. **B.** The singular subject "filtering" requires the singular verb "permits."

Lesson 10: End of Sentence Punctuation
Drill 1
1. ! The sentence is an interjection.
2. ? The sentence includes a direct question.
3. ? The sentence includes a direct question.
4. . The sentence reports a fact.
5. . The sentence reports a fact.
6. . The sentence includes an indirect question.
7. ? The sentence includes a direct question.
8. . The sentence reports a fact.
9. ! The sentence is an interjection.
10. . The sentence expresses a desire.
11. . The sentence includes an indirect question.
12. ! The sentence is an interjection.
13. . The sentence reports a fact.
14. ? The sentence includes a direct question.
15. **B.** A period is needed since the question is indirect. A uses a confusing word order, suggesting a question is being asked.
16. **A.** A period is needed since the question is indirect. D uses a confusing word order, suggesting a question is being asked.
17. **B.** The tour guide asks a direct question, so a question mark is needed. D is not a direct question and is not a complete thought.
18. **C.** C presents a direct question that is answered afterward. D is not a complete thought.
19. **A.** A period is needed since the question is indirect. B confusingly adds "it."
20. **B.** A period is needed since the question is indirect. D confusingly uses "will" in a way that suggests a question is being asked.

Lesson 11: Within Sentence Punctuation

Mini Active Learning Activity
1. The colon should follow "types" in order to signal the clarification on what the two types of attentional processes are.
2. A colon should generally follow an independent clause, which it does not in this case.
3. The simplest approach is to simply delete the colon. A second would be to make the information before the colon an independent clause. Potential revisions are shown below.
    - Sabrina learned an ironic **lesson:** meddling in people's lives out of a desire to help them can have unforeseen consequences that merely exacerbate their problems.
    - Sabrina learned the ironic **lesson that** meddling in people's lives out of a desire to help them can have unforeseen consequences that merely exacerbate their problems.
4. A colon should generally follow an independent clause, which it does not in this case.
5. It should follow the word "common." This way, there is an independent clause before the colon, and the information after the colon explains the independent clause (clarifying what invasive species have in common).
6. A dependent clause follows the colon, which is not appropriate.
7. The colon should be changed to a comma. When a dependent clause beginning with "although" follows an independent clause, a comma is appropriate.
8. One approach is to simply delete "although" so that an independent clause follows the colon. This would provide an elaboration that somewhat expands on what came before the colon (making clear why his expectations were low). A new sentence could then explain how the party exceeded Tomas's expectations. A better revision would be to add a comma at the end of the sentence followed by an independent clause explaining how the party exceeded his expectations. Possible revisions are shown below.
    - Tomas enjoyed his high school reunion party more than he thought: although he was initially concerned it would be awkward, he enjoyed catching up with his friends and reminiscing about old times.
    - Tomas enjoyed his high school reunion party more than he thought: although he was initially concerned it would be awkward, his doubts were relieved when everyone was friendly.
    - Tomas enjoyed his high school reunion party more than he thought: he was initially concerned it would be awkward.

Drill 1
1. **C.** A semicolon is needed to separate the two independent clauses about Mark Twain.
2. **A.** The colon separates the independent clause from the explanation clarifying why improved infrastructure was needed.
3. **B.** No punctuation is needed when an indirect quotation is being reported.
4. **B.** A semicolon is needed to separate the two independent clauses. ("Advocates…natural gas" and "nevertheless…safety").
5. **B.** A colon is needed to introduce a list. "Including" is not needed due to the presence of the colon.
6. **D.** A colon clarifies what the adaptation is after the independent clause.
7. **C.** C correctly separates the items in the list with commas without adding additional punctuation. A colon should not follow the preposition "with," as in A. B uses a colon inappropriately since the second part of the sentence does not elaborate on the first. D uses a semicolon inappropriately since there is no independent clause on each side of it.
8. **A.** The semicolon separates the independent clauses.
9. **A.** A colon after the independent clauses signals the explanation about why the launch went better than expected.
10. **A.** The semicolon separates two independent clauses.
11. **B.** The dashes function as commas setting off nonessential information about radioactive materials.

12. **A.** The dashes function as commas setting off nonessential information about Norman Rockwell.
13. **B.** Only a comma can link the introductory dependent clause to the independent clause that follows.
14. **D.** The dash emphasizes the three listed ships at the beginning of the sentence.
15. **D.** A colon introduces a list. There is no need for "which included."
16. **C.** A colon introduces the specification of one of Leni's favorite topics (elaborating on the independent clause). "That being" is not needed, as it is confusing and unnecessary.
17. **A.** A colon introduces the list after the independent clause.
18. **C.** A colon introduces an explanation for why fruit flies are ideal candidates for genetic studies after the independent clause.
19. **C.** The dashes function as commas setting off the nonrestrictive information about the components of nucleotides.
20. **C.** A comma is needed to link the dependent clause to the independent clause that follows.
21. **D.** No punctuation should follow "such as."
22. **C.** A semicolon connects two independent clauses.
23. **B.** The nonessential information is set off by commas.
24. **D.** The dash provides the needed pause to emphasize the end of the sentence. Since independent clauses are not being separated, a semicolon is unacceptable.
25. **C.** A participial phrase describing the changes after the independent clause should follow a comma, creating a loose sentence.
26. **A.** The colon appropriately sets off the information that clarifies what is still needed, the need for unique content. There are already two dashes setting off the nonessential information ("whether online or offline"), so no additional dashes are needed.
27. **C.** A comma should separate the introductory participial phrase from the independent clause that follows.
28. **B.** A colon is needed to signal the elaboration about how tipping varies between cultures.
29. **B.** The independent clause follows the list preceding the dash.
30. **C.** A colon should follow "extraordinary" to introduce the elaboration about what the extraordinary discovery was.
31. **A.** A dash functions as a dramatic pause, highlighting why Seattle is a great place for people interested in the tech industry.
32. **B.** A colon should precede the independent clause that elaborates on the solar industry being viewed positively.
33. **C.** The introductory phrase should be separated from the independent clause that follows with a comma.
34. **B.** A colon should signal a description of how the lake turned blood-red after the independent clause.
35. **D.** No punctuation is needed before the prepositional phrase beginning with "for" that modifies "desire." No punctuation should separate the preposition "for" from the rest of the prepositional phrase.
36. **B.** Though D is grammatically acceptable, the colon is a better stylistic choice for introducing the clarification (it would make sense to plug in the word "specifically" after the comma in D, so a colon is a good choice). Had B been grammatically incorrect, then D would have been best by default.
37. **B.** A comma should connect the dependent clause beginning with "as" to the independent clause preceding it.
38. **C.** A colon introduces the independent clause clarifying the unique aspect of the narrative structure.
39. **B.** The colon signals the elaboration about what method revolutionized the field of genomics.
40. **A.** The complete sentence of equal importance should be separated by semicolons. The second clause is not an explanation of the first, so a colon or dash would not be appropriate.

Lesson 12: Items in a Series

Drill 1
1. **C.** Commas are needed after the first two food items in the series.
2. **D.** Commas are needed after the first two skills listed in the series.
3. **C.** Commas separate each city from the state in which it is found. Semicolons separate the first two states from the following cities.
4. **B.** A comma is needed after "Sophocles" in the list of names.
5. **A.** Commas are needed after "pencils" and "erasers" in the list of supplies.
6. **B.** Commas are needed after the states "Washington" and "Oregon" in the list of states.
7. **A.** Commas are needed after the first two movies in the list of movies.
8. **B.** Semicolons are needed between each meal since commas are included between the different food items constituting the first meal.
9. **A.** Semicolons are needed between each responsibility since some of them include commas within them.
10. **B.** Commas must separate the two workplaces, which are "academic institutions" and "government agencies."
11. **C.** Commas should separate the specialties. No punctuation should follow "including."
12. **D.** Semicolons are needed between each person since there are already commas between each name and its corresponding title.

Lesson 13: Possessives

Mini Active Learning Activity
1. The underlined portion incorrectly suggests the grade book belonged to multiple teachers instead of one.
2. The underlined portion should say "teacher's."
3. The underlined portion incorrectly suggests the forecasts belonged to one forecaster instead of many.
4. The underlined portion should say "Meteorologists'."
5. Nothing belongs to the projects, so it should not be possessive.
6. The underlined portion should say "projects."
7. Student B is correct. "Students" is an indirect object and "many chances" is a direct object, so no apostrophe is needed.
8. Sentence 1 suggests Fei and Eli performed their research together. Sentence 2 suggests they did separate research projects that happened to be on the same topic.

Drill 1
1. **C.** The singular noun "family" in possessive form is "family's" (the plantation belongs to the family).
2. **B.** The possessive form of people is "people's" (the candidate belongs to the people).
3. **B.** "Alliances" is not possessive (nothing belongs to them). Multiple alliances are discussed, so the plural noun is needed.
4. **C.** The possessive form of one group is "group's" (the latest song belongs to the group).
5. **A.** The apostrophe is only needed after the second name because Watson and Crick performed the research together (the research belongs to Watson and Crick).
6. **C.** The possessive form of the plural noun "girls" is "girls'." The noun "reactions" is not possessive but belongs to the girls.
7. **B.** The possessive form of the singular "Fitzgerald" is "Fitzgerald's." "Stories" need not be possessive, as they belong to Fitzgerald.
8. **C.** The possessive form of the plural noun "students" is "students'." The feedback belongs to the students.
9. **B.** The possessive form of the name "Suzuki" is "Suzuki's." "Method" belongs to Suzuki.
10. **A.** The possessive form of "Simone" is "Simone's." "Musical performances" belong to Nina Simone.
11. **C.** The possessive form of "Crater Lake" is "Crater Lake's." "Weather" belongs to Crater Lake.
12. **D.** Both scientists must be put into possessive form since they worked on separate projects, which each belonged to them.
13. **D.** The possessive form of "Tanzania" is "Tanzania's." "Mount Kilimanjaro" is NOT possessive (it is the noun belonging to Tanzania).
14. **B.** "Men's" is the possessive of "men." "Basketball" is not in possessive form (the team does not belong to the basketball, but the basketball team belongs to the men).
15. **A.** The dog belongs to the cousin, so "cousin" is possessive ("cousin's"). The cousin belongs to the mother, so "mother" is possessive ("mother's"). The mother belongs to Alistair, so "Alistair" is possessive ("Alistair's"). "Dog" is not possessive since nothing belongs to it.
16. **B.** The possessive adjective "your" modifies the gerund "questioning."
17. **D.** The possessive pronoun is needed. The responsibility belongs to the councilwoman.
18. **C.** The possessive determiner "our" modifies the gerund "protesting."
19. **A.** "Students" is modified by "studying," so no apostrophe is needed.
20. **B.** "Parks" should not be possessive. The possessive determiner "their" is already present.
21. **C.** No possessive is needed because "coach" functions as a verb, not a noun.
22. **A.** "Claim" is a noun that belongs to the speaker, so only "speaker's" is possessive.
23. **D.** "Claim" acts as a verb introducing the quote. "Author" need not be in possessive form since this noun does not own anything.
24. **C.** "Water's" is the possessive form of "water." "Health benefits" belong to the water.

25. **B.** No possessive is needed because "walking" is a participle describing the children.
26. **B.** "Brain's" is the possessive form of "brain," to which the "neurotransmitters" belong. "Neurotransmitters" is not possessive since nothing belongs to them.
27. **A.** "Executive's" is the possessive form of "executive." The thoughtful efforts belong to the executive. "Company's" is the singular possessive of "company." "Practices." belong to the company. Note that "its" signals "company" must take the singular possessive form.
28. **D.** The adjective "chicken" describes the noun "eggs." No apostrophes are needed.

Lesson 14: Restrictive and Nonrestrictive Punctuation

Mini Active Learning Activity
1. A dash is needed after "Humphrey Davy" to isolate the nonessential clause between dashes.
   - The Davy lamp—which was named after its inventor Humphrey Davy— consisted of a wick lamp that had a flame enclosed inside a mesh screen.
2. The synonym for slander should be set off by commas.
   - It is dishonorable to slander, or defame, other people's characters.
3. The nonessential participial phrase "displaying telltale signs of submission" should be set off by commas.
   - With its body in a crouched position and its tail tucked between its legs, the younger wolf, displaying telltale signs of submission, showed the more dominant wolf it did not mean to challenge its authority; rather, it just wanted to play.
4. The appositive for Walter Cronkite should be set off by a comma.
   - In 1981, Jimmy Carter awarded the Presidential Medal of Freedom to journalist Walter Cronkite, one of the most trusted voices in news.
5. The participial phrase should be set off by commas.
   - Sans-culottes, literally meaning "those without breeches," were common people during the French Revolution, many of whom were urban laborers who became militant partisans.

Drill 1
1. **C.** "Needless to say" is a parenthetical expression that should be set off by commas.
2. **D.** The restrictive clause starting with "that" should not be set off by commas.
3. **C.** Commas must surround the nonrestrictive relative clause ("who is a great salesman"). It is clear that the subject is Esteban.
4. **A.** The fact that the person who completes a background check is able to become a Foreign Service Officer is essential to understanding the sentence. The relative clause should not be set off by commas.
5. **C.** Commas must surround the nonrestrictive clause ("which ….years"). Social media is clearly the subject of this sentence.
6. **A.** Commas must surround the nonrestrictive phrase ("a dystopian… Orwell"). "*1984*" is clearly the subject of the sentence.
7. **B.** A colon can only follow an independent clause ("The three central crops of various Native American groups" has no main verb and does not express a complete thought). The actual names of the crops are nonessential. They should be set off by dashes rather than commas since the nonessential information itself is in a list.
8. **D.** No punctuation is needed with the restrictive clause beginning with "that."
9. **C.** Stockholm is defined as the city where the Nobel Prizes are awarded, so the relative clause beginning with "where" is restrictive. A comma should follow "Sweden," which is nonrestrictive (countries following a city are nonrestrictive).
10. **B.** The end of the sentence is nonrestrictive, so it should be set off by a comma. The fact that French toast is the subject's favorite breakfast food is supplemental information.
11. **A.** "One…Egypt" is a nonrestrictive appositive that should be set off by commas.
12. **B.** An independent clause ("Jefferson designed it himself") cannot interrupt a sentence without being set off by appropriate punctuation. The information should be set off by parentheses.
13. **D.** The restrictive clause beginning with "that" requires no punctuation.
14. **C.** "Or supporter" is a nonrestrictive appositive that renames "proponent," so it should be set off by commas.
15. **B.** "Bill Gates" is a restrictive appositive that is needed for the sentence to make sense, so the name should not be set off by punctuation. "Founder" cannot act as the subject. If the sentence had said "the founder of Microsoft" or "Microsoft's founder," then "Bill Gates" would be nonrestrictive.

16. **A.** "Fiorello La Guardia" is a nonrestrictive appositive because it follows "New York's 99th mayor." The sentence makes sense without the name, so commas around the name are needed.
17. **D.** "Also known as a natural minor scale" is a nonrestrictive appositive that renames "Aeolian scale." It should be set off by commas.
18. **B.** "Who have obtained doctorate degrees" is a restrictive relative clause that defines "people," so it should not be set off by punctuation. The meaning of the sentence is not clear when the relative clause is deleted.
19. **D.** The nonessential appositive ("also…stone") that renames "philosopher's stone" should be set off by commas.
20. **A.** The restrictive relative clause beginning with "that" is interrupted by a nonrestrictive clause set off by commas ("in addition…Pulitzer Prize").
21. **C.** The nonessential phrase ("though very thorough") should be set off by commas.
22. **B.** The nonessential appositive ("millions…United States") cannot be set off by one dash and one comma. The same punctuation should be used throughout.
23. **C.** The nonessential appositive ("a physicist from the United Kingdom") should be set off by commas.
24. **D.** The "prelude" is the nonessential appositive renaming the "first song" and should be set off by commas.
25. **C.** The nonessential appositive "named after…Eiffel" should be set off by commas. Within the appositive, there should be no commas between "engineer" and "Alexander Gustave Eiffel" because the name of the engineer is needed in order for the sentence to make sense.
26. **A.** "In many versions of the story" is nonessential and can be removed from the sentence, so it is set off by commas. "Who has an evil stepmother" is an essential relative clause that is interrupted by a nonessential prepositional phrase.
27. **B.** The participial phrase "designed to improve health standards for pesticide use in banana production" interrupts the dependent clause "when the project was developed." In order for the relative pronoun "which" to have been acceptable, it would need to have followed a comma.
28. **C.** The nonessential appositive "both immigrants" can be set off by commas.
29. **D.** The participial phrase "known for its fast running speed" should be set off by the same punctuation throughout. Since a dash is used at the end of the phrase, it must also be used at the beginning.
30. **B.** The nonessential participial phrase should be set off by dashes. When the elements set off by punctuation in A and D are ignored, the resulting sentences are not complete.
31. **D.** The definition for "beholden" ("or indebted") should be set off by commas. When the definition is ignored, the result is a complete sentence.
32. **C.** The nonessential appositive phrase ("a process…conditions") defining collective bargaining should be set off by the same form of punctuation on both sides of the appositive. Since a dash is used at the beginning of the phrase, it must also be used at the end of the phrase.
33. **B.** The nonessential appositive for "painter" ("mural artist Diego Rivera") should be set off by commas. Within the appositive noun phrase, the name "Diego Rivera" is essential for knowing the identity of the "mural artist," so no comma between "mural artist" and "Diego Rivera" is needed.
34. **C.** The parenthetical "he says" should be set off by commas.
35. **A.** The parenthetical "some psychologists argue" should be set off by commas.
36. **D.** The parenthetical "some experts contend" should be set off by commas.
37. **B.** The coordinating conjunction "but" should join the independent clauses to avoid a comma splice.
38. **C.** The nonessential phrase "such as the amount of the initial investment" should be set off by commas.
39. **C.** The parenthetical phrase "among other places" should be set off by commas.
40. **C.** No punctuation should precede the restrictive clause beginning with "that." "Well" modifies "is" and should be a part of the same sentence.
41. **B.** Parentheses are needed on both sides of the parenthetical element.

42. **C.** The parenthetical element beginning with "if not" and ending with "concerns" should be set off by dashes on both sides. The sentence is complete when this information is ignored.
43. **D.** The nonessential appositive "a professor of international relations at Georgetown University" should be set off by commas. The sentence is complete and logical when this phrase is ignored.
44. **D.** No punctuation is needed because the fact that the lobby was decorated with colorful lights is essential information for understanding the sentence.
45. **D.** The phrase beginning with "such as" is nonessential (the given examples of factors themselves are not essential to understanding the sentence), so it should be set off by commas on both sides.
46. **B.** The nonessential phrase "unable to discriminate between fact and fiction" should be set off by commas.
47. **B.** The nonessential participial phrase should be set off by the same punctuation on both sides. A pair of parentheses is one acceptable option. The comma after the parentheses introduces the independent clause after the opening phrase.
48. **A.** The nonessential relative clause beginning with "which" should be set off by commas on both sides. No additional punctuation within that clause is needed since the information is essential for understanding the clause.
49. **D.** No punctuation is needed. The name of the organization is essential because without this information, the sentence can be misinterpreted to suggest all nonpartisan organizations seek to promote transparency in the news. Also, the fact that there is no comma after the "Center for Media and Democracy" means that no comma should precede "such as" (either both commas are needed if the information is nonessential or neither if it is essential).
50. **B.** The definition of "compressed workweeks" should be set off by dashes on both sides.
51. **D.** The names are essential, so no commas are needed.
52. **A.** The nonessential appositive naming Dr. Adil Najam should be set off by commas. Within the appositive, no commas are needed before the parentheses that give the acronym for World Wildlife Fund.
53. **C.** The nonessential conjunctive adverb should be set off by commas on both sides (not dashes).

Lesson 15: Unnecessary Punctuation

Mini Active Learning Activity
1. No comma should separate the elements of the "verb + that clause" that reports on a state of affairs, namely a benefit of coding.
2. No comma should separate the subject ("girls") from the verb ("quit") that follows.
3. The compound verbs in the predicate should not be separated by a comma. Note that had "they" appeared after "and," the comma would have been acceptable (in that case, "and" would be connecting independent clauses).
4. Since the order of the adjectives can be switched, a comma is needed after "swift."
5. No comma is needed before the comparative preposition "than."
6. No comma should separate the cumulative adjectives whose order cannot be reversed.
7. No comma should separate the noun "appearance" from the prepositional phrase "of impropriety" that modifies it.
8. No comma should separate the adjective ("silent") from the noun ("films") it modifies.

Drill 1
1. **D.** No comma is needed between the adjective "important" and the noun "works" or between the preposition "of" and its object "world literature."
2. **B.** No comma is needed between the verb "promote" and the object "the economic development" or between the preposition "of" and its object "the areas."
3. **D.** No comma is needed between the cumulative adjectives "many" and "prestigious." No comma is needed between the adjective "various" and the noun "performances."
4. **A.** The compounds subjects connected by "and" do not need to be separated by commas. No comma should precede "both formed" since "formed" is the main verb after the subjects. A comma should introduce the dependent clause beginning with "though" at the end of the sentence.
5. **D.** No comma is needed after the verb "appointed" and its object "his horse." No comma is needed between the preposition "to" and its object "the Senate."
6. **D.** No comma is needed between the adjective "professional" and the noun "consultants." No comma is needed between the preposition "of" and its object "their business practices."
7. **C.** The nonrestrictive phrase "popular during the eighteenth century" should be surrounded by commas. The compound elements joined by the conjunction "and" should not be separated by a comma.
8. **B.** No comma before the intensive pronoun "herself" is needed. Commas are needed surrounding "a skilled entrepreneur herself" because the phrase is a nonessential appositive.
9. **D.** No comma is needed between the preposition "of" and its object "the 1950s" or between the verb "rejected" and its object "traditional middle class values."
10. **C.** No comma is needed between "director" and the restrictive appositive "Lee Daniels" or between the subject ("Lee Daniels") and the verb "is."
11. **B.** Commas cannot separate compound subjects (the two music halls). No comma between the subjects and the verb "are" is needed.
12. **B.** No comma between the items joined by the coordinating conjunction "but" is needed.
13. **D.** No comma is needed between the subject "Yalta Agreement" and the verb "was." No comma is needed between the preposition "between" and its objects (the listed names).
14. **B.** The main verb "is" should not be set off by a comma, as it is part of the main clause containing the subject "ability."
15. **A.** A comma is needed after the introductory participial phrase. No comma is needed between the adjective "architectural" and the noun "techniques."
16. **B.** Neither a comma nor a semicolon can follow "such as."
17. **D.** No comma is needed between the cumulative adjectives "delicious" and "chocolate." No comma is needed between the adjective "chocolate" and the noun "cake."

18. **A.** Commas are needed between the coordinate adjectives but not between the adjective "intelligent" and the noun "teacher."
19. **C.** No comma is needed before the reflexive pronoun "itself." The comma is needed after "creative" to separate the dependent clause from the independent clause that follows.
20. **D.** No comma is needed to connect the compound elements ("architects" and "environmentalists") separated by "and."
21. **C.** Commas are needed surrounding the parenthetical "though" that is found between the dependent clause ("while…person") and the independent clause that follows ("the…significant").
22. **B.** A comma is needed after the introductory dependent clause ("as a…leader"), and "and" should be removed ("and" can't join a dependent clause to an independent clause that follows). There should be no comma between the subject "George Clemenceau" and the verb "helped."
23. **B.** The nonessential phrase "always the opportunist" should be set off by commas. The compound predicates connected by "and" should not be separated by commas.
24. **D.** A comma is needed after the introductory appositive. No comma is needed between the verb "is" and the object "a symbol."
25. **C.** Commas separate the items in a series. No comma is needed between "washing" and "machine," since a washing machine is one item. No comma is needed between "air" and "conditioning," since air conditioning units represent a single type of item.
26. **A.** A comma should separate a city from a country. The country is nonrestrictive since the name of the city is included.
27. **D.** No comma is needed between the subject "firm" and the verb "will make." Since the subordinating conjunction "if" is present, the coordinating conjunction "and" is not needed.
28. **D.** No comma is needed between the cumulative adjectives "horn's" and "mellow" or between the subject "sound" and the verb "is."
29. **B.** There is no need for punctuation to set off the technical term "banana state."
30. **C.** Commas should not precede an open parenthesis. The participial phrase "carved representations of spiritual messengers" should be set off by parentheses.
31. **B.** There is no punctuation needed between the participle "called" and the technical term "memes."
32. **D.** There is no comma between the participial phrase "known as" and the nickname "The Grape State." No comma is needed before the short dependent clause beginning with "because."
33. **C.** There is no comma between the adjective "Stewart's" and the noun "performance." There is no comma between "Actor" and "James Stewart's" within the noun phrase "Actor James Stewart's performance" because the name is restrictive. If the sentence were reworded as "Actor's performance…," the sentence would be unclear.
34. **B.** The prepositional phrase "in an article" should precede the colon. The direct quotation clarifies which line from "Hamlet" was quoted. The prepositional phrase "in an article" modifies the participle "quoted," so no comma should precede or follow the preposition "in." The phrase "in an article" should not be set off by commas because the sentence does not make sense when the phrase is removed from the sentence.
35. **B.** No comma is needed between the verb "ensure" and its object beginning with "that."
36. **A.** All of the information after "more" is essential, so no punctuation is needed.
37. **B.** No punctuation is needed to introduce the partial quote that is integrated in the sentence's syntax.
38. **D.** No punctuation is needed since "around 1300" essentially modifies "sometime."
39. **B.** No punctuation is needed between the subject clause and the main verb.
40. **B.** No punctuation is needed between the adverb "highly" and the adjective it modifies "stylized." A comma is needed between "highly stylized" and "purple-toned" since their order can be reversed. No comma is needed between the adjective "purple-toned" and the noun "hair. **Note: While color is typically treated as a cumulative adjective, a previous exam treated it in a sentence with a similar grammatical structure as coordinate. Even so, none of the other choices makes sense. C and D use a comma between an adjective and a noun, while A uses one between an adverb and adjective.**

41. **D.** No punctuation is needed to introduce a quote after "that" that is integrated in the sentence's syntax.
42. **A.** No punctuation should appear between the adjective "topped" and the prepositional phrase "with cilantro" that modifies it. The prepositional phrase is essential because the meaning of the sentence is unclear when this phrase is deleted.
43. **C.** No punctuation should separate the independent clause from the dependent clause beginning with "if." No comma is needed between the compound subjects "individuals" and "businesses" connected by "and."
44. **B.** No comma is needed between the verb "identify" and its object.
45. **B.** No comma should set off the prepositional phrase "of the local newspaper," which modifies the headline. This phrase cannot be deleted without changing the meaning of the sentence. A comma should follow "declared" to introduce a direct quotation.
46. **C.** The compound objects "unorthodox" and "controversial" should not be separated by commas. The dependent clause ending with "controversial" should be separated from the independent clause that follows by a comma.
47. **A.** A colon introduces a long quote after a complete sentence.
48. **B.** A comma is needed after "commented" to introduce the quote. The correlative conjunctions "so…that" should not be separated by commas. A incorrectly makes it appear as if the information between the commas is nonessential.
49. **A.** No comma is needed before the essential relative clause beginning with "that" or between the compound predicates connected by "and."
50. **B.** A colon should signal a description of what the wedding planner does best. While a dash could also work, no comma is needed between the verb "engaging" and its object.
51. **D.** No punctuation should separate the elements of the "verb+that clause." No colon is needed after "that" since the information before the colon does not express a complete thought.
52. **A.** No comma should introduce the partial quote integrated within the sentence's syntax.
53. **C.** No punctuation should separate the subject from the verb phrase "can lead to" that follows, nor should any commas separate the verb from its object "widespread misunderstandings."
54. **B.** No punctuation is needed between the verb "is" and its object "home." No comma should introduce the prepositional phrase modifying "home."

Punctuation Unit Quiz

1. **D.** No punctuation is needed to separate the preposition "of" from its object.
2. **B.** B creates a loose sentence, appropriately using a comma to set off the participial phrase that elaborates on Arcesilaus's claim in the opening independent clause.
3. **C.** No apostrophes are needed. "Of" does not belong to the "stories" and "from" does not belong to the "exile."
4. **B.** No punctuation should set off the name of the reviewer whose name is essential to the sentence (the sentence does not make sense when "Justin Chang" is ignored). No comma should introduce the partial quote integrated within the sentence's syntax.
5. **C.** A colon follows the independent clause to signal the elaboration on why people are more creative in coffee shops.
6. **D.** D logically ends the sentence with a direct question that is answered in the following sentence. It makes clear there was a mystery to be resolved.
7. **D.** No punctuation should separate the title from the essential name. No comma should separate the subject from the verb "showed."
8. **A.** The nonessential "both flora and fauna" should follow "resources." A semicolon should follow this phrase to punctuate the list of national parks' functions and maintain consistency with the semicolon between the second and third functions of national parks in the list.
9. **C.** A semicolon should separate what could stand alone as complete sentences. "However" is a supplementary adverb ending the first independent clause.
10. **C.** "Iodic oxide" is a nonessential appositive for "a gas form of iodine" that should be set off by commas.
11. **C.** A colon should follow the independent clause to signal the elaboration for how Cannon did more than she was hired to do. Note that "though" ends the independent clause by creating a supplementary adverb clause for dramatic effect.
12. **B.** The "unique genome" belongs to the platypus, so only "platypus" should take the singular possessive form "platypus's."
13. **D.** The name of the title is essential for understanding the sentence, so it should not be set off by punctuation, as is the case with the first novel.
14. **A.** The nonessential appositive should be closed off by a comma on the right of "manganese trichloride ($MnCl_3$)" since there is a comma on the left. Within the appositive, no comma should precede the parentheses.
15. **C.** The three initiatives should be separated by semicolons. For each initiative, the optional phrase about the year it occurred in is introduced by a comma.
16. **C.** The nonessential elements should be set off by dashes.
17. **A.** No punctuation is needed to separate the independent clause from the dependent clause that follows beginning with "whenever."
18. **D.** No punctuation should separate the verb from its object. No commas are needed within the "verb + that" clause.
19. **A.** "Generated by wind" essentially modifies "energy" and should not be set off by commas. "At velocities as low as 2 meters per second" essentially modifies wind and should not be set off by commas.
20. **D.** The nonessential information should be set off by dashes.
21. **B.** No punctuation should set off the restrictive appositive needed to avoid vagueness.

Lesson 16: Transitions

Drill 1

1. **A.** "In broad terms" can introduce a general definition.
2. **C.** A contrast transition shows the difference between needing to exercise at an intense level and not exercising too hard.
3. **A.** A sequence transition (the steps in the interview process occur in a certain order) is needed.
4. **B.** A transition showing a relationship of addition is needed to show that Kipling was known for more than one type of writing.
5. **C.** A transition of emphasis is needed to clarify how a healthy corporate culture contributes to business success.
6. **A.** A contrast transition is needed to show the opposing views of Jefferson and Hamilton.
7. **C.** An example transition is needed to illustrate one application of distillation.
8. **C.** An example transition is needed to show examples of how objects are named in terms of Mach numbers.
9. **C.** A cause and effect transition is needed to show a result of the Green Revolution.
10. **B.** A cause and effect transition is needed. "Therefore" ("for that reason") explains why light seen from the sky is from four years ago.
11. **C.** A similarity transition is needed to show another technique that had the effect of making art appear three-dimensional.
12. **B.** A cause and effect transition is needed. Because consumers pay more attention to the internet, television advertisements are less effective at attracting customers.
13. **A.** A contrast transition is needed. Despite the fact that the precise function of the building isn't known, there is evidence that suggests what the function might be.
14. **B.** A transition showing a relationship of addition is needed to introduce a second benefit of kale.
15. **D.** "In fact" is needed to signal the elaboration on Neil deGrasse Tyson's love for astronomy.
16. **C.** "Then" is used to show that the conclusion that studying abroad is worthwhile is logical because of the aforementioned personal and practical benefits.
17. **C.** The transition "still" shows the contrast between the students' lack of experience and eagerness to learn despite that fact.
18. **B.** "Initially" (meaning "at first") shows the correct time relationship to clarify when the continental drift theory was not widely accepted (in contrast to its later acceptance).
19. **A.** "On the other hand" shows the correct contrast between a way not to motivate and ways to motivate employees.
20. **B.** "In effect" clarifies the impact of the technology.
21. **D.** "In other words" is needed because the second sentence restates the first sentence using different words. Strikes limit the authority of managers (their ability to control their businesses).
22. **B.** The addition transition "what's more" is needed to provide a third benefit of physical therapy for student athletes.
23. **C.** The second sentence reveals what the candidate did to achieve her goal of galvanizing first-time voters ("to this end" means "to achieve this goal").

Lesson 17: Rhetorical Synthesis

Drill 1
1. **D.** Only D gives details about the length of the canal.
2. **C.** Only C indicates something both story collections have in common, namely that they depict people in supernatural situations.
3. **A.** Only A directly compares the lengths of the journeys.
4. **B.** Only B mentions a specific factor (pesticides) that is causing bee numbers to decline.
5. **C.** C puts the focus on the 2008 piece, introducing it with a modifying phrase. It also presents a brief description of the artist for people not familiar with Hernandez.
6. **D.** D most clearly indicates the scope of the work done by the museum by referencing what it does to preserve India's history. It references the diversity of manuscripts in terms of their languages, ages, and mediums.
7. **C.** C provides an overview of what the novel is about and makes clear who the author is. It provides an important detail about the author, effectively introducing him.
8. **A.** A describes a specific advantage sand batteries have over lithium ones, namely that they are less polluting.
9. **D.** D both mentions what the researchers did in the study (their methodology, which included a chemical analysis of the skull) and reports on its findings (conclusions about how the triceratops died).
10. **B.** Only B reports on what the study was designed to help the researchers learn.
11. **A.** A mentions both leaders' contributions to the Selma march and how their contributions differed.
12. **C.** C both explains the definition of "combine" and notes one specific artwork that is an example of it.
13. **B.** B clarifies how a specific accomplishment of Tubman's was unique (by mentioning something she was the only woman to do). It also clarifies that she was a notable (important) member the Underground Railroad.
14. **B.** B gives specific details about the methods the research team used to gather data.

Expression Unit Quiz

1. **C.** The second sentence presents an effect (consequence) of the walrus's clapping, so "consequently" is needed.
2. **C.** The traditional (established) view is that people today suffer sleep deprivation more than earlier humans did, but new research mentioned in the next sentence challenges this contention.
3. **D.** A transition showing a relationship of addition is needed since a second example of problems caused by open office settings is mentioned.
4. **C.** "Conversely" is the most precise contrast transition, highlighting an opposing characteristic between pre-Renaissance and Renaissance artists.
5. **A.** The second sentence gives an example of an artist who does hybrid works.
6. **A.** "Currently" shows the correct time relationship, indicating how researchers can rearrange bones now.
7. **B.** The second sentence highlights a difference between hares and rabbits.
8. **D.** "Though" highlights the contrast between a trait that is beneficial for zebras and one that is not helpful for researchers.
9. **B.** "Increasingly" signals a change relative to tradition, highlighting a finding from the previous sentence.
10. **A.** The sentence shows a reason why the ability for the praying mantis to rotate its head without moving its body makes it a formidable predator.
11. **B.** The contrast transition "still" (meaning "despite this") is appropriate. It highlights that despite the fact that some jobs require in-person workers, those that don't should consider hiring remote employees.
12. **C.** C highlights a contrast between mass and weight, showing how they are different.
13. **A.** The sentence highlights a similarity between how customers in different areas rallied behind a small business.
14. **C.** C makes a broader point about how statistical analyses are used to answer broader research questions about authorship, going beyond the specific case study of *Wuthering Heights.*
15. **C.** C indicates what the research team sought to find out (the study's aim).
16. **B.** B both mentions the aim of the study (what researchers wanted to find out about geese migration) and the methodology they used to answer their research question (attaching trackers to geese).
17. **D.** D explains what the researchers wanted to learn in their study.
18. **A.** A gives a brief synopsis of what the book is about without explaining what Wall Street itself is, as the reader is already familiar with Wall Street.
19. **C.** C both explains what mother culture proponents argue and gives a clear overview of where and when the Olmec civilization existed, orienting the readers.
20. **A.** A emphasizes the work LaDuke does and provides a sense of how long she has been doing such work.